The Animals' Freedom Fighter

The Animals' Freedom Fighter

*A Biography of Ronnie Lee,
Founder of the Animal
Liberation Front*

JON HOCHSCHARTNER

McFarland & Company, Inc., Publishers
Jefferson, North Carolina

ISBN (print) 978-1-4766-6818-5
ISBN (ebook) 978-1-4766-2746-5

LIBRARY OF CONGRESS CATALOGUING DATA ARE AVAILABLE

British Library cataloguing data are available

Front cover: Ronnie with Wyre Forest Vegans & Veggies
stall at an animal sanctuary fundraising event in Stourbridge,
United Kingdom, May 2016 (courtesy Ronnie Lee)

Manufactured in the United States of America

*McFarland & Company, Inc., Publishers
Box 611, Jefferson, North Carolina 28640
www.mcfarlandpub.com*

To my beloved wife Amanda,
without whom nothing would be possible,
our companion animals, Max and Teddy,
who bring so much joy to our lives,
my parents and sister—
Selden, Hock, and Lucy—
who have always been there for me,
and my mother-in-law, Judy,
for welcoming me to the family

Acknowledgments

I'd like to thank Ronnie Lee. A first-time biographer couldn't ask for a better subject. Ronnie was always cheerful and prepared for our weekly interviews by conducting significant amounts of his own research. In many respects, he is an uncredited co-author of this book. I'd like to thank Josh Harper, formerly of the SHAC 7, who helped proofread the manuscript for historical accuracy.

Finally, I would like to thank the following people, who donated to the crowdfunding campaign that enabled me to write this biography: Hayley Dunk, Doug Hine, Katy "Bones" Lowe, Jacky Owen, Paul Crouch, Melissa Mallen, Joolz Hatton, Ted Grant, Skye Hollywood, Colin Avolve, Yolanda Raymond, Sharon Kirby, Barbara DeGrande, Natalia Pérez, Andrew Lee Wright Barnes, Amanda Holtey, Kathy Goss, Michael Beasley, Neil W., Glenys Isaacs, David Bastien, Fiona D., Steven Peters, Angela Lynch, Brian Foster, Steve P., Animal Concern, Dipen Ramesh Patel, Michelle Walsh, Faye Thatcher, Angela "Wear Your Voice" Tubb, Marc and Sarah Nelson, Veda Stram, Jocelyn and Lisa Fragniere, INVSOC Invercargill Vegan Society, Craig Hollingsworth, Alwynne Cartmell, New Zealand Anti-Vivisection Society, Rob Sheppard, Mark "Muzzy" Muschamp, David Hochschartner, Polly Holt, David and Bella, Trish Smith, Robin Howard, Angie Hamp, Bobby Balfour, Andrew Willgoss, Jan Glover, Emmy Amers, Jake Hobbs, Sue Baumgardt (Dickens), Liz Layton, Dan Doherty, Audrey Garcia, Nigel Davies, Eric Moreau, Genevieve Cottraux, Mary R. Crumptom, Bernie Wright, Pat Wainwright, Angie Wright, and Wendy Alf Fletcher and many others.

Table of Contents

Preface

This project began in late 2015. Since college, I'd been interested in animal rights—and, more recently, animal-rights history. I was surprised and disappointed by the dearth of biographies and memoirs of animal-rights activists. So I set out to write one.

Choosing Ronnie Lee as a biographical subject was a no-brainer. These days—while I'm awed by the courage of Animal Liberation Front activists and deeply sympathetic to the despair that drives them—I believe only a mass movement can free animals. But, as a younger man, I was a great admirer of this underground organization. To be able to speak with Ronnie would be a dream. Plus, I knew that my own development, from an advocate of individualist attacks to one of electoral engagement, in some ways mirrored Ronnie's own.

Thankfully, Ronnie agreed to cooperate in the writing of his biography. With the help of many generous backers on Kickstarter, we raised the funds that allowed me to take on the project. Every week, typically on Sundays, I would interview Ronnie over Skype. I estimate we recorded about 60 hours of conversation. Over this period, I experienced personal highs and lows. My fiancée Amanda and I set a date to get married, while my cat Max suffered an inexplicable injury, requiring the tip of his tail be amputated. All this and more made it into my discussions with Ronnie, whom I came to consider a friend. But the interviews did more than this for me. They reaffirmed my view of Ronnie as a heroic figure.

For some time, I've been a reader of Louis Proyect's blog, "The Unrepentant Marxist," which displays two quotes prominently. The first is from Max Horkheimer: "A revolutionary career does not lead to banquets and honorary titles, interesting research and professorial wages. It leads to misery, disgrace, ingratitude, prison and a voyage into the unknown, illuminated by only an almost superhuman belief." The second is from I.F. Stone, and

1

begins: "The only kinds of fights worth fighting are those you are going to lose, because somebody has to fight them and lose and lose and lose until someday, somebody who believes as you do wins."

Ronnie has been this kind of fighter on behalf of animals. I hope you enjoying reading his story.

1

Family History
and Early Years

Ronald Anthony Denis Lee—founder of the Animal Liberation Front (ALF), who would serve three prison sentences for his activism—was born in Gloucester, England, on February 17, 1951. He is best known and will be hereafter be referred to as Ronnie.

Ronnie's ideas and example, whatever one might think of them, have been undeniably influential. The "leaderless-resistance" model, as used in defense of animals, has spread across the globe. ALF is active in over 40 countries, according to the *Palgrave Dictionary of Public Order Policing, Protest and Political Violence*. In this writer's own nation, the United States of America, the Federal Bureau of Investigation ranked ALF and groups like it as the foremost domestic-terrorism threat facing the country, as recently as 2005.

And yet, Ronnie's origins were fairly inauspicious.

Margaret Tierney, Ronnie's mother, was born on a small farm in Newtownhamilton, Northern Ireland, on January 7, 1920—the same year Frank Aiken led 200 men from the Irish Republican Army in an attack on the Royal Irish Constabulary barracks in that village. Her parents were Mary and Patrick Tierney. Margaret was the second eldest of seven children and lived with her family on what was primarily a dairy farm. "They did have pigs and chickens there as well," Ronnie said, adding they also grew some vegetables. As Catholics in Northern Ireland, the Tierneys were part of a religious minority.

Margaret left school at 14, helping at home, and traveled to England three years later with an older friend of the family, who was marrying a doctor in Oakworth, West Yorkshire. "Basically, they employed my mum to help in the doctor's surgery with small tasks, such as bandaging patients," Ronnie said.

3

When the Second World War began, Margaret went back home, believing it to be safer than Oakworth. "Where she was working—although it was out in the country—it wasn't too far from some big industrial cities in the north of England," Ronnie said. "They thought if there were bombings, she might be effected."

But she was called up for military service and had to return to England. After working in a factory testing electrical equipment, Margaret began military training in Pirbright, Surrey. "One of the things a lot of women did in those days was working in the [Women's] Land Army, which was growing crops, because the men were away at war," Ronnie said, before adding his mother didn't want to do that, having grown up on a farm. Instead, she volunteered for the Auxiliary Territorial Service, the women's branch of the British army. "They didn't serve as troops," Ronnie said, adding much of the ATS' work was clerical. "She processed the soldiers' applications for home leave. That was her main job."

Following the 1943 Allied victory in Italy, Margaret was sent to Naples and Rome, where she did more clerical work in support of the occupation forces. When the war ended, she was sent to Vienna, Austria, where she was stationed at Schönbrunn Palace, which had been requisitioned by the Allies. "That actually, in many ways, was the high point of her life," Ronnie said. "She always talks about that period with great fondness. Because she never really traveled after that."

In 1947, she returned to Ireland, but, in the wake of her wartime adventures, life there felt dull, and her employment prospects weren't good. So she moved to Moreton Valence, Gloucester, and lived with her sister, Elsie Tierney, at a former airbase, where people squatted. "My mum's recollection is that people moved into the empty buildings," Ronnie said. "They were eventually allowed to stay there legally." On the strength of her record in the ATS, Margaret got a job with the Ministry of Defence in Quedgeley, Gloucester, where she managed military stores. Elsie's home was very cold in the winter, so Margaret moved to a room on Linden Road in Gloucester.

It was shortly after beginning work at the Ministry of Defence that Margaret almost died. While on a tour of a facility associated with her job, she became lost. Seeing double doors at the end of a particular corridor, she walked through them. "There was nothing on the other side," Ronnie said. "It was used for deliveries and she fell several stories. Luckily, there were sandbags at the bottom and she landed on the sandbags. That's what saved her life. Otherwise she certainly would have been killed—she fell a long way." Margaret walked away from the fall relatively unscathed. "My legs nearly went up into my body," she said. "I was very shaken up." Still, she went straight back to work, not telling anyone, as she was ashamed of what happened.

Harry Ronald Lee, Ronnie's father, was born on April 9, 1919, in Ropley, Hampshire, and raised in the Church of England. "When he was 3-years-old, his mother and father fell out, and his father left," Ronnie said. Ronnie's father disliked the name Harry, the name of Ronnie's paternal grandfather, Harry Lee, and, as a teenager, would change his name to Ronald Henry Lee. For the sake of clarity, I will refer to him going forward as Ron, as he was known, as opposed to Ronnie, the name I'll reserve for his son, the subject of this book. After his father left, Ron's mother, Ellen Louise Robbins, known as Lou, got a job as a housekeeper to a farmer who operated Cherry Orchard Farm, not far from Bristol.

The farmer also worked as a butcher in Kingswood, a suburb of Bristol. "He would kill pigs on his farm and sell the meat in the shop," Ronnie said. "It's kind of ironic that both of my parents were brought up on farms where animals were kept and killed." Ron attended Kingswood Grammar School, but, like Margaret, left school at 14. When the farmer bought a house in Gloucester, Ron and his mother—who was still in the farmer's employ—followed him there, living in the same home. "The farmer … had split up from his own wife and sons," Ronnie said. "He was very fond of my dad. He more or less treated my dad as his own son."

Eventually, when the farmer got older, he entered a care home. Ron and his mother stayed at the large house on Midland Road. Lou made a living taking in lodgers, while Ron began training as a hairdresser. "But then a friend of his mum's, my grandma's, got him a job at a company called Rotol," Ronnie said. "They were a company that made propellers for aircraft, especially military aircraft." Ron worked as a draftsman, drawing up plans for new propellers. "He was quite a clever guy, my dad," Ronnie said. "He obviously left school at 14, so he wouldn't have had much education in that direction. But he was very, very good at designing technical stuff."

When the Second World War broke out in 1939, Ron was called up and began army training. However, his health was not the best and his mother, concerned with his welfare, pestered the military to allow Ron to serve in a non-fighting capacity. Eventually army administrators conceded, and Ron worked on the airfields in the Gloucester area.

"When the aircraft flew out," Ronnie said, "he used to check them over and go underneath them with a torch—make sure the undercarriage was all right and everything." Ron was very fastidious in this. According to Ronnie, later in life, his father said many of his wartime colleagues were not so careful. "They'd often say they checked the planes, when they hadn't actually done so," Ronnie said. "My dad said some pilots actually lost their lives because planes weren't checked properly by people."

While checking planes during the Second World War, Ron had ideas for improving the mechanisms of the aircraft. After the fighting was over, when he went back to work at Rotol, he passed these ideas along. "Some of his suggestions for improving the mechanics of the planes were actually taken up by the aircraft industry," Ronnie. "I don't think my dad got paid for any of them." That said, Ron was awarded a promotion.

During this period, he was living with his mother, and as a result, didn't have many expenditures. So he was able to save up enough money to buy a flamboyant vehicle. "The Lord Mayor of Gloucester was selling his car, which was a Daimler," Ronnie said. "It was quite an old car.... I don't think it was necessarily, massively expensive." After Ron purchased the vehicle, he left the flags on it, which signified the mayor's office. When he drove around, Ronnie said, police would stop traffic for his father, believing he was the Lord Mayor.

Margaret and Ron met at a dance in Guildhall in the late 1940s. The pair were married in May 1949 at Saint Gregory's Church in Cheltenham, Gloucestershire. Ronnie didn't recall religion being a source of tension in the house, but he speculated his mother might have had some prejudice to overcome on the matter, despite her Catholicism being a minority faith in England. "In those days, if somebody was a Catholic, it was frowned upon by the Catholic Church if they married a non–Catholic," Ronnie said. For her part, Margaret said religion wasn't a disputed topic because Ron didn't put much stock such matters. "He didn't care what he was," she said, adding some Catholics in Ireland, though, would have taken issue with Ron's Protestant background.

Still, Margaret and her husband didn't get along particularly well. "We didn't separate or anything," she said. "He liked looking at the other women sometimes." According to Ronnie's younger sister, Patricia Lee, known as Patty, Margaret and Ron were not very physically affectionate. "I don't remember our parents ever kissing, holding hands or even sitting next to each other," Patty said. "They didn't have very much in common apart from Ronnie and myself."

Ronnie, Margaret and Ron's first child, was born prematurely at the Gloucester Royal Infirmary. He only weighed 4 pounds and 13 ounces. "Also, I was a breach baby," he said. "In other words, I came out ass-end first. I probably was trying to get away from the world even then." He was a difficult baby, crying all of the time. "There was an occasion when my mum was changing my nappy, and my dad was looking on, curious, and I pissed in his eye," Ronnie said, laughing. "There was one occasion when my dad had to take a lampshade down from the ceiling, because I wanted it. I was crying so much that he had to get a stepladder and get the lampshade down for me to stop me from crying."

After his parents married, they lived together in the house on Midland Road, with Lou. But when Ronnie was born, Margaret and Ron wanted a place of their own. According to Margaret, she didn't have a good relationship with Lou, who saw Margaret as a rival for Ron's affection. So Ron sold the Daimler, and used the money for a deposit on a cottage in Ashleworth, where he and his new family moved. "It was quite a distance for him to go to work at Rotol," Ronnie said of his father's commute, which Ron suddenly had to complete without a car. "He bought a motorized bicycle. In those days, you could get these bicycles that had a little motor in the rear wheel."

The commute was onerous, and Ron and his wife felt isolated in their new surroundings, so after a few months, they moved back to Gloucester, to a house on Sandycroft Road. Ron's mother moved in with them. "As she was getting older, she wasn't really able to cope with running the place on her own," Ronnie said. "My grandma was kind of contributing to the upkeep of the house, in the way of the money she received. But then she went to live with two of her brothers." Without the additional income provided by Ron's mother, he and his wife decided they needed to downsize their housing. Staying in Gloucester, they moved to a house on Lea Crescent.

Ron was offered a job with an engineering company,

Ronnie, about 1 year old, with neighborhood girls in Gloucester (photograph Ron Lee, courtesy Patricia Lee).

called Armstrong Whitworth, in Coventry. In the spring of 1953, he accepted and moved with his a family to a house in that city on Brackenhurst Road. Again, they moved after only a few months. "My dad didn't like it," Ronnie said. "He didn't like the people in Coventry. I think, perhaps, he found them to be unfriendly, and he didn't like working for this company." So Ron got a job at an English Electric factory in Stevenage, and he and his family moved to a house on Shephall Lane. At English Electric, Ron worked on guidance systems for nuclear missiles, in particular, a battlefield missile codenamed Blue Water. "If it came to repairing anything on his car, he was absolutely useless," Ronnie said of his father. "But when it came to that kind of work—his actual work—he was very, very good. It's very strange that it was confined to this kind of area."

Patty, Ronnie's only sibling, was born about 18 months after him on July 27, 1952. According to family lore, when his mother first introduced him to Patty, Ronnie was unimpressed, advising his mother to put the newborn away in a drawer. "We've always gotten on very well, even as kids," Ronnie said of Patty. "There may have been the odd squabble. But we always had a very-good, really, a very-friendly relationship." Patty was a much happier and easy-to-manage baby than her brother. "She was good," Margaret said of her daughter. "Nobody even knew she was there."

Still, Patty was involved in typical, childhood mischief with Ronnie. Their father had always been musical. For instance, as a boy, Ron sang in the church choir and learned various instruments. So, when Ronnie and Patty were young, he kept two violins in the house, which they played with. Ronnie remembers he and his sister breaking the strings. "We also had fun playing tricks on our parents," Patty

Ronnie (left), about age 2, with Patty (photograph Ron Lee, courtesy Patricia Lee).

said. "One day we exchanged clothes to see if they would notice. They did, of course, but it made them laugh."

Ronnie said Ron and Margaret were good parents. "We were very well cared for," Ronnie said, speaking for his sister and himself. "The food would always be there for us. We were kept warm and looked after very well." Patty agreed, adding that, as a stay-at-home mother, Margaret did most of the childcare, and kept phenomenally busy. "Mum seemed to be continually washing, cleaning, ironing or polishing shoes," Patty said. "She would cuddle and attend to us tirelessly when we were sick."

While Margaret managed the house, Ron was the breadwinner. "I don't think my dad played a huge part in dealing with me, really, as a baby," he said. "To some extent, that was the culture in those days. That was left for the woman to do rather than the man." Patty struck a similar note, saying her father was rarely home. "He smoked Player's cigarettes and would sit at the dinner table when he came home, scribbling long mathematical equations on the packet," Patty said. "His mind was usually elsewhere, inventing new and revolutionary projects."

Still, Ron was involved enough to make his son a special toilet—as Ronnie didn't like sitting on an ordinary one—after growing too big to use a potty. According to Ronnie, this was compromised "of an orange box with a potty inside and a hole cut in the top, together with a broom handle and a piece of string as a pretend flush. When we went to see relatives, this contraption had to come with us, much to the amusement of my cousins." Ronnie said his father was also very good at yo-yo, demonstrating tricks for his son.

By the summer of 1953, the Lees had a television, as Ronnie knew his family watched the coronation of Queen Elizabeth II on it. But there weren't many shows aimed at children in the years before Ronnie entered school. "There was very little," he said, referring to what was available on television for kids his age. "It was more the radio." Ronnie enjoyed a radio program, produced by the British Broadcasting Company, called Listen With Mother, which featured stories and songs. As the title suggested, he would listen to the program whilst sitting on Margaret's knee. He recalled the program's signature opening, in which a presenter said, "Are you sitting comfortably? Then I'll begin."

Incredibly, Ronnie remembered the moment, when he was only 3, that Margaret received the news her mother had died. "I remember this telegram boy coming to door, and my mum looking out the window, saying, oh my God, it's the telegram," Ronnie said. "Because, often, if you got a telegram, it was bad news—that somebody died." And so it was in this case, as the telegram informed Margaret of her mother's passing. Ronnie probably retained the memory, he said, because it was a traumatic event.

Patty recalled her brother as shy and introverted. "Ronnie didn't like talking to people, especially adults, and rarely smiled," she said. "This got him disliked by some of the neighbors." Ronnie enjoyed pedaling about in a toy car, given to him by his father. Patty would join him. "We would pedal up and down—along the large, paved area at the back of our house—making up stories about where we were going," she said. Ronnie also had a beloved soft toy. This was a skinny bear that Ronnie called Batty, because, for whatever reason, as a child, he believed the creature looked like a bat. "Batty used to travel everywhere with me, often inside my jacket," Ronnie said. "I don't know where he is now, but I remember still having him up until the early 1980s."

Interestingly, in the period before he entered school, Ronnie's family didn't have companion animals. And there was nothing unusual in their view of non-humans. Neither of his parents, for instance, were anti-vivisectionists or vegetarians. "Each day was a particular meal," Ronnie said. "Sunday would be a Sunday roast. Monday would be what was left over from that. Tuesday would be something else. We'd always have fish on Friday because my mum was Catholic." His father placed a high value on convention when it came to his diet, not even wanting to eat foreign food. "They weren't involved in anything really cruel," Ronnie said of his parents. "But they weren't particularly concerned about animals either."

2

Roebuck Primary School

Ronnie attended Roebuck Primary School in Stevenage, funded by the local education authority, from age 5 to 11, approximately between 1956 and 1962. At first, it was a hard transition for him. "Nowadays, children will go to what's called a preschool or a nursery school," Ronnie said. "They'll maybe start off going just a few hours a week. They're gradually introduced to it." But when Ronnie started school, it wasn't like that. "One minute you're at home with your mum, and the next minute you're at school for the most part of the day," Ronnie said, describing his experience. "It's really quite a shock to the system."

He remembered crying a great deal when his mother dropped him at school. But gradually he grew accustomed to the new environment and routine. "I did well at school, really," Ronnie said. "Once I got over the initial shock of being separated from my mum, I settled into it, and I think I quite enjoyed being there." His sister, Patty, after walking Ronnie to school every day with their mother, Margaret, joined her brother at Roebuck a year later, in the grade below.

During their time in primary school, Ronnie said he suspected Patty might have seen him as dull. "She was more outgoing than me," Ronnie said. "She was more friendly. She was more happy-go-lucky. I was more serious—shyer than she was." He enjoyed collecting things, including stamps, coins, matchboxes, and other items. "She was more interested in outdoor activities," Ronnie said. "Whereas I was more interested in that kind of indoor thing…. I think she thought I was a bit boring, a little bit of a stick in the mud, to be quite honest."

Indeed, certain aspects of his nature did annoy Patty. "When we were given a new board game, Ronnie would spend time reading through the lengthy instructions and would halt the game to check it was being played according to the rules," she said. Similarly, when they played chess, Ronnie

11

would deliberate for so long she would lose patience and do something else.

Still, they were quite close. The siblings even had their own vocabulary. "For some reason, we thought this mop looked like our grandma," Ronnie said. "[So] we called the mop Lou. And we'd talk about Lou. You know, where's Lou? And my parents would think, what the hell are you talking about?" Similarly, there was a scratch on a door, that again reminded them of their grandmother, which they called Lou as well. "We made up different words for things, most of which I can't remember now," Ronnie said.

They played imaginative games together. For instance, the Lees had an inordinately-large, mesh stocking to hold Christmas presents. While he was still small, Ronnie would climb inside this and lie on a mat before the fireplace. "I thought, well, this mat's blue," Ronnie said. "That will be the sea. I'll be a whale in the stocking." Patty would cautiously approach the mat and Ronnie, imagining himself as a killer whale, tried to grab her. They called it the whale game.

Similarly, in the family garden, Ronnie and Patty pretended to be racehorses in the Grand National. "My sister and I used to set this course up and we used to make jumps in the back garden out of broom handles resting on chairs, and things like that," Ronnie said. Later, he would view such competitions as appalling, because of the routine killing of horses involved, but at the time he appreciated the races. "Because our garden was on two levels, it was more interesting," Ronnie said. "We'd be able to go up the hill, and then jump down the rockery and go over the [other] jumps. We used to quite often amuse ourselves doing that."

They collected stamps as well. According to Patty, her brother took this very seriously and she helped buttress his collection. "Occasionally I would swap my stamps with friends and obtain one that Ronnie wanted," she said, adding he would offer her worthless stamps in exchange, featuring butterflies or flowers. "I would hold out for a while, but [ultimately] agree to swap as it wasn't that important to me."

Also during this period, in which he attended Roebuck, Ronnie concocted an elaborate plan—which he and his sister carried out—to steal extra presents from Santa Claus, or Father Christmas, as they called him. "I stretched a trip wire across the stairs," Ronnie said. "And I stretched another trip wire across the bottom of the chimney…. The idea was to trip him up, so he'd fall over, presumably knock him out. Then we'd have all the presents out of his sack that were for the other kids." Of course, Ronnie made the mistake of telling his parents he'd done this, so they were very careful to avoid the trap when depositing gifts. "I was very disappointed the next morning when Santa wasn't lying there," Ronnie said, laughing. "It's quite a wicked thing to do really."

But their mischief extended beyond this. He and his sister stole cherry brandy from their parents' liquor cabinet. "It was very sweet," Ronnie said. "My sister and I used to have a drink of it secretly." They never had enough to get drunk, and probably wouldn't have enjoyed it at all, were it not so saccharine. "I think it was curiosity and because we knew we weren't really supposed to do it," Ronnie said, further explaining the brandy's appeal.

The Lees suffered a number of health problems, in Ronnie's time at Roebuck, such as the one discovered during his first year of school. "I don't know whether this was a problem that arose because I was born prematurely," Ronnie said. "On one of the sides of my neck, I had a tight muscle." As a result, his head was pulled down and to the side—especially when he was tired. Margaret took Ronnie on a bus to see a London specialist, who said the boy needed an operation, which Ronnie didn't want. "My mum kind of conned me, really, that I wouldn't have to be away from home," Ronnie said, adding the prospect of even temporarily leaving Shephall Lane scared him. Of course, when Ronnie arrived at Great Ormond Street Hospital, staff informed him he would need to stay a few days. "They kind of dragged me off, crying and screaming," Ronnie said, laughing.

The next year, Ronnie got in an accident on a tricycle while speeding down a hill. "I fell on my face and broke my front teeth," he said, adding his mouth was filled with gravel and blood. "When my mum cleared the gravel out, she realized two of my teeth were broken. One was slightly chipped, but the other one—half of it was broken." This caused Ronnie a number of dentistry problems. He was provided a plastic cap to cover his broken tooth, which frequently broke and had to be replaced. Additionally, Ronnie said, "my teeth had been knocked backwards a bit, so I had to wear this brace inside my mouth … with this wire on it to push my teeth outwards." He had all of this in his mouth for 2–3 years.

Ron had a number of health issues as well, while his son attended Roebuck. First, he entered a diabetic coma, leading to his diagnosis with diabetes. "He came home one night from work and fell in through the door," Ronnie said, adding his father was sent to the hospital in an ambulance. "He was quite some while in a coma—it was a few days before they got him right." Ron would spend a couple of weeks in the hospital, and would take big doses of insulin for the rest of his life. "Practicing the injection, he had to do it into an orange," Margaret said. Later, Ron suffered severe appendicitis. Again, he was rushed to the hospital in an ambulance, this time to have his appendix removed. "He was in really terrible agony," Ronnie said. "He was more or less rolling around on the floor with that."

Also during this period, Margaret suffered a miscarriage, and was in bed for a week as a result. "I didn't really know," Ronnie said. "It was something more my sister was aware of, rather than me." While Margaret recovered, a woman the Lees knew from church cared for the children. "My dad was no good at cooking or anything like that," Ronnie said, explaining the woman's presence. "She came and looked after us."

In addition, though Patty was generally easy-going in comparison to her brother, she began experiencing panic attacks. "Everything seemed to race in my head and normal voices became louder and faster," Patty said, adding she could make the attacks dissipate by spending time alone. "I would call them 'fasts' as it was the only way to describe them. I tried to say how I felt but I don't think anyone understood."

The school day at Roebuck always began with an assembly in the school hall, at which teachers would make announcements and the children recited prayers. The hall had a sloping floor, from the back to the front. "Quite often, I'd looked down and I'd see piss running along the floor, where a kid behind me had pissed himself," Ronnie said, adding it probably happened about once a week. "I was really worried that it would go on my shoes—it never did."

Ronnie was an anxious child. He recalled himself being intimidated by various forms of seemingly benevolent authority at school, from crossing guards—called lollipop men—to the lunch ladies who monitored children on the playground. As an example of this, he cited a particular meeting with the school's health visitor, who worried him. "She'd take our pulses, listen to our hearts with a stethoscope, and go through our hair to see if there were any lice," Ronnie said, adding she once reported he had a heart murmur. "I went to see the doctor, and when the doctor checked me, they couldn't find anything. They put it down to me being so nervous, so frightened of the health visitor."

One year, Ronnie was cast as one of the three shepherds in Roebuck's nativity play. His father, with the help of his coworkers at English Electric and the equipment there, made Ronnie a lovely, wooden crook to serve as a part of his costume. "I think I only had two words to say in this [play], which I forget," Ronnie said, laughing. "I spent ages learning these words, so worried that I'd get them wrong."

During this period, Ronnie's parents argued frequently about the amount of time Ron spent working. "He'd often come home late," Ronnie said. "My mum used to be annoyed about this…. Maybe she'd have made his dinner and it would be spoiled." Ron had gotten a promotion to junior management, and enjoyed his work. "I'd be running in between them, trying to stop them arguing," Ronnie said, adding he worried they might separate. "Whereas my sister would just go up to her bedroom and play with toys, or, maybe at some stage, listen to a radio…. My sister would try and block it out."

Towards the end of his time at primary school, Ronnie became more aware of the work his father did at English Electric, on guidance systems for nuclear missiles, and it frightened him. "I was really shocked," Ronnie said. "I just knew he went to work at this company and it was to do with engineering." Ronnie recalled attending an open house at his father's work, which featured a buffet and children's games, around a life-size model of the rocket in development. Ronnie disapproved of what his father did, but Ron sought to justify it, telling his son such weapons were necessary to protect Britain from Russia.

This terrified Ronnie. "I used to look up in the sky quite frequently to see if there were nuclear missiles coming along," he said. "I became really paranoid about that." During this period, Ronnie watched a fictional program on television, which began with a 'newsflash' announcing an unidentified, flying object spotted over London. "I immediately thought, oh my God, it's a nuclear bomb," Ronnie said. "And I fainted. I just collapsed."

For all his anxiety, though, Ronnie was at times able to stick up for himself, his family and his beliefs. For instance, when he was about 8, Ronnie was jumping over hurdles that had been set up for an event at school. However, he was approaching the obstacles from the wrong direction, and as a result could have damaged them. Five older girls, perhaps 11 years old, surrounded him, saying Ronnie was in trouble for jumping the hurdles incorrectly, and they were going to take him to the headmaster. "They all grabbed hold of me," Ronnie said, adding he was likely the smallest child in his class. "I just fought my way out—I punched my way out."

In another instance, during this period, he was playing conkers with some other boys. Conkers is a traditional children's game in the United Kingdom, in which two players—having threaded horse chestnuts with string, creating a "conker"—take turns attempting to break their opponent's conker with their own. A school bully approached, and, impressed with the strength of Ronnie's conker, demanded Ronnie hand it over. "I closed my eyes and I just swung for him," Ronnie said. "I knocked him down…. I probably instinctively knew I had to make a stand, although I was frightened and I was only little."

Less dramatically, when the Lees went to visit Lou or she visited them, sometimes Ronnie and Patty were allowed to stay up and watch television, until the transmission ended with the national anthem. "Grandma would make us stand up," Ronnie said. "She'd say, stand for the Queen, stand for the Queen! We'd have to stand and she would be saying, oh, I love the Queen." Eventually, according to Ronnie, he stopped standing.

Similarly, when he was about 10 or 11, a conservative teacher asked Ronnie's classmates what newspapers they had at home. Many of the kids said their parents read right-wing newspapers, like the *Daily Express* and the *Daily Telegraph*. In contrast, Ronnie said his father read the *Daily Mirror*, a left-wing newspaper. The teacher suggested this was a bad publication. "I ended up having an argument with him," Ronnie said. "I think it was more in defense of the family than political… [But] we never liked the conservatives in our house, so there was probably a political aspect to it as well."

Ronnie had a range of interests during this period, but girls, at least in a romantic sense, weren't really one of them yet. "I used to be friends with girls," Ronnie said. "Most of the girls I knew were my sister's friends. [But] I didn't have a girlfriend." This changed slightly during his final years at Roebuck, when he began to develop crushes. "There were some girls in the class where I thought, you know, they look nice or they're nice," Ronnie said. "But it didn't really go further than that."

One of Ronnie and his friends' favorite activities, while they were in primary school, was trainspotting. "In Stevenage, there was an industrial area, where they had all the factories," Ronnie said. "On the way to the industrial area, there was a bridge over the railway line." This location, called the Bailey Bridge, was where Ronnie and his friends would go trainspotting. "You were up on a high embankment and you could look down on the trains," Ronnie said, adding the pastime was particularly exciting in those days because most of the trains were powered by steam. "We had these books—basically, I suppose, trainspotting books—that had all the numbers of the trains. If you saw a particular train, you would put a tick against that number."

Ronnie enjoyed sports, and he was disappointed his father didn't share this enthusiasm, especially after Ron's long hours at English Electric. "When my dad was home from work, he just wanted to rest," Ronnie said. "I used to drag him out sometimes to play sports. But it used to be so arduous trying to get him out of the chair and come out and kick a football." In contrast, fathers of Ronnie's friends were more engaged with athletics.

During this period, Ronnie was fascinated by astronomy. "My dad bought me this telescope for looking at the moon," Ronnie said, adding he mounted the 3-inch refractor onto an open-window frame in his family's living room. "My mum, my dad, and my sister would always complain because I'd do this on a really cold night and they'd be sitting in there freezing." For her part, Patty recalled being intrigued by the telescope as well. "I know my mother hated the cold, but I don't remember complaining myself when the window was open," she said, noting that she loved to use the refractor and think about the wonders of space. "I remember the first time I looked. The moon looked so incredible it made me feel sick." Margaret recalled taking her children to a London planetarium. Despite Ronnie's passion for astronomy, when an arithmetic teacher at his primary school began a discussion about the space race, Ronnie argued against it, on the grounds associated funding could be better spent on Earth.

Perhaps unsurprisingly, given his interest in astronomy, Ronnie was a fan of science fiction. In particular, he loved Quatermass, a British television, radio and film franchise, which debuted in the early 1950s, centered on a fictional scientist battling hostile, alien forces. "My mum wouldn't let me see it, and I'd always nag her, even though I was really frightened of the program," Ronnie said. Meanwhile, Ron was a member of a science-fiction book club, receiving a new title every month. "I don't know whether he really read these books," Ronnie said. "He used to put them in the book case. And I started reading them."

The Lees were a strongly–Catholic family. "Around the house there would be religious icons," Ronnie said. "There would be religious statues that my mum would have, and religious pictures. At one time, I think there was even a bowl attached to the wall of holy water, where you could bless yourself when you came in the house." Margaret would always tell her children what to say in confession, according to Ronnie, and this would usually include them being spiteful, selfish, angry, and disobedient. "And I thought, sometimes, well I haven't really been disobedient," Ronnie said. "But I used to say it anyway."

Ronnie struggled taking communion, which, in the days before the Second Vatican Council, was delivered in Latin. "You weren't supposed to let it touch your teeth," Ronnie said of the host, which Catholics believe to be the body of Jesus Christ. "But it used to get stuck to the roof of my mouth. The thing is, you weren't supposed to leave the altar until you swallowed it, and there were people waiting. I thought, oh my God, I can't bloody get this thing off the roof of my mouth…. You're not allowed to poke it—you're not allowed to poke Christ." Ultimately, after much exertion with his tongue, Ronnie would successfully swallow the wafer.

Interestingly, according to Ronnie, his father—who, again, was raised in the Church of England—grew to become a more passionate Catholic than his mother, in some ways. For instance, at night Ron would pray with his son to a picture of Saint Theresa, when Ronnie wanted to go to bed. At the end of these prayers, Ron would ask the image of Theresa to smile, as a sign his prayers would be answered. "He was looking at this picture to see if she smiled, or if he imagined that she smiled," Ronnie said. "Sometimes, we would be there for ages. I'd be thinking, for fuck's sake, smile, so he'll bugger off and I can get to sleep." Though Ronnie was a believer while in primary school, he still thought this was odd at the time.

Similarly, Ronnie found his mother's prejudice against his Protestant peers to be strange. She would say his non–Catholic classmates were going to hell. "I thought, that can't be right—can it?" Ronnie said. "That kid, who hadn't really done any harm, just because he's not Catholic, is going to burn in the fires of hell?"

Perhaps predictably, given her fire-and-brimstone views, Margaret was the family disciplinarian, not Ron. "If we'd been naughty, my mum would sometimes say, wait until your father comes home," Ronnie said, adding this wasn't a convincing threat because Ron never punished them. "We knew he wouldn't really do anything." The worst Ron did, when he was tired from a day at work and watching television, was throw slippers at his children when they misbehaved. "He couldn't be bothered to get up," Ronnie said, amused. "We used to duck out of the way." If Ron fell asleep on the couch, one of the siblings would tickle his feet, while the other tried to hold him down. "He couldn't stand it, and that's why we did it," Ronnie said. "But he never got cross with us."

Ronnie, about age 7, with father Ron, on a family holiday at Weston-super-Mare (photograph Ron Lee, courtesy Patricia Lee).

Margaret was very concerned with outside opinion, according to Patty, closing the curtains long before the children went to sleep, in order to give the impression she put Ronnie and Patty to bed earlier than she did. "Mum

Ronnie, about age 8, with Patty, on a family holiday at Looe (photograph Ron Lee, courtesy Patricia Lee).

liked to keep our business to ourselves and avoided talking too much to the neighbors," Patty said. "I was always getting into trouble for talking too much and would have to tell her every word I had said. I would get a few sharp smacks, but it wouldn't stop me from being friendly to people."

While Ronnie was at Roebuck, the Lees owned a number of companion animals. The first of these was Sally, a small, black-and-white dog who Ron and Margaret adopted when their son was about 5 or 6. But they found her hard to cope with, and, after only a few months, they either found her a new home or returned her to the rescue center. Ronnie hypothesized his parents might have done this because Sally was boisterous and damaging the Lee's house. "I was fond of her," Ronnie said, "and I was upset that she had to go back."

Later, when Ronnie was about 7, the Lees had a black-and-white rabbit named Frisky, who lived in a hutch at the end of the family's garden, and sometimes allowed to run about the yard. "He wasn't very tame and he used to bite my mum," Ronnie said, adding his mother believed this was a sign of Frisky's frustration with confinement. So one day, Ron and Margaret took him to the local park and let him go. "Whether he would have survived out in the wild, I don't know," Ronnie said. "But I think my mum thought he would." Again, Ronnie was upset.

Approximately a year later, Ronnie received a pair of tumbler pigeons from an older cousin, in Gloucester, who raced pigeons at the time. "They were supposed to be a male and female," Ronnie said, adding they were named Bill and Queenie. "There used to be eggs, but none of them ever hatched. I think, in actual fact, they were both female." Ron built a pigeon loft in a corner of the Lee's backyard, where the pigeons lived. They were free to come and go during the day, but at night Ronnie would shut the loft, so Bill and Queenie wouldn't be attacked by predators. Additionally, he would provide them with fresh water and pigeon corn. These birds were the first animals for whom Ronnie was primarily responsible. "They had, really, quite a nice life," he said.

That same year, the Lees adopted a medium-sized mutt from a Blue Cross rescue center, a few miles from their home in Stevenage. "Because he was a golden color, we called him Sovereign," Ronnie said, adding the name referred to former British currency. A few months after adopting the dog, garbage men were emptying bins nearby, and Sovereign created a commotion. As it turned out, one of the garbage men had been the animal's previous owner. "He'd been the companion of this refuse man, and he'd traveled in the lorry with him," Ronnie said, adding one day Sovereign had run off, leading to his adoption by the Lees. Hearing this, Ronnie was heartbroken, and, in tears, begged the man not to take the dog away. Ultimately, the man agreed.

When Ronnie was about 10, Ron and Margaret purchased a black-and-white, cocker-spaniel puppy, Snowflake, for Patty. "The problem with these breeders is there is a lot of interbreeding," Ronnie said, adding that this effected Snowflake. "If she was a person, she'd be described as having learning difficulties. She wasn't full ticket. And she had a lot of health problems." The Lees paid for multiple operations to address these problems, an expenditure which, according to Ronnie, wasn't particularly unusual at the time. "There would have been some people who would have had Snowflake put down, rather than

Ronnie, about age 7, with his pigeons, Bill (foreground) and Queenie, outside their loft at the Lees' home in Shephall Lane, Stevenage (photograph Ron Lee, courtesy Patricia Lee).

pay the money for the operation," Ronnie said. "But, of course, she was my sister's dog, and we were very fond of her…. So that was never a consideration."

But these weren't the only animals Ronnie came in contact with while attending Roebuck. For instance, Ronnie enjoyed going to the house of another friend, whose family owned a budgerigar, a common pet parakeet.

"You can teach them to talk a little bit." Ronnie said. "This budgie used to swear. It would go, fuck off, and, get out of here.... I used to love going round to [my friend's] house and listen to the budgie."

One day, in Ronnie's primary school years, a racing pigeon with an identification ring landed in the Lee's garden. Ronnie contacted the pigeon association, in charge of racing, which gave him the number of the bird's owner in Kent. When Ronnie called him, the owner advised Ronnie to wring the pigeon's neck. "I said, you horrible man, I'd love to wring your neck," Ronnie said. "I remember saying it on the phone." Ronnie gave the bird to some boys on his road, who raced pigeons and would take care of the animal.

During the same period, the family would visit a zoo and safari park, nearby Stevenage. At the latter attraction, Woburn Safari Park, exotic animals like lions ran loose, so visitors were not supposed to leave their cars. On one occasion the Lees had an interesting run-in with another primate. "A monkey jumped on the bonnet of the car and my dad was laughing," Ronnie said, adding the monkey began assailing the window screens in order to attack Ron. "My dad stopped laughing and became terrified— with the monkey trying to get in! So that was quite amusing."

Occasionally, while in Ronnie's primary school years, the Lees traveled to Northern Ireland, to visit Margaret's younger brother, Denis Tierney, who inherited the family farm in Newtownhamilton. During one such

visit, Denis' greyhound caught a rabbit. Denis was pleased, saying they would eat the animal for dinner. "I was kind of horrified about this," Ronnie said, adding he was an omnivore at the time. "Obviously, we'd had a rabbit as a companion, the one that my mum let go." In addition, an unprepared corpse elicited a more visceral reaction from Ronnie than cooked flesh. "You don't associate the meat with being an animal,"

Ronnie, about age 9, with the family's dog, Sovereign, in their back garden at Shephall Lane (photograph Ron Lee, courtesy Patricia Lee).

he said. "You're not encouraged to think of it that way. So when you actually see the animal, the rabbit that was killed, it's different." Ultimately, the Lees didn't stay for dinner as they were returning to England that day.

One day, during the same period, he was at a friend's house, shooting cans with an air gun. "Then some birds landed in the yard," Ronnie said, adding his friend wanted to shoot the birds. "But he'd run out of ammunition. He said, I'm going to go inside and get some more pellets and shoot these birds. So, when he went indoors, I threw some little stones and frightened the birds away." When Ronnie's friend came back, the birds were gone. Not mentioning his own involvement, Ronnie said the birds had flown off.

Similarly, while Ronnie attended primary school, a friend of his decided to poke a wasp nest with a stick. Ronnie tried to stop him, but to no avail. "These wasps just covered him, and stung him everywhere," Ronnie said. "We took him in the house and he was crying and screaming, stung all over his face, in his hair—everywhere." Ronnie believed his objection to disturbing the wasps was more than just self preservation; he sensed an injustice. "I thought, just leave them alone," he said. "They're not doing any harm. Why do you want to go poking a stick in there?"

Ronnie, about age 10, with his mother, Margaret, and Patty, on a family holiday at Weston-super-Mare (photograph Ron Lee, courtesy Patricia Lee).

According to Ronnie, during the period he attended Roebuck, roughly between 1956 and 1962, from age 5 to 11, he didn't care about animals any more than his peers. "A lot of kids are fond of animals," Ronnie said. "And a lot of my friends were fond of animals—you know, some more than others." Perhaps this is true. But, arguably, we can see signs of the man he would eventually become.

Towards the end of this period, Ron got a new job at International Computers and Tabulators at their premises in Luton and Stevenage. This was a step up for Ron, as he was paid more and given a management position. His son was pleased with the change as well. "I just thought it was wrong for somebody to be working on weapons of mass destruction, really," Ronnie said.

3

Saint Michael's College

Ronnie attended Saint Michael's College in Hitchin, nearby Steve-nage, from age 11 to 18, approximately between 1962 and 1969. At the time, secondary schools were divided between grammar schools, for children who passed the 11-plus exam, and secondary modern schools, for children who didn't. Ronnie, having passed the 11-plus exam, was entitled to go to a grammar school.

"Saint Michael's wasn't the nearest grammar school," Ronnie said. "There were one or two nearer than that. There was a grammar school in Stevenage that a lot of my friends went to. But, you see, Saint Michael's was a Catholic school." His mother, a staunch Catholic, applied for her son to attend Saint Michael's, an all-boy's school about 6 or 7 miles away. Ronnie was accepted, starting at the grammar school in September of 1962.

Though Saint Michael's College was obviously a religious institution, Ronnie's education there was state-funded. "If you passed the 11-plus, it was free of charge," Ronnie said. "But they did allow other boys to go there if their parents paid." Though Ronnie was a day student, the grammar school boasted dormitories where students could live. "There weren't all that many Catholic, secondary schools around," Ronnie said. "Some of the boys may have come from some distance. So they would stay as boarders. They would actually live at the school and just go home at the school holidays." Ronnie took a bus to school, using a free pass provided by the local authority.

During his earlier years at Saint Michael's College, Ronnie was a dili-gent student. His grades always landed him at or near the top of his class. "I always got good reports from school," Ronnie said, adding there were three exceptions to this rule: art and wood working—neither of which he was very good at—and physical education. Despite enjoying soccer and cricket, Ronnie loathed his physical-education instructor. "He was a very nasty piece of work," Ronnie said, adding a frequent activity in the class involved jumping various obstacles. "Because I was only small—I was probably the smallest in the class—I had problems jumping over these things." The instructor verbally abused those students, like Ronnie, who couldn't manage the jump. Once, the instructor even hit Ronnie. "He had a big ring and it made a big mark on my leg," Ronnie said.

Similarly, the instructor would take his class to an outdoor swimming pool, which was very cold. "He would just push people in the water, whether they could swim or not," Ronnie said. "I often used to get my mum to write a note to the school [saying] that I'd had a bad leg or something—trying to get out of the swimming, because I absolutely hated it." When his father bought him a punching bag and boxing gloves, setting the former up in the Lee's garage, Ronnie drew a picture of the instructor which he attached to the bag. "It used to encourage me to hit the punch ball harder," Ronnie said. This instructor was so universally reviled, according to Ronnie, that when it was announced the instructor had been in a car crash—ending his teaching career at Saint Michael's College—students openly celebrated at a school assembly. "All the boys cheered because he was so hated," Ronnie said, adding the instructor's replacement was much nicer.

Intramural sports at the grammar school were organized by houses, named after Catholic martyrs. These weren't physical houses, but, essentially, teams that players were divided amongst. "I was in Fisher House, named after Blessed John Fisher," Ronnie said. "We had a blue vest top and black shorts to play football." Students would play soccer even in snow. "We used to play in, really, quite bad weather conditions," Ronnie said, adding that, during warmer months, students would play cricket.

While attending Saint Michael's College, Ronnie's fears of nuclear annihilation remained strong, and were particularly heightened during the Cuban Missile Crisis in October 1962, despite the fact his father was no longer working on such weapons. Once, during the 13-day standoff, the grammar school's administration held a special assembly to address the issue. "The headmaster said at the assembly, boys, let's all have a moment of quiet now, when we all confess our sins, because this could be the day we all die and the world ends," Ronnie said. "I was absolutely shitting myself. I spent the whole day looking out the window to see if I could see a mushroom cloud."

When he was 14, Ronnie stopped attending Mass with his family. "I just came to the conclusion that it was a load of rubbish," Ronnie said of Catholicism, adding this was a gradual realization. Of course, he still had to attended Mass at school. "I think there were one or two times when I got out of it," Ronnie said, adding he'd hide with other students who wanted to skip the service. "We'd kind of skive off, but you'd get in trouble if you were caught."

As a joke, one day, while reciting the Confiteor in a school Mass, Ronnie pounded his chest with both hands—like King Kong—instead of striking it with a single fist, in penance, as he was supposed to. "All the boys around me were laughing," Ronnie said, adding the priest saw him do it and threatened to report him to the headmaster. However, the priest misheard Ronnie's last name, believing it to be Leaver, instead of Lee. "He obviously went to see the headmaster and said there's a boy called Leaver who'd done this," Ronnie said. "Of course, there wasn't a Leaver. So they weren't able to find who it was and I escaped."

However, he did not always get away unscathed. Once, the headmaster caned Ronnie and others for disrupting a Greek class from the outside. "Along the side of the classroom there were glass panels where you could look out into the corridor," Ronnie said. "We were making faces through the glass panel and kids in the class were laughing." Unfortunately, the headmaster caught them in the act, and brought them up to his study to receive four blows each from his cane. "You'd bend over and he'd hit you on the backside," Ronnie said. "It hurt. There wasn't a lot of mercy with it."

Sometimes, during their lunch break, students, including Ronnie, would play cards on the English teacher's desk. Afterwards, when the teacher came to start class, the students would quickly hurry back to their desks, occasionally, in their haste, leaving the cards behind. Finding these on his desk, the teacher would tear up the cards and throw them in the trash. "So what we started to do was glue the cards onto the teacher's desk," Ronnie said. "He'd spend about half of the lesson in this mad frenzy, trying to rip these cards off the desk."

While attending Saint Michael's College, there was a classmate with whom Ronnie frequently shared his lunch, which Margaret had made. "I think he was quite greedy," Ronnie said. "He'd always try to scrounge sandwiches off me, as well as having his own dinner." One day, as a prank, this classmate put a plastic worm in Ronnie's food, which Ronnie bit into. So when he got home, Ronnie made his classmate a sandwich with every hot ingredient he could find, from mustard to horseradish. The next day, per usual, Ronnie's classmate asked for food. Ronnie made a show of refusing the request, but ultimately agreed, handing his classmate the special sandwich. "He just stuck it straight in his mouth, like he always did, and started scoffing," Ronnie said, laughing. "Then he began coughing, choking, and running around the classroom looking for water."

He and the same classmate wrote poems for charity. The pair would each write a poem and put it up on the school notice board. Underneath each poem would be a receptacle, and the pair would ask their classmates to vote for their favorite poem by putting money in the corresponding container. "It was probably something for children abroad that the money went to," Ronnie said.

In connection with his geography class, Ronnie posted the weather report for nearby Stevenage. "My dad bought me this kit for doing weather forecasting," Ronnie said, adding this included a wind gage, barometer, and other tools. "Every morning I used to check on my equipment and do my weather report. There was a weather report notice board, where we'd all pin our weather reports up. I used to be the one who did the weather report from Stevenage." This report included inches of rain since the previous report, wind speed and other measurements.

Despite his small size, Ronnie said he suffered only one real incident of bullying during this period, after which he was never bothered. "I was just talking to some other boys, and this bully came up and grabbed hold of me," Ronnie said, adding this ended similarly to an earlier confrontation, at primary school, in which another classmate tried to take his conker. "I did the same thing again. I just punched him. And the same thing happened. He went down on the ground and ran off. I never had any trouble from him again either."

While attending Saint Michael's College, Ronnie ran a small business, renting out issues of DC Comics—centered on Superman, Batman, and Green Lantern—to his classmates. "I used to buy these comics," Ronnie said, adding he owned a big collection. "I used to hire them out to kids at school. They could hire them for a penny. They were allowed to keep them for a few days and then they had to give them back." Ronnie said the arrangement was mutually beneficial. "It did us both a favor," Ronnie said. "It made me a bit of money and it saved them [from] buying them."

When Ronnie began paying to eat school lunches, he and his friends had a competition, which they called Gut of the Week, to see who could consume the most. "I was probably the smallest kid in the class, but I used to eat more than any other kid," Ronnie said, adding he won the Gut of the Week competition every time it was held, except once, when he was sick at home. "I used to be able to eat a lot. I don't know what happened to it. Because I didn't put any weight on."

Ronnie didn't have much romantic experience with girls while in grammar school. The most of that sort of interaction he had occurred at the social club associated with the local soccer team. "There was a bar there, and all that kind of thing," Ronnie said. "There was a group of us, boys and girls, that used to go there together. That was sort of my first romantic involvement." This didn't result in anything particularly serious, and he didn't have a girlfriend. "I always used to put my studies first, before anything else," Ronnie said, adding that while he was interested in girls during this period, his mind and priorities were largely elsewhere. "I was into sports. I enjoyed playing sports to some extent, but I enjoyed watching sports as well."

Near the end of Ronnie's time at Saint Michael's College, the grammar school hired a new headmaster, a priest, who questioned some of the Catholic Church's teachings. "He didn't agree that masturbation should be a sin," Ronnie said as an example. "We found this quite amusing that he was saying this." Ronnie said he and his classmates liked this headmaster, who was younger and less conservative than his predecessor. "The problem was, of course, some of the boys went home and told their parents," Ronnie said, adding some parents reported the headmaster to the school governors, who were intent on dismissing him. "So we got a petition up and we all signed." This, however, was ignored by the school governors.

Ronnie was impressed by the political radicalism of students he saw while visiting universities he was interested in attending. "Marxist this and socialist this—all that kind of thing," Ronnie said. "They were selling magazines and giving out leaflets. There was a lot of hubbub going on. It seemed to be very radical. It really struck me." For a Catholic school student, it was quite the culture shock. "A lot of the [university] students would be dressed in hippie-type stuff in those days," Ronnie said. "I thought, wow, am I going to get into that if I come to these universities?" But, in the end, Ronnie didn't do well enough on his A-level exams to attend a university.

While Ronnie attended Saint Michael's College, Patty attended two different schools. After hearing a staff member she had particular distaste for would be her teacher again at Roebuck Primary School, Margaret and Ron sent their daughter to Sacred Heart Convent School in Hitchin. Then, after passing the 11-plus exam, Patty attended Saint Francis College in Letchworth. "My school life became very difficult when I attended Saint Francis College," Patty said. "Although I had earned a scholarship, I felt intimidated by the fee-paying, high-society girls in my class. Most of them were boarders at the school as there parents were diplomats and lived abroad. This effected my confidence and I no longer had much interest in education."

Early in this period, Ronnie and his sister watched *Doctor Who*, a British television show in which there were particular creatures which terrified Patty. "So I got the head of a mop, draped it over my head, dressed myself up as one of these monsters and burst into her bedroom," Ronnie said, adding Patty was so terrified, his mother reprimanded him, saying he could have given Patty a heart attack. "I was kind of quite devilish in that way, really."

Following an obscenity-trial verdict, which allowed more-explicit material to be published in Britain, Ron brought home books of a sexual nature, loaned to him by coworkers. While his wife was not aware of this, his son, apparently, was. "I took my sister's Bible out of its brown-paper cover, and I put this sexual book in," Ronnie said, adding Patty almost got into trouble at school for this, but the nuns ultimately believed her claim of ignorance. "When she came home, she was very angry.... And I was laughing." This was the first Margaret had heard of the books, which she immediately burned—much to Ron's chagrin, as the paperbacks belonged to other men. Hearing this, Margaret said her husband's coworkers needed to be burnt as well, according to Ronnie.

While working for International Computers and Tabulators, during this period, Ron designed a superior high-speed printer, using technology similar to the typeball in IBM Selectric typewriters. He would travel to the United States a number of times to sell the printer to various businesses. "Because he invented it, and because he knew such a lot about it, rather than send someone from the sales team to the United States, they sent him," Ronnie said, adding his father made quite a lot of money from such trips. "He was obviously paid his ordinary wages while he was there, but he also got an allowance to stay in hotels, which he very rarely used." Instead, Ron would stay at the houses of friends.

Ron was actually offered two jobs in the United States, and nearly took one of them, though Ronnie couldn't recall where it was located. "They even had a house lined up for him," Ronnie said. "They even had places lined up for us for schools." But Margaret and didn't want to go, disliking what her husband told her about American sociability. "My dad used to say, oh, it's really friendly," Ronnie said, adding his father claimed Americans from different families frequently shared meals together. "Where a lot of people would have thought that was a good thing, my mum didn't." Patty wanted to go, but Ronnie didn't particularly care either way.

In retrospect, Ronnie wondered how moving to the United States might have effected the course of his life. "The different things that happened over here, that kind of set me off campaigning for animal liberation—would that have happened in the United States?" Ronnie said, noting the British animal movement was more dynamic than its American counterpart. "I don't know. I really don't know."

Ron remained overly dedicated to his work, which had a negative effect on his health. "Because he was now in a management position, he was responsible for what got done and getting things produced in time," Ronnie said, referring to his father's stint at International Computers and Tabulators. "They had a very important deadline to meet, and I think things got behind, and he worked two days and two nights non-stop. He just ended up collapsing from exhaustion and ended up in a hospital."

During this period, when Ron's blood sugar was low, Margaret would burst into her son's room at night, asking for Ronnie's help. "My mum would normally make him a sweet cup of tea, but he hated sugar, because he didn't normally eat sugar," Ronnie said. "So we had to get this into him, but he'd be fighting and swearing, because he wasn't in his right mind." Ronnie helped Margaret administer glucose to his father every couple of months. "I'd have to basically hold my dad down," Ronnie said. "I'd have to kneel on his arms. He'd be shouting and swearing, and trying to shake me off." This was traumatic for Ronnie.

But Ron's hypoglycemia was most frightening to his family when he drove them in a car. When Ron began showing symptoms of diabetic shock, the other Lees would shout at him to stop the vehicle, which he'd refuse to do. "We'd almost be grabbing the steering wheel to pull the car over, because it had an effect on his mind," Ronnie said, adding this was a particularly bad time in his father's struggle with diabetes. "Things weren't in balance, so it was worse."

Ronnie began learning to drive in his father's white Ford Corsair. On one occasion, while Ronnie was practicing under his father's supervision, Ronnie jokingly wondered whether this would be the day he crashed the car. Ron scolded his son for raising the possibility, which turned out to be remarkably prescient. "He wasn't the best of driving instructors," Ronnie said of his father. "He told me to do about six different things, all at the same time." Overwhelmed, Ronnie crashed the Corsair into the side of the road, denting the car. His father drove them home, castigating Ronnie the entire way. "He almost thought we'd crashed because I made the joke about it," Ronnie said. Not wanting his own vehicle to suffer further damage, Ron gave his son an old, black Ford Popular, which he'd purchased for 20 pounds.

Ultimately, the Ford Popular required expensive repairs, so Ronnie sold the vehicle to a man for 5 pounds. "He was kind of a dodgy character," Ronnie said, adding the police came to visit the Lee's house about a week or so later, inquiring about the Popular, which they'd found dumped. "Of course, it was still in my name, because this guy hadn't changed it." Thankfully, Ronnie wasn't prosecuted. He believed the man had purchased the car, believing he could repair it, and finding he couldn't, abandoned the vehicle on the side of the road. After Ronnie had passed his driving test, Ron purchased another used car for his son, who was, again, without a vehicle. This time it was an Austin Mini, which cost 100 pounds.

During his years at Saint Michael's College, Ronnie had a number of small jobs. One of these was at the social club, associated with the local soccer team, which he visited with friends. "It was basically washing up the beer glasses from the bar," Ronnie said, adding he preferred this to working on the club's dance floor, which was too noisy for his taste. "I don't think I got paid a lot for it." His father also got him a job working at International Computers and Tabulators. "Because he was in management, he could pull a few strings," Ronnie said. "I was taking components off a circuit board with a soldering iron ... so they could use them again." Finally, Ronnie received commission for selling lottery tickets door to door.

After selling tickets, one of Ronnie's friends would buy lager, despite being under the legal drinking age. "They would serve him, because, although he was probably only about 15 or 16, he looked 18," Ronnie said, adding he appeared younger than his friend. "I'd hide around the corner." The pair would return to the Lee's house and find the complimentary cigarettes Ron received on business trips. "My dad didn't smoke those," Ronnie said. "So he'd just, basically, put these cigarettes in the cupboard." Ronnie and his friend would drink the lager, smoke the cigarettes, and play poker for pennies. Margaret and Ron turned a blind eye to this. "They knew we were doing it," Ronnie said. "I think they thought we were safer at home." Ron sometimes received sherry as a gift from business partners. Because of his diabetes, he couldn't drink it. But Ronnie could and did. "I used to swig it down, just in one," he said. "Then I'd spin around, because that would make me feel more drunk."

At the beginning of Ronnie's time at Saint Michael's College, the Lees moved to a new house in Stevenage, on Fellowes Way. This was more costly than their previous home on Shephall Lane, only about half a mile away. "Where we lived on Shephall Lane was semi-detached," Ronnie said. "In other words, it was joined onto another house, if you see what I mean. Whereas the house on Fellowes Lane stood on its own, obviously a more expensive property."

Ronnie's pigeons, Bill and Queenie, were lost in the move, when his mother refused to bring their loft to Fellowes Way, viewing it as an eyesore. "My dad got this dovecote for them to roost in, which is a much smaller construction," Ronnie said, adding he wasn't happy about this. In particular, Ronnie was worried that because the new house wasn't very far from the old one, his pigeons would return to Shephall Lane. His parents' plan was to keep Bill and Queenie in a large crate, for a couple weeks, in the hope Bill and Queenie would grow accustomed to Fellowes Way and not go back to the old house.

"But that didn't actually work," Ronnie said, adding that when the birds were released, they disappeared. So Ronnie went looking for them on Shephall Lane. "I think I saw one of them, but I wasn't able to catch the one that I saw," Ronnie said. "Somebody said that they thought they'd found the body of the other one, that had been killed by a cat or something. All of that was rather vague. But they never came back again." Ronnie was devastated by this, and ignoring signs of the bird's passing, hoped the pair were living in contentment somewhere else. "I was angry with my mum and dad," Ronnie said. "I thought they should have been more responsible."

Of course, the Lee's dogs, Snowflake and Sovereign, made the trip to Fellowes Way. Also, during the time Ronnie was in grammar school, the Lees briefly owned a guinea pig named Ozzie, who they adopted from a

Ronnie, about age 16, with Patty, and Sovereign, in the back garden of the Lee family home at Fellowes Way, Stevenage (photograph Ron Lee, courtesy Patricia Lee).

friend of the family. "He had a run in the garage," Ronnie said. "He used to come outside when it was a nice day." But one of Ron's coworkers took a liking to Ozzie, and asked if he might keep the animal, to which the Lees agreed. This decision didn't particularly effect Ronnie. "I think, at the time, my sister and I were getting older and were interested in other things," he said.

Because of the grammar school's Catholicism, on Fridays, Ronnie and his fellow classmates would go to a nearby restaurant to get fish and chips. "To go to the fish-and-chips shop, we had to go past the local abattoir," Ronnie said. "I remember the sound of the animals, the cries of the animals. I used to always hate it." Similarly, Ronnie's walk to the bus station required he pass a tanning factory. "There was the most horrible, sweet smell that used to come from this place," Ronnie said. "My nostrils used to be full of that as I walked back to catch the bus."

Despite his discomfort, at the time, Ronnie, who still ate meat, believed killing animals was inevitable. "Obviously, I must have known that animals were being killed, because I'd heard their cries in the abattoir," Ronnie said. "I suppose I just thought that they had to be killed—that it was necessary. Because I hadn't really heard of anyone being a vegetarian or anything like that. It was just one of those sad facts of life. But I didn't find it very pleasant."

While Ronnie attended Saint Michael's College, his father started taking him fishing. "My dad had a fishing rod, which he hadn't used for years," Ronnie said, adding Ron purchased him a rod and the pair started fishing in local rivers and a nearby reservoir. "I took a dislike to it, because it didn't seem right to me about the hook going through the fish's mouth. I suppose I came to the conclusion it was cruel." Ronnie stopped going, informing Ron of his reasoning. "He was fine with it," Ronnie said. "He used to just take me for something to do, really. So when I said I didn't want to go, he probably thought he could just have more time watching television."

On a visit to Woburn Safari Park, the Lees witnessed a guide use an oar to club a seal attempting to climb aboard their tour boat, where a bucket of dead fish was kept. "I immediately had a go at him," Ronnie said, referring to the guide. "I said, what the hell are you doing, you cruel so-and-so? I think I swore at him." Everyone else in the boat sat in silence, as Ronnie threatened to report the guide and make sure he lost his job. "[Ronnie] shouted at him," Margaret said. True to his word, Ronnie phoned up the park administration the next day and told them about the incident, over his parents' objections. "They said, we'll treat this very seriously, and we'll look into it, " Ronnie said. "Whether they did or not, I don't know."

A few years later, while walking Sovereign at Shephalbury Park, Stevenage, Ronnie spotted the caretaker of a nearby school mistreating an animal. "He had an Old English Sheepdog, and he was viciously beating this dog with the dog's lead," Ronnie said, adding he quickly confronted the caretaker. This culminated in Ronnie uttering the most horrific threat he could imagine. "I said to him, if I see you beating that dog again, I'll pour petrol over you and I'll set fire to you," Ronnie said. "I verbally attacked him to such a degree that he was actually shaking." The next day, Ronnie got news the caretaker had died of a heart attack the night before, which didn't phase the teenager one bit. "I said, good, I'm pleased he died," Ronnie said, adding he didn't know if the timing of the attack was coincidental. "I wasn't sorry for him at all."

Similarly, while vacationing in the seaside village of Blackrock, Ireland, Ronnie came across some children selling crabs to eat. "I persuaded my dad to buy one of these crabs," Ronnie said. "I went and released the crab back into the sea." He found it disturbing these animals would be boiled alive. In retrospect, Ronnie said he knew such seemingly merciful purchases only encouraged further animal exploitation. And he wasn't sure where this early passion came from for defending animals. "I don't really know," Ronnie said. "Obviously it came from somewhere, but I don't really think it came from my parents. There wasn't anything about them that was like that."

4

Vegetarianism
and Working Life

In the summer of 1969, shortly after Ronnie left grammar school at the age of 18, Sovereign died. Margaret called the dog inside for his dinner, but he didn't come. "She looked over the fence and he was lying in the field," Ronnie said. "So she shouted to me and I went over the fence." Examining Sovereign, Ronnie knew there was something seriously wrong with the 10-year-old animal. "Between us, we managed to get him back into the house and we called the vet," Ronnie said. "The vet came and he ended up being taken into the veterinary surgery." Sovereign was diagnosed with a ruptured spleen, with significant internal bleeding. The veterinarian wasn't able to save him.

"It was kind of a mystery how this had occurred," Ronnie said, noting the Lees asked if their dog might have been by a car. "The vet said, well I don't think so. The area of the injury isn't big enough. It's more like somebody kicked him." Ultimately however, the veterinarian didn't know what caused Sovereign's injury. The Lees were totally devastated. "I remember my mum throwing herself on the floor with grief," Ronnie said, adding this was a feeling the family shared. "It was really traumatic. Often with animals, they grow old and they may end up having to be put to sleep to stop them suffering. You get a period to get used to the fact those animals are going to die." This was obviously not the case with Sovereign. As Ronnie put it, one moment he was a healthy dog and the next moment he died.

"He'd become a really wonderful dog," Ronnie said of Sovereign while the Lees lived at Fellowes Way. "When we had him at Shephall Lane, he wasn't very well behaved. He'd run away; he'd fight with the dog up the road; and he hated people in uniform." This all changed when the Lees moved to Fellowes Way. Ronnie wasn't sure if this was merely a function of Sovereign getting older, but the dog mellowed. "If we were going somewhere quiet, we could take him for a walk—[and] he didn't need to be on the lead," Ronnie said. "He'd come back as soon as he was called. He became, absolutely, a real pleasure."

Perhaps mercifully, Snowflake, the Lee's pedigree cocker spaniel, did not take Sovereign's death particularly hard. "She did not have any kind of relationship with Sovereign," Ronnie said, speculating this resulted from her low intelligence, produced by inbreeding. "Snowflake would be just quite happy sniffing around the garden and doing her own thing. Sovereign would be off playing with his friend." He had a much closer relationship with the dog who lived next door. Snowflake died of kidney failure a couple of years later, according to Patty.

Shortly after Sovereign died, one of Ronnie's friends showed up on the Lee's doorstep with a puppy. "We weren't intending to get another dog, at least straight away," Ronnie said. "We were still grieving." But Ronnie's friend thought the black mutt might cheer the Lees up. The family adopted the dog, calling her Mandy. This addition helped Ronnie manage his grief over losing Sovereign. "I loved her very much and used to play with her and everything," Ronnie said.

At approximately the same time, the Lees adopted a kitten. The animal originally belonged to the neighbor's daughter, who quickly lost interest in her. "The kitten kept coming over our garden fence," Ronnie said, noting Patty grew especially fond of the visiting cat. "My parents asked the people next door, would it be okay if we adopted the kitten? And they said, yeah." The Lees called the tortoiseshell-and-white animal Toots. Mandy and Toots, who were about the same age, got along fabulously. "We used to love watching them play," Ronnie said. "They grew up together."

That summer, Ronnie and a friend decided to embark on a road trip across Ireland in Ronnie's Austin Mini. With the car's roof rack piled high with their belongings, the pair set off, taking a ferry from Stanraer, Scotland, to Larne, Northern Ireland. "We had a really big culture shock, when we drove from Larne into Belfast, because the Troubles in Ireland had begun," Ronnie said. "There was some civil unrest and there'd been some rioting. The troops had just been sent over there." Ronnie was stopped by British soldiers, but as soon as the men heard Ronnie's English accent they allowed him to pass.

Signs of the ethno-nationalist struggle were everywhere. "I remember one road, where there was four or five burnt-out baker's vans, all turned over on their side," Ronnie said, adding they were used as a barricade. "All these baker's vans were from the same company. So I felt really sorry for the baker.... Obviously it must have ruined that business." Flags and painted slogans, indicating opposing loyalties, lined the streets. Ronnie knew there was trouble in Northern Ireland, but this was the first time he grasped the extent of it. "I was surprised at the military presence," he said. "I was surprised at the scenes of damage that there was there from the civil unrest."

Still, Ronnie's sympathy had always been with the Republicans, a feeling he traced to his mother's Catholicism. "My mum wasn't a staunch Republican," Ronnie said. "She wasn't really politically-minded. But she hated the Unionist side." Growing up, Margaret would tell her son about repression carried out by the Ulster Special Constabulary—a Protestant, quasi-military force, with a particularly vicious reputation. "I was much more aware of the situation in Ireland than most of my friends were, because they didn't have anyone in their family who was connected with that," Ronnie said, adding that while Margaret's family wasn't directly involved in the Republican struggle, they knew many people who were.

When Ronnie and his friend left Belfast, though, signs of the conflict became much less ubiquitous. "Even before we left Northern Ireland, we had a bit of a crisis," Ronnie said, describing his car skidding into a ditch. "To get the car out, we had to take all the luggage out of the car to make it lighter, then take it all off the roof rack, remove the roof rack, and make the car as light as possible." After all this, the pair finally managed to push the Mini out of the ditch, before repacking the luggage and continuing on their journey.

Ronnie and his friend, having crossed into the Republic of Ireland, began camping at seaside locations. "We kind of went around the coast," he said. "We went to Donegal. We went to another place called Sligo, and we went to a soccer match there." Following this, the pair travelled to Galway and then Connemara, where their tent was destroyed on Achill Island. They had only needed a two-person tent, but this friend had borrowed luxury, family tent from relatives. Due to its size, the tent was less resistant to wind than a smaller tent would have been. "There was this tremendous storm in the night," Ronnie said. "We both woke up in the morning with the tent on top of us—all of the tent poles buckled and broken."

This put an abrupt end to Ronnie and his friend's ability to camp outside. So, for a few days, they stayed in a rented caravan in Galway. "We'd spend our time playing cards and going out," Ronnie said. "We still had the car obviously. We were able to go around the local area. But our plan to go around the whole of the coast camping was scuppered." Finally, the pair travelled back to Northern Ireland, where they briefly stayed with some of Ronnie's extended family in Crossmaglen, before heading back to England. Only a few miles from home, the loaded roof rack on Ronnie's car blew off, and bounced down the motorway. "We had to stop, pull over onto the hard shoulder, and I had to run back and retrieve all this stuff," Ronnie said, laughing. "There wasn't as much traffic in those days. It would be a nightmare if that happened now."

Despite the setbacks he encountered, Ronnie believed this trip was a step toward greater autonomy for him. "It was the first time I'd been on a holiday like that without my parents," Ronnie said. "So I think that kind of helped me with independence. It was enjoyable. It also gave me an insight into how serious the situation was in Northern Ireland." Still he was happy to be back, and laid on the floor to greet Mandy, who jumped all over him.

It was about then that Ronnie received the results of his A-levels, which were disappointing and meant he couldn't attend a university. Still, there was a possibility he could pursue a career as a solicitor. "What they called it was taking articles," Ronnie said. "It meant you signed a contract with a firm of solicitors, and they would take you on as what was called an articled clerk. They were supposed to train you, and then you would go to college and take exams. After five years from the date that you signed articles, if you passed your exams, you would then become a qualified solicitor."

Ronnie didn't have a burning desire to follow any particular career path at that point. But his parents wanted Ronnie to work as a professional, and he was good at English, Latin, and mathematics, which he thought would translate best into a solicitor job. "They weren't particularly science-based subjects," Ronnie said. "And the maths is handy in terms of being a solicitor because you have to know accounts—accounting is part of it." Ron and Margaret were pleased by their son's decision to pursue an articled-clerk position, because solicitors often boasted prestige and comparatively-high remuneration. "It was a way that I could eventually get a well-paid job without having secured very-good qualifications in school," Ronnie said.

He began writing letters to dozens and dozens of local law firms. Some refused Ronnie outright, but others demanded he pay to work. "They weren't going to pay me a wage, because they were training me," Ronnie said. "That was costing them money, so they wanted my dad to pay them money to take me on." This was simply not financially feasible for the Lees, and made for a frustrating period for Ronnie, as he spent months writing firms and taking Mandy for long walks. "I didn't get any sort of other job, became, of course, I thought that at any moment I might get a letter through the post saying I could start work," Ronnie said.

It was also during this period, while he searched for a job, that Ronnie became a vegetarian. Patty was dating a fellow student at Stevenage College. "I remember my mum saying, your sister has an even worse bloke now than the previous two," Ronnie said, adding he asked his mother what was wrong with Patty's boyfriend. "She said, oh, this one's a weirdo. I said, why's that? She said, he's one of these bloody vegetarians." This intrigued Ronnie, as he hadn't really heard of vegetarians before. So Ronnie discussed the issue with Patty, who said her boyfriend was a vegetarian of many years, and didn't believe in killing animals.

This rationale struck a chord with Ronnie, and was harder to ignore because Patty's boyfriend, who represented the county in track-and-field events, was so clearly healthy on a meat-free diet. "I thought, well, it hasn't done him any harm," Ronnie said. "If he'd looked really ill and hadn't looked healthy, I'd have thought, it's obviously not doing him any good—we're meant to eat meat." Ronnie struggled with the vegetarian argument, trying to justify his continued omnivority. "I spent about three nights staying awake thinking about this, and it playing on my mind, and me trying to find some excuse to carry on eating meat," he said, adding that only a few days after speaking to his sister, he gave up and decided to become a vegetarian.

This was welcome news for Patty, who was interested in becoming a vegetarian as well, but was worried about her mother's reaction. When Ronnie and his sister went in the kitchen for breakfast one morning, Margaret asked what they'd like to eat. "Normally we'd have egg and bacon for breakfast, or something like that," Ronnie said, adding he answered they would have cornflakes. "Straight away, my mum twigged it. She said, oh no, don't tell me that crank's gotten to you. Don't tell me you've become bloody vegetarian." According to Ronnie, when he confirmed both he and his sister were now vegetarian, Margaret told them to eat the grass in the backyard, which needed cutting. "I was terribly uncomfortable with it," Margaret said, referring to her children's vegetarianism.

"My mum had been brought up in a very traditional way, where eating animals went without question," Ronnie said, before noting Margaret did end up cooking her children flesh-free meals. "Invariably, these things would still contain animal products. They wouldn't contain meat or fish, but there would still be animal products in the things that she made. So whether or not we helped save any animals by going vegetarian I think is quite doubtful." At the time, Ronnie was not aware of the slaughter and suffering created by the egg and dairy industry. He believed, for instance, that cows needed to be milked.

Margaret continued to mock her children's vegetarianism and complain about having to cook separate meals, but eventually she accepted Ronnie and Patty's choice. "My dad didn't really say anything," Ronnie said. "As long as he could go to work [and] watch the telly, he wasn't that bothered. I don't think he particularly liked it, that we were vegetarian. But it didn't annoy or upset him as much as it upset my mum." Ronnie's life was largely the same after becoming vegetarian. He still attended soccer matches and went to the associated club with friends, who teased Ronnie about his decision. There was no fundamental shift in his long-term goals or social circle.

While Ronnie looked for work, his father also began to drink alcohol in a manner which concerned his family. "Pubs started stocking a lager called pils," Ronnie said, adding pilsner had a comparatively-low sugar content, which allowed his diabetic father to drink it. "So he went a little bit crazy on it." Ronnie suspected this was because for years his father hadn't been able to drink at all. "He'd be driving his car and drinking," Ronnie said. "I used to worry, because I thought, well, he's not safe to drive. He's gone and drank this beer and it's quite strong. He never crashed, but it was always a real worry." Ronnie noted this was at a time in which drunk driving was not prohibited the way it would be later. While Ronnie didn't think his father was an alcoholic, his mother was concerned by Ron's behavior as well. "My mum wasn't very happy about it," Ronnie said. "Sometimes he became argumentative when he'd had a drink. He didn't become violent or anything."

After a long search, in early 1970, Ronnie accepted a job at Machin and Company, a solicitor firm in nearby Luton, where he was paid 5 pounds a week. "I very much enjoyed it there," Ronnie said, adding he was the youngest male worker. "There were quite a lot of young women—you know, the secretaries and women doing other jobs." This was a change Ronnie appreciated after having attended an all-boys school. While firms were supposed to train their article clerks, for the most part, Ronnie just received tasks no one else wanted. For instance, Ronnie would sit in court on the solicitor's behalf. "There would be no point in my boss going, because he'd done his part of the work," Ronnie said. "So he used to send me to go and just sit behind the barrister and take notes. Because it wasn't worth his while."

This was fine with Ronnie, as he made more from the travel expenses he was provided than his wages. "I used to get paid a shilling a mile," Ronnie said. "This added up, because some court cases would last for a week and I'd be going every day. The allowance was more than it cost for the petrol." The court cases were generally uninteresting, despite assumptions to the contrary, because of the repetition involved. "Even the most interesting case can actually become boring," Ronnie said, noting he attended robbery, fraud and other sorts of cases. He remembered a particular case regarding a parking offense. Ronnie had been out with friends the night before and fell asleep in court, which led to a public scolding from the judge. "I was quite embarrassed at the time," Ronnie said, laughing. "I woke up and everyone was looking at me."

While in the office, Ronnie would socialize on the third floor with secretaries and other workers. On one occasion, he spilled a boiling cup of coffee on his lap, which caused him a great deal of pain. Unfortunately, the bathroom—the nearest source of cool water—was in the basement. "So I had to run all the way down from the third floor to the basement, with this boiling-hot coffee that had gone through to my balls," Ronnie said. "I had quite a burn down there from it. Of course, when I came back upstairs, they were all rolling around laughing. They were saying, you'll be no use to anyone now."

Ronnie didn't have a steady, romantic relationship during this period. "I loved to kiss and cuddle with girls, and maybe a little bit more," Ronnie said. "I wasn't really into going out with anyone as a serious girlfriend." He thought this was because he prioritized hanging out with male friends at the time. "I was very much into going around with my mates really," Ronnie said, noting they enjoyed playing cards and attending soccer matches. "Occasionally, one of them would get a girlfriend, and then they'd be saying, well, I can't come tonight; I can't come to this; I can't come to that.... I thought, I don't want to be like that." And there was no pressure from his parents to settle down.

Ronnie was frequently tasked with making photocopies in the basement, where two of his female friends worked. "I'd have a really good laugh with them," Ronnie said. "We were all very fond of each other." Unfortunately, an older receptionist was a bit of a busybody, and would deliberately leave the intercom on between reception and the print room, so she might eavesdrop on the younger women's conversation. Ronnie and his friends working in the basement hated this. "We thought, next time I come down here, we'll give her something really good to listen to," he said, adding the group pretended—for the sake of the receptionist listening—to have wild sex. "We were thinking of the most dirty things to say." According to Ronnie, the receptionist was unable to report what she heard, because doing so would reveal her misuse of the intercom.

In 1970, both Mandy and Toots were pregnant, as Margaret and Ron were not diligent in getting their animals spayed. "They left it too long," Ronnie said. "It's a common mistake. People don't understand how young dogs and cats can actually get pregnant." Mandy had nine puppies, with Patty assisting in the birth. "When the puppies come out, they're covered in a membrane," Ronnie said. "The mother licks the membrane and gets them breathing, but there were so many [Mandy] wasn't able to cope with it." Patty tore the membrane and got the puppies suckling, saving a number of lives, according to her brother. "We found homes for all them," Ronnie said. "I homed one of them with one of the young women at work who was in the print room."

Meanwhile, Toots had three kittens. One of them was born without a tail and only lived a few hours. Ronnie was very upset, and took the dead animal to a veterinarian, who said the kitten hadn't properly developed. "His organs weren't right," Ronnie said. "That's why he died." The Lees kept the other kittens, who they named Timmy and Pickle. Both were male tabbies. Margaret and Ron were okay with keeping the kittens because they were less work than puppies.

In 1971, Ron grew interested in horse riding, after being exposed to the activity by his secretary and her husband. "Sometimes my dad used to go with them to the stables," Ronnie said, adding his father would pay to ride. "He bought all the equipment. There was one particular horse that he was fond of that he used to ride all the time, and he ended up buying this horse." Ron frequently went to the stables to care for the animal, called Noah, who he saw as a status symbol. Ron spoke frequently about Noah in a conspicuous manner. "It used to amuse me," Ronnie said. "I used to quietly laugh, really. We'd be with a group of people, and he'd start saying, I have a horse and I enjoy riding. I thought he was bragging a bit."

One day, Ron returned to the house covered in mud, with cuts on his face, holding a broken riding crop. He explained Noah had thrown him off before rolling on top of him. Ronnie thought Noah's behavior was hilarious. "I said, well, he wanted to make sure, didn't he?" Ronnie said, adding he roared with laughter. "My dad said, it's not funny—it's not funny! I could have been killed." This incident was a blow to Ron's confidence, and afterward he sold Noah and stopped riding.

In March of 1971, Patty gave birth to a boy named Anthony. Her vegetarian boyfriend was the father. "My mum and dad were quite distressed about it," Ronnie said, adding in particular Margaret worried what people would think of Patty, an unwed mother. "While my sister was pregnant, my mum made sure she hardly went out, or—if she went out—she wore a big coat. Because my mum was terrified of the neighbors seeing [Patty] was pregnant." Immediately after Anthony's birth, Margaret arranged for him to be put in foster care. "I was absolutely heartbroken when Anthony was

taken from me," Patty said, noting she was only 18 years old. "I had a Cae-
sarian operation and cared for him brilliantly for two weeks." Margaret
hoped the baby would be adopted, while Patty planned to get Anthony
back, visiting him in foster care every day. "The woman who was fostering
Anthony was very sympathetic to Patty," Ronnie said. "She understood
that Patty was at some stage going to have him back and that he wasn't
going to go for adoption." Patty regained custody of her son in June.

By this point, Margaret and Ron temporarily separated. "My mum
and dad's relationship had been getting worse," Ronnie said, adding his
father moved out to live with a work colleague in Hitchin. "I thought it was
a shame. I did feel sad they felt they had to separate. But I noticed they'd
been arguing a lot." Had he been younger, Ronnie would have been devastated. But now he had a life of his own, and to some degree saw his parents' split as a good thing for both Margaret and Ron. "I felt there were
probably faults on both sides," Ronnie said, noting he didn't favor one parent during the split. After Ron moved out, he sold the Lee's house on Fellowes Way, in Stevenage, and bought a smaller house in Meppershall, where
his wife, children, grandchild and five animals lived. It was a two-bedroom
bungalow, with Ronnie getting his own space—while Margaret, Patty, and
Anthony shared a room. "My dad would still pay, but I think my mum actually did get a job," Ronnie said. "She went to work at a supermarket for a
while."

During this period of marital conflict, Ron launched a company called
Data Controls, though he still worked at International Computers and Tabulators, by then known as International Computers Limited. "He designed
some sort of clutch mechanism for engines," Ronnie said. "While he'd been
working at all these firms, and designing different things, they used his
designs to make profit for themselves. And he thought, well, I'm going to
make some money myself out of one of my designs." Ron opened his own
office, but ultimately the plan fell through, likely because of investment
problems, according to his son.

In early 1972, Patty and Anthony moved out of Meppershall to live
with Patty's boyfriend. "We lived in Hitchin for a short while until we
were allocated a council house in Stevenage," Patty said. She also married
her boyfriend, with her future mother-in-law making the arrangements.
"They got married at the register office in Stevenage," Ronnie said, noting
the groom's parents were the only ones in attendance. "My parents didn't
go to it. I didn't go either—I think I had to work that day or something. It
was on a weekday and I wasn't able to go." The low-key nature of Patty's
wedding made him sad. Ron and Margaret deliberately skipped the event

because they disapproved of the groom. "He got Patty pregnant," Ronnie said, explaining his parents' distaste. However, Patty said there was more to it than that. "My parents did not like my boyfriend because they could see he was a jealous and controlling person," she said. "I was frightened of him, as he became violent after a while. I was not able to understand or deal with his behavior."

Shortly after Patty moved out of Meppershall, Margaret and Ron reconciled. This simply hadn't been possible before, as the Lee's house had no space for Ron. "I think my dad got in touch with my mum and said, look, I'd like to come back," Ronnie said, adding he believed his father had grown sick of living with his colleague. Margaret had her own reasons to reconcile. "She was too embarrassed to say that she had split up from her husband," Ronnie said. "She'd told the neighbors that she was married, but her husband was working away from home. Of course, after a while, the neighbors started wondering, where is your husband? When is your husband coming home? My mum thought, well, what am I going to do? Because I can't keep this charade up." Margaret agreed for Ron to come back on that basis. Ronnie didn't particularly care that his parents reconciled, and was under no illusions about what it meant. "I knew it wouldn't turn into an affectionate relationship," Ronnie said. "I knew they would still not get on very well, even though he was living there."

Ron continued to drink pilsner in excess, and Margaret often tasked Ronnie with retrieving his father for dinner from a nearby bar, after she'd phoned the establishment in vain. This was an arduous process which Ronnie loathed. "I'd go to the pub and say, Dad, you need to come home," Ronnie said. "He'd say, oh, I'll just have another pint. And I'd say no, Dad, you've got to come. I sat there ages with him. He'd say to me, you have a drink. And I'd say, no, no, no, I've come to bring you home." Ronnie knew if he didn't succeed in bringing his father home, he would be in trouble as well. "It used to be real torture trying to drag him out of the pub," Ronnie said, adding, in the end, he and his father would be about two hours late for dinner.

5

Veganism and the Hunt Saboteurs Association

In the period lasting from the spring of 1972 to the summer of 1973, for the first time, Ronnie became truly aware of the scope of animal suffering, and his life changed accordingly. In his early 20s, he kept incredibly busy—juggling activism, work, school, and family commitments.

In early 1972, Ronnie took time off from Machin and Company to begin studying for the first part of the Law Society's examinations. "I went down to the College of Law in London for lectures," he said, adding he attended classes on a number of subjects. "I know in part one there was criminal law. There was contracts. There was what you called tort, which is where you sue somebody for damages." This was just a selection of the subjects he learned. The institution had guidelines indicating how much work an average student would need to complete to pass the first examination. "I calculated that the amount of work I would have to do, according to the guidelines, was eight hours a day, every day of the week," Ronnie said, adding this was in addition to the time spent in lectures.

He worked doggedly to hit this mark. So, if he didn't complete eight hours of studying one day, those missed hours would carry over into the next day. "I would just do as much as I could—within reason," Ronnie said. "Some days, I might do 11 hours, which meant the next day I didn't have to do so much. I'd study on the train going to and from London." He attended lectures at the College of Law about three or four days a week, while much of the remainder of his time was spent studying at the Lee's house in Meppershall. "I was determined to pass these exams and do well," Ronnie said, adding his small bedroom had essentially become a study. "I organized my time very, very carefully." Unsurprisingly, this had an effect on Ronnie's social life. He rarely saw his friends.

That said, one day he took a break from his studies and traveled to Stevenage, where he saw a health-food store advertising vegetarian food. This intrigued Ronnie. "Obviously I'd been eating vegetarian food that my mum had been cooking up—which might just have been a fried egg, or something made from cheese, or something she'd bought in the supermarket which happened to be vegetarian," Ronnie said, noting these meals were incidentally flesh-free. "I thought, what does vegetarian food mean? Is that something I don't know about?" So he went inside and bought some items which weren't available at the supermarket. But more importantly, he purchased a copy of the Vegetarian Society magazine, which exposed him to broader animal-rights concerns.

"I got home, and when I had a chance I started reading this magazine," Ronnie said, adding he learned from this one issue about vivisection, factory farming, hunting, and other forms of animal abuse. "There were either articles about these subjects or adverts from national societies that campaigned against these things." There was also mention of the Vegan Society, which made Ronnie aware of violence involved in dairy and egg-production. He'd never heard the term vegan before, and suddenly his vegetarianism felt insufficient. "I was kind of rattled to the core," Ronnie said, noting he was overwhelmed by the amount of animal exploitation not directly related to meat production. "Once you realize that, you know you have to make a much more fundamental life change—or I felt that."

Ronnie immediately wrote to the organizations named in the magazine, including the Vegan Society, for more information. "Over the course of the next few days, all these letters began arriving," Ronnie said, adding he joined these organizations—from the British Union for the Abolition of Vivisection to the League Against Cruel Sports—using the wage he still received from Machin and Company. "One of the first things I read was the information from the Vegan Society, about the importance of being vegan and the reasons for being vegan." Ronnie vowed to become vegan, and, following the instructions provided by the organization at the time, did so gradually.

This advice proved to be more difficult to follow than simply going vegan. "I started trying to do that, and thinking, well, I'll have less milk today or I won't have an egg today," Ronnie said. "But I found it really complicated." After a few days he just became vegan, at which point he finally told his mother about the change. Predictably, given her reaction to Ronnie going vegetarian, Margaret was not pleased. "She said to me, you've just gone completely mad now," Ronnie said, adding Margaret refused to cook or pay for vegan meals. "She said, you'll be dead within a year." Ron had a similar, if less pronounced, reaction, blaming Patty's vegetarian husband for the shift in Ronnie's thinking.

About 10 days later, Ronnie walked into the Lee's kitchen and caught Margaret breaking an egg into the food he was cooking. "I said, oi, mum, what are you doing?" Ronnie said, adding Margaret knew he didn't want to eat eggs. "She turned around and said, I've been breaking an egg into it for the last week; I'm keeping you alive." Following this, he kept a close watch on his simmering food, despite securing a promise from Margaret not to add animal products to what he ate. "She said, all right, I won't do it anymore—if you die, you die," Ronnie said, amused by his mother's mortal fear.

At the time, explicitly-vegan options were few and far between. "A lot of the vegan products were actually made for the Jewish community," Ronnie said, noting he consumed many kosher products which were free of animal ingredients. For instance, he used a kosher margarine, called Tomor, and ate kosher ice cream made by a company called Snowcrest. "If a Jewish person wants a beef sandwich, they can't have butter on the bread," Ronnie said, referring to strict Jews. "They have to have vegetable margarine. And if they have a dinner that contains beef or chicken, then, if they have a dessert, that can't contain milk."

Around this time, Ronnie saw a news segment on television about hunt saboteurs. The saboteurs were dousing the foxhounds with anti-mating spray, which was generally used to mask the scent of female dogs in heat. However, in this case, the saboteurs were using the substance's powerful aroma to mask the smell of foxes. The hunters, of course, were furious about this and whipped the saboteurs with riding crops. Watching this, Ronnie became enraged on the saboteurs behalf. "I thought, this is absolutely disgusting that these people are trying to save foxes from being torn apart and they're being whipped by these appalling people on horseback," he said.

As a result, Ronnie decided to get involved with the hunt saboteurs. So he contacted the League Against Cruel Sports, who gave him the contact details of the Hunt Saboteurs Association, who put him in touch with the local saboteurs group. "Strangely enough, it was the same people who were being whipped on the telly," Ronnie said, adding the group was based in Northampton. "I went out there and met them. I'd spoken to them on the telephone first. They were pleased to see me."

When they went to the home of the group's leader, Ronnie found him to be quite a character. "I was really shocked," Ronnie said. "He was a witch, or a male-witch, warlock, I suppose. He followed the Wicca religion." This local leader had a room in his house with a pentangle and various Wiccan artifacts. Perhaps noticing Ronnie's disquiet, the leader assured the new recruit he only did white magic—not black magic. "I said to him, can't you magic the hunt away?" Ronnie recalled, laughing. "He said, oh no, it doesn't stretch to that."

The group was primarily made up of people in their early 20s, like Ronnie, while the leaders were about 30. The group, which included both men and women, varied in size. "There were people there with different levels of commitment," Ronnie said. "There would be people who would go out every Saturday and sometimes in the week to sabotage the hunts, and there were other people who didn't go so often. But they were probably able to call on eight or 10 people, I would say." The Hunt Saboteurs Association was fairly new, having been formed a less than a decade prior, and some of the saboteurs Ronnie met had been involved since the organization's founding.

Dave Wetton, a longtime saboteur, said there were no political requirements for involvement at the time, aside from an opposition to the hunt. "My credo was always—and still is—based on the fact it wouldn't make any difference at all to the fox whether the person trying to save it from being killed by the hounds was a vegan leftie [or] a meat-eating righty," Dave said. "Having said that, I guess political allegiances did come up to a certain degree in the early days of the HSA, in the shape of radical Young Liberal and Young Socialist groups who often came out sabbing." He said conservative groups would have been welcome to participate, but they never did.

Despite his busy schedule, Ronnie began throwing himself into animal activism. This agitation had to fit between the eight hours of study he still completed on a daily basis. "My whole life became—more or less—studying and campaigning for animals," Ronnie said, adding this was motivated by his horror at the treatment of animals. "I was a little bit frustrated that I had all of this studying to do, because obviously that took up so much time." But he remained committed to passing the Law Society's examinations, reminding himself that, once he went back to work, he'd have more time for activism.

The Northampton saboteurs, of which Ronnie was an active member, used other tactics in addition to dousing the backs of foxhounds with antimating spray. "We'd put stuff down on the ground, as well, to cover the scent of a fox," Ronnie said, adding some of these substances would be homemade. "We'd have hunting horns, and we'd blow the hunting horns to call the hounds in our direction—to call them off the trail of a fox." Some of the saboteurs were as adept with the horns as the hunters themselves.

At the time, Ronnie was the only vegan in the group. There were a couple of vegetarians, but most members ate meat. "This was very much the same, I learned, with all these organizations I joined, obviously apart from the Vegan Society," Ronnie said. "These organizations which campaigned against animal experiments, against the fur trade, and against hunting—the people that ran these organizations were meat eaters." Killing animals for food was taken for granted, even in these groups. "They'd be holding a placard in one hand and eating a chicken sandwich in the other," he said, adding his presence gradually made his comrades consider veganism.

However, the vegans Ronnie knew at the time were an odd bunch—perhaps more strange than the Wiccan leader of the Northampton Group. For instance, the Vegan Society put him in touch with a vegan family that walked everywhere barefoot—including around town. "I did meet them, but I had nothing in common with them," Ronnie said, adding he saw himself as just an ordinary person who cared about animals. "I used to think, the trouble is anyone seeing them will think vegans are weird." Similarly, when Ronnie attended a party thrown by the Vegan Society, he met a number of people with bizarre health notions. One man hung upside-down several hours a day, believing this nourished his brain, while another wore several overcoats in the summer heat, believing it kept his aura from dissipating. "I thought—oh, my God—they're all mad," Ronnie said, noting many vegans at the time had mystical beliefs.

Shortly after joining the Northampton group, the Hunt Saboteurs Association told Ronnie there were several people close to Meppershall, where he lived, who were interested in hunt sabotage. "So I got in touch with them, and we formed a group," Ronnie said, adding the group was centered around nearby Luton. By then, the 1972 fox-hunting season was over, and the otter-hunting season had begun. Otter hunting was less common than fox hunting, so the Luton group had to travel significant distances to engage in their activism. Of course, tactics they'd used previously were less effective. "It was harder to cover the scent of the otter, because the otter was in the river," Ronnie said, noting the hunters would be in the water, poking the river banks with large poles. "We'd basically try and make a lot of noise, so the otters would run and hide, or we'd attempt to physically get in the way of the hunters."

The saboteurs were generally quite close to the hunters, in a physical sense, sometimes right amongst them. "There would be pushing and shoving, and sometimes there would be fisticuffs," Ronnie said, noting most of the violence came from hunters. "The hunt saboteurs really tried to remain non-violent." That said, he recalled one confrontation which ended with a saboteur breaking a hunter's nose. When the police came, this saboteur provided the authorities with false information and escaped prosecution.

For the most part, Ronnie and his fellow saboteurs were not subject to criminal sanction for their activism. "There was a possibility you could be done for damaging property if you sprayed a foxhound," Ronnie said, mentioning he found this to be unlikely. "It was really the civil law—the law of trespass. These hunts would go across farmers' land. The farmer would have allowed the hunt on their land, but that permission would not extend to the hunt saboteurs." So, sometimes, the police would remove the Luton group from private property.

Ronnie recalled one otter hunt, in which his band of saboteurs was prevented from pursuing the hunters further. The hunters—dressed in blue, as opposed to the red worn during fox hunts—were very pleased by this turn of events. The huntmaster taunted the saboteurs before turning to leave. "He climbed over this fence that had barbed wired at the top, and he caught the ass of his trousers," Ronnie said, adding the huntmaster ripped the rear of his pants, exposing his underwear. "He was so embarrassed that he tried to carry on as if nothing had happened…. We were just absolutely roaring with laughter."

While disrupting otter hunts, the Luton group and others frequently came across anglers. Ronnie would release fish from their keepnets. "There were some occasions where I would run up, let the fish go, and I'd be chased by the angler," Ronnie said. "In the end, I always managed to get away." But other saboteurs disapproved of this. "We were still in the time when a lot of those guys ate meat," Ronnie said, adding many of his comrades viewed fishing as fundamentally different from the hunting of mammals, and thus acceptable. "So that did cause a bit of friction."

By the autumn of 1972, when the fox-hunting season started afresh, Ronnie successfully passed the first part of the Law Society's examinations, and was back working at Machin and Company. "Of course, everyone was pleased at work," Ronnie said. "I had some drinks and celebrated." Patty gave Ronnie her Hillman Imp, after he sent his car to the scrapyard. She didn't have much need for the Imp, as she stayed home with Anthony. Besides using the vehicle for work, he also used it for animal activism, which resulted in hunters damaging the Imp.

The leader of a particular hunt smashed the car's front window while Ronnie and a friend were inside. "The glass went all over us," Ronnie said, noting he and his friend had been following the hunters. "They didn't want us following the hunt and trying to sabotage them. They used to get very angry." This was just be one of a number of incidents, throughout Ronnie's work with hunt saboteurs, in which his car was damaged by hunters. He didn't report it to the police because he believed authorities would take the hunters' side.

This assumption proved correct not much later, when Ronnie and his fellow saboteurs were arrested, following a physical confrontation with hunters. "They kept us locked up all day," Ronnie said, adding he asked the police what the saboteurs were charged with. "They said, we're going to charge you with conspiracy to disrupt a lawful activity. I thought, well I've never heard of that charge before. When the hunt was over, they let us out. So, basically, they just used it as a pretext to keep us in." This was Ronnie's first arrest. And, although the saboteurs were released, they still had the possibility of prosecution hanging over them. "I didn't tell the people at work about it," Ronnie said, noting he spoke instead to a London lawyer who advised the hunt saboteurs. "He said this could be quite a serious case if we ended up charged with this." Luckily, nothing came of it.

Margaret and Ron learned of their son's arrest when the police took Ronnie's name and address and verified this information with a visit to the Lee's home in Meppershall. When Ronnie got home, his mother was distraught—more so over the neighbors' opinion than the arrest itself. "She said, you brought the police to the door," Ronnie recalled. "She said, the neighbors would have seen a policeman at the door…. Little did she know what was to come." Ron, of course, was not happy about his son's arrest either. Neither supported his involvement with the saboteurs. "They were worried about me getting into trouble with the law," Ronnie said. "I think they were also concerned that I might get physically injured." Beyond this, his parents were conventional people and his unconventional activism made them uncomfortable, according to Ronnie.

But Ronnie's commitment to hunt sabotage was unshaken. When hunts were held during the work week, he would take the day off from Machin and Company and attempt to disrupt the hunt on his own. "I'd be very careful to avoid them, obviously," Ronnie said, referring to the hunters, "because I was on my own and probably would have been beaten up." Ronnie would also call the newspapers and try to get coverage of the Luton group's activism. When he was successful, Ronnie served as the group's spokesman. "There would be stories in the local newspaper—and sometimes my picture would be in there, blowing a hunting horn," he said. "My mum hated this. She hated it. My dad didn't like it either. Their son was in the paper and what were people going to think?"

Ronnie kept a scrapbook of all his newspaper clippings until one day he returned from work to discover Margaret had vandalized it. "My mum had written all over it," Ronnie said. "She'd written, you're a lunatic; you'll end up in prison; you brought the police to our door." Margaret had written these things over the clippings, effectively destroying the scrapbook. "I can't remember saying anything to her," Ronnie said. "I just thought, there's no point having an argument with her. I didn't bother with the scrapbook after that." He assumed she would just write all over it again.

In addition to hunt sabotage, Ronnie also helped stop the cull of squirrels in a North London park. The local government had received complaints about the animals and tapped a shooting club to exterminate them. He and his friends distributed a poster calling those opposed to the killing to invade the park on the day of the shoot. "We went around the local area putting these posters up everywhere," Ronnie said. "We thought, they're soon going to be taken down, but hopefully some people see them." On the day of the slaughter, Ronnie was surprised by the number of protesters there—about 30–40 people, which was a comparatively good turnout. The local government had to temporarily call off the shoot, as it was too dangerous with so many people in the park.

Having achieved this, about 12 protestors, including Ronnie, invaded the local government offices and demanded to see the senior official. Once granted an audience, they convinced this official to conduct a survey as to whether the cull should move forward at a later date. "We were certain if they took the survey it would come out in favor of the squirrels," Ronnie said. "They did the survey. Most people were opposed to [the shoot] and it never happened. But that was only because we went in the offices."

Ronnie also became involved in the Reform Group of the Royal Society for the Prevention of Cruelty to Animals. "The RSPCA, at the time, was not opposed to hunting," Ronnie said. "They actually had a number of hunters on their ruling council and a lot of hunt supporters were members of the RSPCA." The Reform Group sought to elect members to the ruling council who, among other things, were opposed to hunting and would change the organization's policy in that regard. "This involved a lot of behind-the-scenes work—lobbying people, persuading anti-hunt people to join the RSPCA," Ronnie said, noting he helped in the effort. "We'd go to the RSPCA general meetings and speak out against hunting. Of course, at these meetings there were a lot of hunt supporters as well. So there would be uproar." This would include scuffling, calls to the police, and ejections from the event.

Late in 1972, Ronnie moved out of his parents' house. Partly, it was due to conflict with Margaret and Ron over his involvement in the hunt saboteurs. But it was also because Ronnie's commute to work was too long for his taste. So he rented a small room in Luton, about half a mile from Machin and Company. But he only stayed there one night. "My dad was taken ill," Ronnie said, adding his father had to go to the hospital for tests. "It was to do with his diabetes. Every now and again, it would become unbalanced." Margaret asked Ronnie to come home and help care for his father, which Ronnie agreed to. He would move out of his parent's home on a more-permanent basis in early 1973, once again renting a room in Luton.

Ronnie would organize the Luton group from the pay phone on the ground floor of his apartment building. "I used to spend hours on this phone, organizing people to go hunt sabbing and arranging where I'd pick them up and everything," he said, adding his quick rise to leadership in the group was the result of simple dedication, and he learned the skills required out of necessity. "People have fears about these things—don't they? People feel nervous about speaking to the media if they've never done it before. People also feel nervous about trying to organize things if they've never done it before." Ronnie overcame these anxieties by force of will. They became less daunting as he dealt with the press and organized more. Before long, he was invited to join the national committee of the Hunt Saboteurs Association, the ruling body of the organization.

"His absolute, single-minded devotion to the welfare of animals was immediately apparent and very impressive to all who met him," said Pete Myatt, a member of the Luton group. "Ronnie could be seen by those not in sympathy with his views as a figure of fun. He was small in stature, with distinctive round glasses, and was compared with the sitcom character Hiram Holiday on several occasions." Despite this, Ronnie would never back down from an argument with these ideological opponents. "I can remember several debates when—surrounded by aggressive hunt followers—self-preservation was never an issue for Ronnie. I am afraid I was more concerned with keeping my boyish good looks."

Ronnie was suspicious of the motives of saboteurs—in other local groups—who he saw as insufficiently serious. "With quite a few of them, there was almost a camaraderie with the hunt people," Ronnie said, noting that some saboteurs and hunters exchanged pleasantries, like opposing athletes after a game. "I thought, what's this all about? This guy's an animal murderer." Similarly, Ronnie believed some saboteurs were too interested in hunting culture, such as how hounds were controlled and the terminology used by hunters. "Some of the hunt sabs were fascinated with all of that," Ronnie said. "All I wanted to know about hunting was enough to be able to sabotage what they were doing."

Activism became a compulsion for Ronnie. "It was an obsession to be quite honest," he said. "My life completely changed. I didn't have anything to do anymore with my old friends. I obviously made a new set of friends, the people involved with the hunt saboteurs." There were a number of reasons for Ronnie's disconnection from prior friends. Initially, the rift was caused by his study for the first part of the Law Society's examination. But it would only deepen as Ronnie entered the animal movement. "Along came this knowledge of animal abuse, and I never went back to my old life," Ronnie said, adding his old friends were moving in divergent directions as well. "One chap became manager of the local ballroom…. Others of my friends were getting girlfriends. So that social group was splitting up anyway." Going to soccer matches and the club felt less important to Ronnie than it had previously.

While Ronnie didn't discuss his arrest at work, he was open about his veganism and involvement with the hunt saboteurs. There was a restaurant, nearby the Machin and Company building, where employees frequently ordered food. Ronnie's coworkers mocked him when he ordered vegan options from this establishment. "They pulled my leg a bit—not in a nasty way," he said. "They said, don't you want to eat a bit of meat today? Don't you want some prawn balls?" One day, however, the police raided the restaurant and found a dead German Shepherd in the fridge. It turned out the restaurateur had been killing stray dogs and feeding them to customers. "Immediately there was consternation in the office," Ronnie said. "I said, you eat pigs, cows, sheep and hens. What's the difference?" Ronnie felt he had the last laugh, pointing out to his coworkers he was the only one who could be sure he hadn't eaten a dog.

During this same period, someone at Machin and Company saw a mouse and the firm immediately called pest control. "They put this poison down," Ronnie said, describing blue warfarin used by the exterminators. "It causes internal bleeding, basically. That's how they kill them." Ronnie's superiors told him that, if he interfered with the poison in any way, he would be fired. "They knew what my views were," Ronnie said, adding he unsuccessfully argued to his superiors that the mice should be left alone. "So I thought, what am I going to do? Because I don't want to lose my job, but I'm not going to [just] sit here." Ronnie hatched a plan. Going early to work one morning, he collected and disposed of the warfarin, which he replaced with blue chalk. "Unless you made a really close inspection—which none of [my coworkers] were going to do—you wouldn't see that there was any difference," Ronnie said, noting eventually his superiors believed the problem had been resolved, as they didn't see more mice.

Ronnie continued going to court on behalf of Machin and Company. One day, he left an anonymous message for a barrister who happened to be an ardent hunter. "I think he was in court, doing a case," Ronnie said. "The case I was on had just ended and I had some spare time. So I snuck into this robing room.... And I put a threatening note in his wig box, saying, we know you're a hunting so-and-so and we're going to get you." Ronnie was amused hearing the barristers discuss the note later. He wasn't caught because he hadn't mentioned his anti-hunting views in the court building.

6

Band of Mercy

In the brief period lasting from the summer of 1973 to the summer of 1974, Ronnie cofounded the Band of Mercy, a predecessor to the Animal Liberation Front. He conducted a number of attacks on the group's behalf, including arson against a pharmaceutical laboratory and seal-hunting boats, ultimately leading to his arrest.

The 22-year-old, still involved with the hunt saboteurs, was especially frustrated by fox-cub hunting. "We couldn't really do anything about that," Ronnie said. "We'd turn up at those things and we'd just be bystanders." In the night prior to the cub slaughter, hunters would block up the foxholes while the animals were outside. Some hours later, hunters would surround the woods with people on horseback and foot, before sending in the hounds. Meanwhile, the hunters would make a great deal of noise, shouting and cracking whips. "So the foxes were frightened to run out of the wood," Ronnie said. "The hounds would just massacre the foxes because they couldn't escape down the holes."

Sometimes, the saboteurs were able to unblock the foxholes prior to the hunt, but this wasn't always possible. So Ronnie racked his brain, trying to imagine a different method of stopping the slaughter. It eventually occurred to him that activists could go to the hunt kennels and sabotage the vans in which hounds were transported. "The problem was we couldn't do that as hunt saboteurs," Ronnie said. "Because hunt saboteurs always tried to operate within the law." The actions needed to be carried out under the banner of a new group. So in the early summer of 1973, before the cub-hunting season began, Ronnie met with five other activists in a London cafe to form the Band of Mercy.

He knew them mainly through the Hunt Saboteurs Association, but not exclusively. Including Ronnie, there were four men and two women, all in their 20s and 30s. "I think I'd already broached the subject with these people, perhaps on an individual basis," Ronnie said. "When I selected the people to get together for the meeting, I knew who to choose." Illegal action against hunt vehicles had occurred sporadically in the past, but this group wanted such acts to become more regular and organized. The question was what to call themselves. "I'd been reading quite extensively about the history of the animal-protection movement, and I was intrigued by a group in the 19th century," Ronnie said, referring to the original Band of Mercy, a youth division within the Royal Society for the Prevention of Cruelty to Animals, which, according to lore, sabotaged hunters' guns. "I thought that was absolutely brilliant. So I said, let's revive that." Ronnie's comrades agreed, adopting the name of a group founded almost a century earlier.

In addition, Ronnie said his conception of the Band of Mercy had more modern inspirations, such as the Angry Brigade, a left-wing militant group which operated in England between 1970 and 1972, and the Situationist International, an organization of left-wing artists and intellectuals which existed between 1957 and 1972. "I thought, can you do really hard-hitting direct action and avoid injury to people?" Ronnie said. "The Angry Brigade had kind of done that." He was influenced by the Situationists' belief in the ability of manufactured situations to create change. "Everyone's just going along, doing the same old thing," Ronnie said. "Then, suddenly, someone does something that's kind of different. You hope that will make people think about what's going on."

According to Ronnie, at the founding meeting of the Band of Mercy, the six activists agreed only actions which didn't pose a risk to humans or animals could be claimed on behalf of the group. This policy would later be carried over to the Animal Liberation Front. "When we discussed what we were going to do with the Band of Mercy, that was our founding philosophy," Ronnie said. "That got passed on to the ALF."

In the autumn of 1973, the Band of Mercy began an illegal campaign against hunters, sabotaging their hound vehicles. "Different groups of us would go in the early hours of the morning," Ronnie said, noting they had a narrow interval in which to carry out actions, between when the kennel huntsman went to sleep and the hunters left for the day. "They'd be up very early to get everything ready." Initially, this Band of Mercy sought to inflict the minimum amount of damage to the hunters' property that would disrupt the killing. So, Ronnie and his comrades would let the air out of the tires on the hound van, taking the valves with them. They would put glue in the locks and ignition, depending on whether the vehicle was open, so hunters wouldn't be able to enter or start the van.

"We'd have these printed notes that we'd leave under the windscreen wipers, explaining why we'd done the action," Ronnie said. "Sometimes we'd spray slogans." The Band of Mercy would telephone the local and sometimes national media to claim responsibility. Unsurprisingly, and often correctly, hunters believed they were being targeted at night by the same protesters who disrupted them during the day, according to Ronnie. "But of course they couldn't prove that," he said. "We'd just say, we don't know what you're talking about."

New members were recruited into the group. One such person was an army veteran who claimed to have been involved in undercover operations. While raiding a hunt kennel, this man took over on the basis of his assumed expertise in clandestine action. He led Ronnie and a friend on a two-mile crawl across a field, in the hopes of reaching the hunters' property. "It was taking ages and we were crawling on our bellies," Ronnie said. "I was getting fed up, really. In the end, we completely missed the kennels and we came out on the road about a mile away." So the group went back to the car, parked it near the kennels, and, while the army veteran stayed with the vehicle, Ronnie and his friend entered through the front entrance. "We just did it the simple way," Ronnie said, adding that, while he found the expedition amusing in retrospect, he was quite frustrated at the time.

Shortly after the cub-hunting season began, Ronnie read an article in a local newspaper about an animal-research laboratory being built in Milton Keynes by Hoechst, a German pharmaceutical company. "There was very big concern over this," Ronnie said, noting anti-vivisection newsletters began covering it. "They weren't just going to do animal experiments at this place. They were going to do experiments involving radiation. Animals were going to be irradiated, which caused increased opposition to this." Ronnie went to see the leader of a local branch of the National Anti-Vivisection Society, which had been campaigning to halt construction of this laboratory.

"We sat and had a cup of tea," Ronnie said. "She told me all about why this place would be really bad and all things they were planning to do there." It was clear to him the lawful campaign to stop construction was not succeeding, so Ronnie and some other members of the Band of Mercy went to scout the facility, which was in an isolated location. They already were proposing to burn it down. "It was the only thing we thought we could do," Ronnie said, adding, however, not enough of the building had been constructed by the first visit to start a ruinous fire.

Pete, who was involved in some Band of Mercy actions, recalled Ronnie asking if he would be willing to assist in the arson. "Fear of getting on the wrong side of the law and ending up behind bars took precedence for me," Pete said. "I made it clear that I was too scared to get involved in anything along those lines."

In November of 1973, Ronnie and another member of the Band of Mercy, Cliff Goodman, returned to the construction site. After waiting for the workers to leave, they inspected the building. "We thought, there's quite a bit of it here now," Ronnie said, noting the walls and flooring had been completed. "It was probably about half built." The pair had a can of gasoline in their car, in case the vehicle ran out of fuel. So they decided to try and destroy the building that very day, entering the unlocked laboratory annex with the can of gasoline. "We just poured the petrol around and set fire to it," Ronnie said, adding he and Cliff drove away as the annex burned, hoping the blaze would spread to the main structure.

They didn't call the media to claim responsibility, because—if the arson wasn't catastrophic, and they had to finish the job at a later date—Ronnie and Cliff wanted to avoid the increased security that would accompany such a claim. In fact, they wouldn't know the results of their action until the next week, when it was reported in the local newspaper, because they feared returning to the scene and viewing the damage might implicate them in the crime. "There was only a small article," Ronnie said, adding he'd hoped for big headlines announcing the laboratory's destruction. According to Ronnie, the newspaper claimed the fire caused over 20,000 pounds worth of damage and was being investigated by police. "There was a theory that somebody who was a kind of down-and-out had been sleeping in the building for shelter and had accidentally started a fire," Ronnie said, noting he was disappointed the building hadn't completely burned. "I thought there probably wasn't enough material in it for the fire to take hold."

Six days later, Ronnie and Cliff struck the laboratory again. They were more prepared than they had been for the previous attack. The duo had several cans of gasoline, makeshift torches, and a plan, perhaps most importantly. The main building had four floors, including a basement. So Ronnie and Cliff planned to burn the top two floors, set fire to the basement, and burn the ground floor on their way out.

In their excitement, however—after making sure no one was inside—they bungled their plan and eventually found themselves in the basement with a fire raging above. Ronnie and Cliff ran up to the ground floor, saw the exit was engulfed in flames, and continued to the next level, where they smashed a window and went down the fire escape. The facility was covered with plastic sheeting, which melted their shoes and got in their hair. Driving away, the pair felt a mix of emotions. "We were delighted we managed to set fire to place," Ronnie said. "But we were also relieved we'd escaped. Because we could have so easily been burnt to death."

Once again, Ronnie didn't know the results of his action until the next week, when he read about it in the local newspaper. There was no coverage of the fire on television or the radio. The article in the paper was brief, and, strangely enough, said the attack had done slightly less damage than the first blaze. "We were gobsmacked," Ronnie said. "The building was totally engulfed in flame. Of course, what we were looking at was the petrol burning. It didn't really take hold of any of the material." Further, according to Ronnie, the paper reported the site would have around-the-clock security going forward. Reading this, Ronnie and Cliff knew they wouldn't be able to target the laboratory again.

So they decided to issue a claim of responsibility to the media, which Ronnie wrote in what he hoped would be unidentifiable penmanship. "I did it in capital letters," Ronnie said, adding he wore gloves to avoid leaving fingerprints. "Every single angle in the writing was a right angle." To prove the veracity of their claim, Ronnie included details in the text which only the perpetrators would know. "I think we left some empty petrol cans behind in a particular location," Ronnie said. "I described where we left them." After using tap water to seal the envelope—as opposed to his saliva—Ronnie traveled some distance to post the letter, trying to avoid detection. The next week, the Band of Mercy's claim of responsibility was on the front page of the local newspaper. "There was a small article about it in one or two of the national newspapers as well," Ronnie said, noting the laboratory's opening was merely delayed, and only by a few weeks.

Still, these attacks on the Hoechst buildings were significant steps beyond gluing locks on hound vans. Ronnie said he and Cliff, who was in his early 30s, were aware of the potential legal consequences. "We were prepared to take that risk," Ronnie said. "It wasn't as if we were married with a family, or anything like that. We were both single guys." Ronnie was still working at Machin and Company, where, perhaps surprisingly, he was learning tricks to further his illegal activism. Ronnie would discuss forensics and other topics with a former police sergeant who worked in the office. "He used to think it was great there was this young chap who was so interested in how the police operated," Ronnie said, adding the man answered questions about fingerprints, how to silently break windows, and other things. "He never found it suspicious."

During this period, Ronnie was still involved in the Hunt Saboteurs Association. In one protest, he and about 20 other activists brought the corpse of fox killed by hunters to the office of the British Field Sports

Society. "We just burst into their offices with this dead fox in a sack," Ronnie said. "We said, you like hunting foxes, so we brought you one. This fox was in a state of decay and it was very, very smelly." The hunt saboteurs then tipped the semi-liquid corpse onto the office's boardroom table. Eventually, the protesters were ejected by police and their photos were taken by Special Branch.

A few weeks after, Ronnie was involved in the occupation of the office of the National Coursing Club. Hoping to avoid scaring the building receptionist, who was unaffiliated with the organization, Ronnie came up with the idea of giving her flowers as the protesters ran inside. "We gave her the flowers and then we charged into the Coursing Club," he said. "Somebody sat against the door and we, more or less, held [the coursing officials] hostage." The protesters, who hung an anti-coursing banner out of the window, sought to force these officials to sign a statement calling for the end of coursing. In retrospect, Ronnie wasn't sure what use such a statement would have, given it would have been signed under duress. "I know it sounds mad, but that's kind of what we were like," he said, laughing. Unsurprisingly, the receptionist called the police—despite his gift of flowers—which came as a great shock to Ronnie at the time. "I was kind of naive, really," Ronnie said. "The police came and we were evicted." Later, he would use smoke bombs to disrupt the coursing itself.

In addition to animal activism, during this period Ronnie was involved in other causes as well. For instance, he became interested in the anti-war movement and began reading a pacifist magazine called Peace News. "There was an advert for it in one of the vegetarian magazines I was reading," Ronnie said, adding he was quite influenced by Peace News. "I even started a local peace group in Luton." On Remembrance Day at the town's war memorial, the group laid down a wreath made of white poppies, symbolizing peace, instead of the customary red poppies. "A guy from an extreme, right-wing movement—the National Front—came along and destroyed the wreath," Ronnie said, adding the vandalism was covered in the newspaper.

Similarly, Ronnie was involved in the British Withdrawal from Northern Ireland Campaign. "We went around to various barracks, giving leaflets to soldiers about how they could leave the army," Ronnie said, noting it was a crime to incite soldiers to leave the military. "At one army base we got arrested and were put in the guard room." He also worked with London Greenpeace and the Campaign Against the Arms Trade.

Finally, Ronnie supported an organization called Women for Life, a self-described feminist group opposed to abortion. "That was totally in line with what my deepest feelings were towards trying to defend those that are the most oppressed and those that are the most vulnerable," Ronnie said. "It's difficult regarding legislation. At the end of the day, if someone wants to have an abortion, you can't really stop them. You have to try to change the culture more than anything." Obviously his pro-life stance was a heterodox view on the left, which put him in a position to which he was unaccustomed to some degree. "I remember going on one big anti-abortion march in London at the time," he said, adding it was a strange experience. "Because there were all these left-wing people protesting against the anti-abortion march." Of course, Ronnie often found the left indifferent or hostile to his animal activism as well.

In the summer of 1974, Ronnie worked against the promotion of an animal circus in Brighton. "They were putting posters up everywhere around the town, advertising this circus," Ronnie said. "We'd go around the shops and try to persuade them to take the posters out of the window." Some of the establishments took these advertisements down and some didn't. But Ronnie was more concerned about the many posters and large banner promoting the circus at a busy railway station in Brighton. So he and Robin Howard, another member of the Band of Mercy, took these down themselves. "I said, look, if we pretend we're entitled to take them down, and don't behave suspiciously, we'll probably get away with it," Ronnie said, adding that's exactly what they did. "We started removing these posters and throwing them in the back of the vehicle. I was shouting to him, are we meant to take this one? He'd be shouting back, yeah, they've told us we have to take all of them down, because the circus has been cancelled." No one questioned their right to remove the advertisements.

In addition, every summer, there was a slaughter of seal pups at an estuary called the Wash on the east coast of England. "They got a license from the government to do this," Ronnie said of the fishermen looking to earn extra money. "They would go and shoot baby seals and sell the skins." Of course, the animals' white coats were highly valued by the fur trade. The previous summer, in 1973, protesters had gone out on inflatable boats to try and stop the killing. "The hunt saboteurs had only limited success in stopping this," Ronnie said, adding he hadn't taken part in those disruptions. "The police got involved in preventing the hunt saboteurs from taking action." So, in the summer of 1974, Ronnie and Robin planned to destroy the hunters' boats.

The pair drove to Long Sutton, where the boats—called the Mitzpah and the Mermaid—were located on a river leading to the sea, according to Ronnie. They climbed into the Mitzpah, which was on the water, and searched to make sure no one was on board. Finding it empty, they poured gasoline all over the vessel, before repeating the process with the Mermaid, which was on the riverbank. Then they lit makeshift torches and flung them into the boats, igniting the vessels in flame. According to Robin, their getaway car was far from ideal. "Every time you steered left the horn sounded and the gearbox rattled like a Gatling gun," he said. "Honestly, we could not have left a better trail for the cops if we had tried." On the drive home, the pair stopped at a pay phone to call the Press Association and claim the arson on behalf of the Band of Mercy. "I'd phone up and say, can I speak to a journalist?" Ronnie said, adding the reporters would ask for his name. "I'd say, well, I don't want to give my name. I'd say what happened and then just hang up."

The next day, the action was covered in the media, including on the radio and television. As it turned out, the Mitzpah had been completely destroyed, while the Mermaid was seriously damaged. "The seal hunt didn't take place," Ronnie said. "I suppose our actions saved a load of fish as well, which I probably didn't think too much about at the time." According to Ronnie, the government hadn't issued licenses for the hunt in the more than 40 years since. He credited this success to a combination of legal protest and underground action.

Shortly after, a sympathizer to the Band of Mercy provided the group with a list of businesses that bred and supplied animals to laboratories. Ronnie thought these establishments would make better targets than the laboratories themselves. The latter had more security, due to the expensive equipment inside. So, in the summer of 1974, Ronnie went with Cliff on two nominal camping trips, lasting a week each, in which the pair struck animal suppliers in rapid succession. "There were probably 20 to 30 of these places in the country," Ronnie said. "Our aim was to attack all of them. In fact, a lot of them did get attacked."

It should be noted that, by this time, the Band of Mercy's philosophy had shifted. Rather than doing the minimum amount of damage required to stop animal abusers, the group hoped to make this abuse as expensive as possible. "The concept of economic sabotage started coming into it, where it would be about causing these people to lose money," Ronnie said. Also, because the Band of Mercy used arson against Hoescht, viewing it as the only means of halting the laboratory's construction, the tactic had become part of group's repertoire.

The Band of Mercy attacks that summer were, to some extent, made possible because Machin and Company granted Ronnie paid time off from work. In between the first and second part of the Law Society's examinations, Ronnie was to be tested on accounting. "I was supposed to be studying for that," he said, explaining his absence from the office, before adding he didn't hit the books as he was expected to. "I had already decided that I didn't want to be a solicitor. Also, I just hated accounts."

By this point, Ronnie's superiors at the law firm looked at him in an unfavorable light, after Ronnie refused to assist in certain cases for political reasons, such as the prosecution of a man for marijuana possession. Ronnie intended to stay on the Machin and Company payroll as long as he could—until he failed the accounting exam and was asked by his superiors to retake it. "So I was stringing it out," Ronnie said, adding Cliff was granted time away from his engineering job as well. "He took it as a holiday."

Embarking on their first week of attacks, the duo drove a station wagon they'd borrowed from a friend. Ronnie's car was either in need of repairs or too small to hold the camping equipment they required. "We would go to one of these places that bred animals for experiments," Ronnie said. "We'd suss it out in the day time." They would try and locate the suppliers' vehicles, which were Ronnie and Cliff's primary target. Having done this, they would set up camp a few miles away in a field or another suitable location.

Around 1 a.m. the following morning, Ronnie and Cliff would pack their equipment back in the car, drive to the supplier and sabotage the vehicles, frequently using arson. "If a vehicle was parked too close to where the animals were, we wouldn't set fire to it," Ronnie said. "We would slash the tires, put paint stripper on it, and stuff like that." Sometimes, these vehicles would be unlocked. So he and Cliff would release the handbrakes, push the vehicles away from the building, and burn them. Having accomplished this, the pair would drive to the area surrounding the next supplier on their list. "We'd set up camp there," Ronnie said. "This was in the middle of the night. It was only a small tent—it was quite easy to set up." After getting some sleep, they would investigate their target and repeat the process throughout each week-long trip.

While raiding a supplier near Salisbury, which bred guinea pigs, Ronnie and Cliff couldn't find the vehicle they spotted during the day. "We thought, what are we going to do?" Ronnie said, adding they hypothesized an employee had taken the vehicle home. "So, basically, we broke into the place and took half a dozen baby guinea pigs." On this particular action, Sue Smith—a founding member of the Band of Mercy, who lived nearby—acted as the pair's driver. "She picked us up afterwards," Ronnie said, adding it was cold for the rescued animals. "To keep them warm, we put them up our jumpers." Sue was driving Ronnie and Cliff back to her residence, where she would allow them to sleep on her floor.

On the way, however, the car was stopped by police. "They said, what are you doing out at this time of night?" Ronnie recalled. "We said, oh, we've been on a camping holiday, but we're staying with a friend tonight." The police told these members of the Band of Mercy the reason they'd been stopped was because there had been a series of burglaries in the area. "That was nothing to do with us," Ronnie said, adding the police requested to search their vehicle. "All this time, we had these guinea pigs up our sweaters, and we were hoping they wouldn't make a noise or move too much." But when the police inspected the vehicle, all they saw was camping equipment, which confirmed the pair's story. The authorities allowed the group to go on their way. And the guinea pigs lived out their lives with Sue, who adopted them.

Of course, Ronnie and Cliff would claim all these actions on behalf of the Band of Mercy. When the guinea-pig breeder heard she'd been targeted, she shuttered the operation. "She said, I'm so frightened that these people will come back that I'm going to close the business," Ronnie said, noting he and Cliff read about this later in a newspaper. "We were really pleased. Because we never imagined that just taking a few guinea pigs would result in a place closing down. Obviously, other places—where we set fire to things—hadn't closed down. It was a very small action that came with a very big result."

While Ronnie and Cliff raided a business called Perrycroft Lodge, which bred beagles for vivisection, the dogs started barking as the duo approached. The operator came out of a nearby house and started shouting at the animals. "This probably wasn't an unusual occurrence," Ronnie said, noting that, if a wild animal approached the kennels, the beagles would likely have barked as well. "The guy didn't come out as if he was suspicious people were there." In his haste to hide, Cliff fell into the animals' cesspit. "He was thrashing around in all this piss and shit from the dogs," Ronnie said, laughing. "It wasn't above his head—so he was able to wade out of it. But he was absolutely stinking." The pair managed to make a narrow escape.

Unchastened, as they drove home at the conclusion of their first week of attacks, Ronnie and Cliff passed a hunting store in the middle of a town center and decided to break the establishment's windows. "We got a load of bricks," Ronnie said, adding he wrote a note on one of the bricks, claiming the action on behalf of the Band of Mercy. "We stopped right outside of the shop, jumped out of the car with all these bricks [and] smashed them through all of the windows." The duo drove away in a hurry. According to Ronnie, this sort of impromptu vandalism was something they repeated. "There was more than one place where we just put a brick through a window," he said.

In the interval before Ronnie and Cliff embarked on their second week of attacks, Band of Mercy actions were receiving quite a bit of publicity, and Ronnie's comrades from the hunt saboteurs strongly suspected he was involved. "People knew what I was like," Ronnie said. "People were saying, I bet that's you. I'd say, well, I'm not saying anything." Of course, traditional anti-vivisection groups were opposed to the Band of Mercy's work. Sidney Hicks, a leader in the British Union for the Abolition of Vivisection, told the media he strongly disapproved of such extralegal action. "He actually said that what we did was worse than vivisection," Ronnie said. "We thought [Hicks' statement] was appalling, but we weren't surprised."

Similarly, Ronnie and Cliff were both on the national committee of the Hunt Saboteurs Association. And the other members of the organization's ruling body, who believed the pair were involved in the attacks, feared Ronnie and Cliff might tarnish the group's reputation. "The hunt saboteurs were meant to keep within the law," Ronnie said. "Pressure was put on us to resign, so we resigned from the committee." However, the Wiccan leader of the Northampton group protested and Ronnie and Cliff were reinstated. Ultimately, when the pair was arrested, the media didn't link them to the Hunt Saboteurs Association.

Dave, who was on the national committee at the time, confirmed that his colleagues suspected Ronnie was involved in illegal activity. "I guess we all knew Ronnie was up to something, because that was clearly his nature," Dave said, noting they didn't know specifics. "It would have been nice to know what was going on, of course. But no one can ever really keep a secret, can they? Sooner or later, someone with a really big mouth will get hold of a secret and then—Bob's your uncle—the police start poking around."

According to Ronnie, both he and Cliff knew they would inevitably be caught. By targeting a limited number of establishments and claiming responsibility after each attack, they were essentially mapping their route for police. "Obviously, we were dealing with an increased risk," Ronnie said. "We were just hoping to get away with it as long as we could." Additionally, he and Cliff hoped, if they were arrested, police wouldn't be able to link them to all of the attacks. It was for this reason the duo parked their vehicle far away from targets. "Because we were doing a lot of places one after the other, there was evidence in the car of other things," Ronnie said, adding this included torches and a list of suppliers. "We had an arrangement with someone else that—if we ever got arrested—that other person would come and get the car."

While in the midst of their second week of attacks, Ronnie and Cliff targeted Oxford Laboratory Animal Colonies in Bicester. A security guard contacted the police. "Within just a few minutes, the place was surrounded—not just by ordinary police, but also by military police," Ronnie said, noting the supplier was located near a military base. "We hid under a building.... But they started shining torches under the buildings. They found us and dragged us out." The pair were arrested and taken to the local police station. With the help of tracking dogs, authorities found Ronnie and Cliff's car, which was about two miles away in a residential area, amongst other vehicles. "It was kind of ironic that it was through animals that we got caught," Ronnie said, adding that, in the car, police discovered evidence linking the pair to many other Band of Mercy actions. Police would find more incriminating information when they searched Ronnie and Cliff's residences.

Of course, Margaret and Ron were distressed to learn what had become of their son. "I phoned my family and told them," Ronnie said, adding he didn't think they were that surprised. "My mum had predicted that I would be jailed." Ronnie believed his parents might have even suspected his involvement in the Band of Mercy attacks, which Margaret and Ron would have likely read about in the paper. By this point, Patty had a daughter named Danielle, born in August 1973. "She was upset, obviously, that I'd been arrested and worried about me," Ronnie said of his sister's reaction.

7

First Prison Sentence

After their arrest on August 23, 1974, Ronnie and Cliff were held at the Bicester police station for about a day. "We were charged with being found on enclosed premises," Ronnie said. "The other one was, I think, going equipped to cause criminal damage." The pair were not yet charged with arson, as the police were still sifting through the related evidence. "They basically wanted to charge us with something whereby they could keep us in custody," Ronnie said, adding the pair was taken to Oxford Prison, a Victorian facility where both unconvicted and convicted prisoners were kept.

"It was a real culture shock for me in this dirty, old building." Ronnie was put in a cell with a prisoner charged with burglary. The space had two metal-framed beds. "On my bed I had a foam mattress," Ronnie said, adding his cellmate's mattress was stuffed with horsehair. "I was pleased I didn't get that one. Because I didn't really fancy sleeping on a mattress made of horsehair." But Ronnie's cellmate liked the mattress, because he smoked the horsehair. "He used to get rolling paper, roll up the horsehair in a cigarette and smoke it," Ronnie said, noting there was a shortage of tobacco amongst prisoners, who didn't have much money. "He offered me a cigarette made of horsehair, which I declined. He said, they're not too bad; once you get used to them, they're okay."

One morning, Ronnie woke up to discover his entire wing of the prison was flooded. "I was on the ground floor," he said, adding his plastic mat and slippers were floating in about 9 inches of water. "I think a pipe had burst or something. We had to all get buckets and mops and clear all this water up." According to Ronnie, a government report had recommended the prison be closed a couple of years before. "The conditions in there were just not good," Ronnie said, adding it remained open due to fiscal considerations. "If you wanted to do a pee, there was just a bucket.... When the cell was open, you could go and empty this bucket. There was a big sluice that you poured it into."

Work was reserved for convicted prisoners, so Ronnie spent most of his time locked in the cell. He was let out for an hour of exercise each day, during which he could walk around the yard and speak with Cliff. "I spent a lot of time reading," Ronnie said. "There was a prison library that we could go to and get books—not a very big library." Prior to his conviction, Ronnie recalled being allowed to write as many letters as he wanted. He took advantage of the opportunity.

On August 30, Robin was arrested for his involvement in the arson against seal-hunting boats, which he and Ronnie had carried out earlier that year. Cliff had spoken to the authorities. "Unfortunately, Cliff, who was arrested with me, talked to the police and sadly told them about Robin," Ronnie said, adding Robin confessed while in custody. "I was disappointed that Cliff had spoken to the police, because I didn't tell them about anyone else." Ronnie hypothesized Cliff cooperated with authorities because he believed doing so would lessen his sentence. "The police are very clever when they question people," Ronnie said. "It may have been that they said, there's obviously other people involved, and—if you don't tell us about other people—then when it comes to court you'll get a longer sentence." The police said something like this to Ronnie.

While Ronnie was angry with Cliff at the time, believing Robin wouldn't have been caught without Cliff's cooperation, his view of those who turned informant was less harsh than that of other activists. "If someone's in the police station and they tell the police about other people, obviously that's a bad thing to do," Ronnie said. "Those people are called grasses and generally become the object of hatred... [But] the Band of Mercy never really gave training to anyone about how to stand up to police interrogation." In contrast, Ronnie said, the police receive a great deal of training about how to crack suspects. Robin was forgiving of Cliff as well. "I wasn't mad," Robin said. "I was shocked when the cops showed me his statement naming Ronnie and me. After that I felt very sad for him. He had clearly been in a very difficult position for whatever reason."

On September 2, Ronnie, Cliff, and Robin appeared in court and were granted bail. Ronnie's bail was set at 1,000 pounds. "My dad was surety for 500 pounds," he said, adding a sympathizer named George Rodgers was responsible for the remaining half. When his son was released, Ron was more relieved than angry. "He was pissed off, but his overwhelming feeling, really, was one of relief that I was out of jail," Ronnie said. "Part of the bail conditions were that I had to live with my parents. So I had to give up my little bedsitter that I had in Luton." Also, every night, Ronnie had to go to the Luton police station and sign in. "This was so I couldn't go very far away," he said, adding if he didn't sign he could have been arrested. "That's how they tried to keep me in my place." At the time, Ronnie didn't have a car. So his father drove him to the station or he took a bus.

On a number of occasions, Ronnie would forget about this mandatory task. "I was busy doing things and I'd suddenly remember that I hadn't signed at the police station," he said, laughing. "My dad would be watching the telly and it might be quite late at night." Ronnie would tell his father he needed a last-minute ride to Luton, which caused Ron to panic. The pair would then drive to the station in a hurry. "That was quite amusing," Ronnie said, recalling his and his father's frenzy.

On one trip to Luton, Ronnie spotted a badly injured cat on the side of the road, who had presumably been hit by a car. Telling his father to stop, Ronnie jumped out of the vehicle to tend to the animal. "Just further down the road, there was a police car that was stopped," he said. "I picked up the cat and ran to the police car. I said—quick, quick—drive as fast as you can; we need to get to a vet." Ronnie knew a veterinarian in the area, Cecil Schwartz, who ran an animal rescue for which Ronnie volunteered. But the police refused to assist. "They said, if it was a dog we could do something, but because it's a cat it isn't protected by law in that way," Ronnie said. "I told them what I thought of them. Then I ran back to my dad and got my dad to drive to the vet."

Unfortunately, Cecil had to euthanize the animal because she was so badly injured. When Ronnie told the veterinarian the police had refused to transport the cat, Cecil was furious. "He contacted the chief of police for that area and complained," Ronnie said. "Because of that, they changed the rules. If a similar sort of thing happened with a cat, they had to give the cat the same priority they would give a dog."

Ronnie remained on the national committee of the Hunt Saboteurs Association, attending the body's monthly meetings in London. Additionally, while out on bail, he continued to participate in hunt disruptions, which understandably distressed his parents. "They were very terrified I would be arrested again and put in prison," Ronnie said, adding, however, he wasn't involved with as many disruptions as he had been prior to his apprehension by police.

Ronnie's superiors at Machin and Company, who had learned of his arrest, didn't want him to work at the law firm anymore. "I didn't want to work there anymore anyway," Ronnie said, adding he and his father organized a meeting at Machin and Company to end his contract. While in the office, Ronnie saw the former police sergeant, with whom he discussed law enforcement tactics and capabilities. "He gave me this very strange look," Ronnie said, noting it wasn't an unfriendly look. "He'd obviously realized that my conversations with him were a bit more than he thought they were."

In need of a new job, Ronnie applied to work for the Luton local authority as a road sweeper. They didn't care he was on bail, so long as the charges against him weren't related to home burglary. "If you're a road sweeper, you do have some opportunity to case people's houses," Ronnie said, adding that because his charges were unrelated to this, the local authority gave him the job. Ronnie commuted to work on the bus, which took about an hour to get to the cleansing department at the council depot from his parents' house. "Because of the time that bus got in—it was the first bus in the morning—I was always five minutes late for work," Ronnie said, adding the time clock, which operated in increments, would record him as being 15-minutes late. "I wasn't happy about this, because I couldn't help it. That was the very earliest I could get to work and I was working 10 minutes for which I wasn't being paid."

So Ronnie went to see the cleansing supervisor, who drove around during the day to make sure the road sweepers were working. "I said, look, could you either pay me for the 10 minutes that I'm working, or allow me to work an extra five minutes at the end of the day?" Ronnie said, noting his supervisor argued that wasn't possible. "I was angry about this." Ronnie decided to extend his breaks to make up for his unpaid work. He did this for a couple of weeks before he was confronted about it by the supervisor. "He said, I noticed that your barrow was unattended for longer than it should have been," Ronnie recalled, adding he then explained to the supervisor why he was taking longer breaks. "He said, oh, that's outrageous." Despite the supervisor's admonition to keep to the assigned schedule, Ronnie continued to extend his breaks.

Discovering this, the supervisor brought Ronnie to the cleansing manager, who was in charge of the depot. The manager said he had no other option but to dismiss Ronnie. In response, Ronnie said he wouldn't leave the manager's office until he was allowed to keep his job, and accused the manager of having done nothing in response to an elderly sweeper's death from pneumonia, which Ronnie believed to have been the result of inadequate clothing provided by the local authority. "I said, I know one thing, you're not going to die, are you?" Ronnie recalled. "I said, because you're sitting in here in your fancy office in your fancy clothes, drinking cups of tea." The manager called the police, and, from the side of the conversation Ronnie heard, it was clear they didn't want to get involved. But the manager eventually cajoled the authorities into responding, exaggerating the threat Ronnie posed.

When the police arrived, the officers said they heard there was a man in the office causing trouble. "I said to the police officers, yes, there certainly is officers—it's this man over here," Ronnie recalled, adding he pointed to the manager. "He said, no, no, it's not me; it's this man. And I said, no it's that man." Looking between the manager in a suit and Ronnie in dirty overalls, the authorities sided with the manager and escorted Ronnie out. So Ronnie went to see his union representative, who said the group couldn't do anything on his behalf. "I said, yeah that's typical of the unions; you're always selling the workers out," Ronnie recalled. "I had a go at the union guy as well." But Ronnie wasn't disheartened. He decided to try and foment a wildcat strike amongst the sweepers.

Ronnie wrote and printed some leaflets, which he distributed to his former coworkers outside the depot. Among other things, the leaflet discussed the sweeper who had died of pneumonia. "It was good stuff," Ronnie said, laughing. "Anyway, they didn't go on strike. I think most of them were more worried about their job. The thing is, I knew I was going to jail, [so] I wasn't particularly concerned. That job was only a stopgap." In need of employment, Ronnie got a job with an office supplier, which provided businesses with everything from desks to printing paper.

While out on bail, Ronnie's social life was limited. He wasn't dating anyone. "I was so focused on the animal issue and on political issues that I didn't really have time for anything else," Ronnie said, adding, however, he socialized with hunt saboteurs and the operators of a left-wing book store. "I'd sit around with them. We'd talk, maybe have a few drinks and that kind of thing. I no longer had contact with my old friends in Stevenage at all."

On October 16, Ronnie appeared in a London police station after receiving a summons. "When I got there, there were like 13 other people there," Ronnie said, adding they were members of the British Withdrawal from Northern Ireland Campaign, with whom he had distributed leaflets at army bases. "We were all charged with an offense called incitement to disaffection." Ronnie phoned his parents to explain the charge and say he would be granted bail. Taking no chances, Ron immediately moved a great number of his son's belongings into the trunk of his car, fearing police might search the Lees' home. "He didn't know what was in my room," Ronnie said, noting there actually wasn't anything incriminating inside. "I thought it was quite sweet of him to do that."

On November 27, Ronnie, Cliff and Robin attended the committal proceeding at Bristol Magistrates' Court for their Band of Mercy actions. Often, in such proceedings, the defense accepts there's enough evidence to warrant a trial. While there was more than enough evidence incriminating the trio, Ronnie sought maximum publicity and contested the committal. Ronnie spoke on his own behalf, despite having a solicitor. "It wasn't going to do me any harm," Ronnie said, noting the evidence against him was over-whelming. He used the opportunity to question the owner of the seal boats he'd torched. "I started asking him, how do you justify slaughtering the seals?" Ronnie said, laughing. "Of course, you're not allowed to ask things like that. So the magistrate kept stopping me from asking questions." Ulti-mately, the trio was sent for trial.

In early 1975, Ronnie read a book by Richard Ryder called *Victims of Science: The Use of Animals in Research*. "I wouldn't say it so much had an influence on me," Ronnie said. "It backed up what I already believed in a philosophical way." Richard's book was where Ronnie first encountered the word speciesism, which he instantly understood. "It gave a name to that prejudice that I was opposed to," Ronnie said. Interestingly, he knew Rich-ard, who was involved in the Reform Group of the Royal Society for the Prevention of Cruelty to Animals, and, to some degree, the Hunt Saboteurs Association. "He wasn't as rough and ready as the rest of us," Ronnie said. "It was obvious that he was an academic-type guy."

In the lead-up to his trial, Ronnie was the subject of a social-inquiry report, designed to help the judge with sentencing. The probation officer responsible for the report seemed to have a military background. "I was hoping I would get some radical, young chap," Ronnie said, describing his disappointment upon meeting the older, conservative-looking man. "I thought, this guy is not going to be the type of person who will be sympa-thetic to me, and he's probably going to recommend big jail time." Still, Ronnie explained to the officer how he felt about animals and his motiva-tion for the attacks. During their conversation, the officer took a lot of notes, but gave no indication of what he thought of Ronnie's explanation. "I was worried," Ronnie said.

A few weeks later, Ronnie spoke with his solicitor, who read Ronnie's social-inquiry report and couldn't understand the recommendation. "He said, I don't know what to make of it; I don't know what we should do," Ronnie recalled. "I said, oh, what's happened? Because, I thought, he's prob-ably said I should have 10 years. The solicitor said, well, he's recommended that you should receive an absolute discharge, which means no punishment whatsoever." Ronnie was flabbergasted as the solicitor read him the report, which described Ronnie as a man of integrity. "My solicitor said, this is brilliant, but the trouble is the judge isn't going to take any notice of that," Ronnie recalled. "He said, there's no way the judge is going to give you no penalty." The officer's recommendation was simply too lenient to be taken seriously. So Ronnie's solicitor persuaded the officer to change his recommendation from an absolute discharge to a suspended sentence.

In February, Robin received a two-year suspended sentence and a 500-pound fine for his involvement in the seal-boat arson. By this point, Ronnie had forgiven Cliff for providing evidence to the police. "It was obvious Cliff realized what he did and was regretful about it," Ronnie recalled, adding Cliff said he was frightened during the interrogation. "That's not an excuse for having done it, but it is a kind of reason, I suppose." On March 24, the two appeared in court together. They both pled guilty, with Ronnie representing himself. "I'd seen barristers speak on behalf of people who had been convicted, and they always groveled," he said, arguing lawyers always claimed their clients regretted their actions. "I didn't want that. I was not apologetic. I did not want anyone to say sorry on my behalf." Ronnie feared a barrister might do this, despite his wishes.

At Ronnie's request, Richard gave evidence to the court about animal experiments and the suffering involved. "He was actually allowed to do that, which was really good," Ronnie said. "Some judges might not have allowed that. But this judge did." Besides serving the defense, Richard's testimony helped publicize the horrors of vivisection. "It was good for what he said to receive media attention," Ronnie said. Cliff's barrister gave exactly the sort of apologetic statement which Ronnie worried his own might have given. "I turned to Cliff and said, this is bloody awful what he's saying," Ronnie recalled. "Cliff said, oh, I know; I know."

When it was Ronnie's turn to speak to the court, he made sure it was clear he had no remorse for the Band of Mercy actions. "I said, I have no apologies whatsoever for what I did," Ronnie recalled. "I said, I acted to save animals from suffering; I don't think I've done anything wrong and I hope people will carry on the fight, in whatever way they can, against animals being persecuted." The room was packed with Ronnie's friends and sympathizers. When he ended his speech they burst into applause. "The judge had to tell people to be quiet," Ronnie said. Despite his unapologetic stance, Ronnie received the exact same sentence as Cliff—three years in prison. This was a lighter punishment than Ronnie expected. According to Ronnie, the case generated sympathetic headlines in national newspapers, including conservative tabloids like *The Sun*, which likened him and Cliff to martyrs. "The report was really sympathetic to us," Ronnie said. "We were really surprised."

The pair was sent back to Oxford Prison, where they began serving their sentence. Before he was convicted, Ronnie was allowed to receive food from outside, rather than consume meals prepared in the facility. This changed following his conviction. He was only allowed to eat prison food, and there were no provisions for vegans. "If you were a Muslim or a Jew, you would get a diet in accordance with your religion," Ronnie said. "If you were a vegetarian, you would get a vegetarian diet. But veganism wasn't recognized." Prison officials sought to give Ronnie the vegetarian meals and force him to pick out those ingredients he found disagreeable. But this wasn't good enough for Ronnie. So he began a hunger strike.

At this point, Ronnie and Cliff's supporters started protesting regularly outside of the facility, both against the duo's conviction and the prison's refusal to provide Ronnie with vegan food. Among these protesters was Ivor Clemitson—a member of Parliament for Luton East, representing the Labour Party. "He came to visit me in prison and he was very sympathetic," Ronnie said, adding he had met the politician before. "I actually went around to see him. I went to his house, I think, while I was on bail. So I knew him quite well." Unfortunately, Ronnie wasn't able to see the protests on his behalf, which lasted approximately until he ended the hunger strike.

After five days without eating, on March 29, Ronnie was moved to Winchester Prison. "Oxford Prison didn't have very good hospital facilities, you see," Ronnie said. "Obviously, if someone's on hunger strike, eventually they may need to end up in a hospital-type environment, although I hadn't reached that stage." Prison officials continued to try and ply him with vegetarian food, but Ronnie refused to eat until he was provided with an undertaking guaranteeing him vegan meals. "It was easy at first," Ronnie said, laughing. "But then I started dreaming of food—in my dreams I was eating food and stuff. Obviously, I felt very weak."

Ronnie ended his hunger strike on April 3, after 10 days without eating, following a meeting with the prison official in charge of the kitchen. "He said, I'm only allowed limited resources, but can we sit down and work something out?" Ronnie recalled. "I had to explain to him what I ate and what I didn't eat." Together they planned a variety of recipes for Ronnie's food in prison. "It was very rudimentary," Ronnie said. "But, I thought, at least I'm being recognized as a vegan." He attributed the prison's change in policy to variety of things, including his petition to the Home Office and pressure applied by Ivor.

On April 29, Ronnie and Cliff were moved to Verne Prison, where they were on friendly terms. "I didn't think anything was gained from being unpleasant to Cliff," Ronnie said, adding their charges were a novelty to other inmates. "I think a lot of them were rather bemused at what we were in prison for. They found it strange someone was in prison for something that didn't involve personal gain. But there was a lot of sympathy. Prisoners did understand we were trying to prevent cruelty to animals." This sympathy didn't just come from prisoners. In private, some prison officials told Ronnie they appreciated his illegal actions. "I'd have prison officers come and talk to me and say, this is just between you and me, but I agree with what you did," Ronnie said, noting a few officials expressed such sympathy. Ronnie got a job in the Verne's workshop, making parts for wooden rocking horses. "Prisons would make money selling these things," Ronnie said. "We were paid. But it was only a very small wage." Ronnie spent the money he earned at the prison canteen, buying supplemental foods like fruit and peanut butter.

During this period, there was a lull in Band of Mercy actions. "Probably Cliff, myself and Robin were the most active people," Ronnie said, adding there were likely no more than 10 members of the group. "We'd been arrested. I think the other people got worried about what might happen to them. Everything went quiet and there were no more actions." This was true while the trio was on bail. But particularly after he and Cliff were sentenced, Ronnie started to believe the fire of illegal action on behalf of animals would be extinguished. "I began thinking to myself, this is the end of it," Ronnie said, adding the prospect filled him with sadness. "We were hoping that other people would join in—that it would grow, that it would escalate. That didn't really happen."

But then on June 18, Mike Huskisson, a national committee member of the Hunt Saboteurs Association, rescued two beagles from an Imperial Chemical Industries laboratory in Cheshire. "These dogs were being forced to smoke tobacco which gave them lung cancer," Ronnie said, adding the rescue wasn't claimed by any group. Two days later, Mike was arrested for attempting to liberate a third beagle from the facility. Another man, named John Bryant, was charged with receiving stolen property for his role in looking after the freed animals. While the first two dogs were never recovered by authorities, unfortunately the third animal was returned to Imperial Chemical Industries. "I was really pleased that these beagles had been taken because someone else had done some direct action," Ronnie said, noting he knew both John Bryant and Mike prior to this. Ultimately, the charges against the two were dropped because the company feared a trial might generate bad publicity.

In September, Ronnie was moved to a London prison, called Wormwood Scrubs, because he was due to go on trial in the city for his involvement in the British Withdrawal from Northern Ireland Campaign. "Wormwood Scrubs was like Oxford Prison," Ronnie said. "I was back at a Victorian prison again, where there was a bucket in the cell to piss in. It was back to those conditions." While there, he met John Walker, one of the six men falsely accused of having carried out the Birmingham pub bombings the previous year, which were attributed to the Provisional Irish Republican Army. "I was talking to him and he said, I'm innocent," Ronnie said, adding John Walker was covered in bruises inflicted by prison officials. "Obviously I didn't know [at the time] whether he was innocent or not, but I was aware that it was really, quite possible the police would frame people." Ronnie recalled John Walker as sympathetic to Band of Mercy actions.

On October 20, Mick Mott, one of Ronnie's friends from the Vegan Society, committed an arson attack against a Bowyers sausage factory in Amersham. Mick claimed the action on behalf of the Band of Mercy, and, in his anonymous statement to the press, demanded Ronnie's release. Correctly believing the perpetrator was someone Ronnie knew, the police questioned everyone Ronnie corresponded with while in prison. However, Mick never exchanged letters with Ronnie and thus evaded suspicion. Ronnie was happy illegal action for animals continued in his absence. But he saw the sausage factory as a strange target, not in keeping with Band of Mercy strategy. "We were seeking to intervene in the chain of animal abuse, whereas setting fire to a sausage factory doesn't do that, " Ronnie said. "The animals are already dead."

The same month, Ronnie and his fellow pacifists went on trial at the Central Criminal Court of England and Wales, the Old Bailey, for incitement to disaffection. The proceedings lasted for about six weeks and once again Ronnie represented himself. "But I had very little work to do," Ronnie said, noting he and others pled not guilty. "Some of the other defendants had barristers. All the leading radical barristers were involved in that case." Because the defendants all faced the same charge, the arguments made by the barristers applied to those who represented themselves. On December 10, the jury returned with a not-guilty verdict after deliberating for only half an hour. This came as a shock to Ronnie, who thought the case might add two years to his sentence, based on an earlier conviction of peace activist Pat Arrowsmith for similar activity.

Following his trial, Ronnie was sent back the Verne. While there, he had frequent disputes with a prison psychologist who saw Ronnie as a corrupting influence, responsible for leading Cliff to prison. "He said, you know, Cliff isn't coping all that well here—he finds it very difficult—and that's your fault," Ronnie recalled. "I said, look, Cliff's nine years older than me. I said, you're talking nonsense." Still, Ronnie agreed he adjusted to prison life better than his former co-conspirator. "Cliff was much straighter than me," Ronnie said. "Cliff was just this normal guy who cared about animals. So that prison environment was more difficult for him. But that wasn't my fault. He was old enough to decide what he wanted to do." Ronnie would argue that point with the psychologist for hours.

On March 29, 1976, Ronnie and Cliff were released on parole, following a demonstration outside the Home Office calling for this. "I think we probably would have gotten parole without the protests, to be honest," Ronnie said. "A really heavy thing in our favor was this was our first offense." Ronnie returned to Meppershall to live with his mother. By that time, his father had moved to Ireland, after accepting a job at an engineering company near Dublin. Margaret would move to join her husband later that year. Patty was caring for a growing family, having given birth to a son named Kyall in January 1975.

8

Animal Liberation Front

Ronnie, by then 25, only lived with his mother in Meppershall for a few weeks. "Basically, the parole stipulated I had to report to a probation officer every so often," Ronnie said, adding there were no restrictions on where he could live. So Ronnie moved to a squat in London, on Nelson Road in Crouch End, along with his friends Liz Davies and Brian Douieb, who ran a left-wing business called Partisan Books, which had—up until that point—operated in Luton. These friends opened another squat for the bookstore on Archway Road. "There was a lot of work to be done at the bookshop—carpentry and that kind of thing," Ronnie said, adding he'd learned a number of practical skills while in prison. "I'd done a carpentry course. So, I thought, I'd be useful to them." In addition to helping at the bookstore, Ronnie received unemployment benefits.

The house which the trio moved into was a three-story building, owned by the London and Quadrant Housing Trust. Other, unaffiliated squatters lived there as well. "Not everyone there was a vegetarian," Ronnie said, adding he had convinced Liz and Brian to give up meat. "But there was a rule that all the food [cooked in the building] would have to be vegetarian." Chores were delegated amongst the residents, with notices posted about whose turn it was clean and cook. Eventually the housing association came to an agreement with the squatters. "They would allow us to stay in the property," Ronnie said, adding the squatters prevented vandals from damaging the building. "They wouldn't charge us any rent or anything like that. But then they would give us a good deal of notice when they wanted to do the place up—to give us time to move out."

Ronnie and his friends started opening other squats on the same street for homeless families and people. When someone needed shelter, Ronnie would break into a nearby house and change the locks. "The population did change quite often," Brian said, adding the trio put notices on newly-squatted buildings, indicating a court order was required for any eviction. "This complied with the law at the time. We had a box full of locks and Yale keys at the ready—day and night." Connecting the utilities was easy, as the companies involved didn't question potential customers. "As long as they knew the bill was going to be paid, they didn't look into whether you were a squatter or what your status as an occupier was," Ronnie said. He viewed his involvement in the squatting movement of the time as an expression of his left-wing politics. "First of all, there were homeless people, and, secondly, there were empty homes those people could live in," Ronnie said. "We were just putting those two together."

Mick lived about a mile away from Ronnie, so the two saw a lot of each other. One day, while Ronnie was busy, Mick got into a conversation with another squatter at the building on Nelson Road. It turned out the squatter, who worked at a university, was engaged in animal testing. Ronnie was appalled when Mick told him this, but Mick promised to do something about it. So before the squatter left on vacation, Mick offered to service the man's vehicle for the cost of materials. "[Mick] put grinding paste in the oil or something," Ronnie said. "Eventually, this got through to the engine and just ground the engine away." During the squatter's vacation, the man's vehicle broke down in the middle of nowhere. "I don't know whether he ever suspected it had anything to do with Mick," Ronnie said, amused.

Around this time, Ronnie, Mick and two other activists met at the home of a sympathizer with a journalist writing an article on the Band of Mercy for an Australian newspaper called *The Age*. To disguise their identities, the activists wore stockings over their faces, which, for good measure, they covered with superhero masks. During the interview, the sympathizer made the group five cups of tea, without realizing the activists couldn't drink without disturbing their disguises. "I looked at the cups of tea and said to the journalist, would you like five cups of tea?" Ronnie recalled with amusement. "He actually included that in his article." Additionally, in the story, the activists were referred to by the superhero identity they'd assumed, which Ronnie found humorous.

On another occasion, a kitten showed up on the doorstep of Ronnie's squat. "We took him in," Ronnie said, adding he placed posters throughout the neighborhood, asking if anyone had lost a kitten. "Nobody came forward. So we ended up adopting the kitten as the house cat, but it was really me who was in charge of him." The squatters named the animal Cyril, after professional soccer player Cyril Knowles, who—a few years earlier—had served as inspiration for Cockerel Chorus' hit song, "Nice One, Cyril." "We got a litter tray for [the kitten]," Ronnie said. "He immediately went to the toilet in the litter tray and somebody said, oh, nice one, Cyril." That's how the kitten got his name.

Ronnie didn't like the idea of feeding meat to Cyril. Uninformed about cats' dietary needs, he went to a health-food store in the area and bought tins of nutmeat for Cyril. "He never ate very much of the nutmeat," Ronnie said, adding that, despite this, the cat seemed fine. "I thought, this nutmeat must be great—because he's hardly eating any of it, and yet he's growing and he's really healthy." Ronnie believed this until a woman, who lived down the road, complained that Cyril was eating her cat's food. "She said, several times a day, your kitten comes into our house when my kitten is having his food, knocks my kitten off his food, and eats my kitten's food," Ronnie recalled, noting Cyril was entering the woman's house through an open window. "So after that I had to feed him ordinary cat food."

As a joke, during a visit from an official representing the Department of Health and Social Security, Ronnie claimed Cyril as a dependent. "[The official] interviewed Ronnie about his finances," Liz said. "She asked all the routine questions. Then she asked about any dependents. Ronnie provided the name, age and all relevant information she requested. She then asked where this dependent called Cyril was. He pointed out his little cat sitting under the chair." Ronnie had kept a straight face the entire time. "It was the funniest moment," Liz said. "She had no idea how to respond."

During this period, Ronnie had a series of brief, romantic relationships which were the most serious of his life so far. One girlfriend was divorced, with two young children. Though she was an omnivore, Ronnie thought there was a chance she might assume a vegan diet. "I talked to her about it," he said. "I used to show her how to cook vegetarian food. I used to cook meals and she seemed to be really interested." However, one day, Ronnie discovered she had purchased her boy fishing equipment. "I said, what's that doing here?" Ronnie recalled. "She said, don't you say anything; I bought that for my son for his birthday." This was a make-or-break issue for Ronnie, so he ended the relationship.

Another girlfriend, who was a hunt saboteur, made the mistake of revealing his past incarceration to her landlord, who banned Ronnie from the property. "He immediately said, you're not allowed to have him in the house," Ronnie said, adding the landlord threatened to throw the woman out if she broke this rule. "I used to meet her at other places, but I wasn't able to go to her home." Finally, Ronnie dated a woman who provided temporary shelter to those animals saved by the Animal Liberation Front, which was soon to be formed. "She had a smallholding-type place and a barn," Ronnie said, adding he sometimes used this location to house rescued animals before moving them to long-term homes. "She didn't go on raids herself. She was too nervous."

By this point, Ronnie had learned romantic relationships could be more than a distraction from animal activism. They could be emotionally sustaining. "Having gone to prison, I thought, maybe it would be nice to take a bit of a break and have a relationship with someone," Ronnie said, adding that, during his Band of Mercy days, he didn't have space in his life for someone else, as he was completely consumed by the horror of animal exploitation. "I kind of got used to that being the situation." Ronnie argued such acclimatization was necessary for activists' mental health. "There are people who have gone crazy, to be honest—people who have killed themselves," Ronnie said. "You can't keep that kind of intensity up. Although I was still pretty intense into it, I did start finding room for relationships. I felt that was a good thing to have. It helped keep me going."

Though, initially, coverage of the genre turned him off, Ronnie became enamored with punk music. "I didn't like what I read," he said. "These bands would be spitting at the audience and the audience would be spitting at them. They would be fighting with the audience. I thought, these are awful people." But then Gary Treadwell, a friend from the hunt saboteurs, played him the Ramones. "I was blown away by it," Ronnie said, adding he loved the American band's rawness and energy. "I thought it was brilliant." So he started following the punk scene in his own country, attending live performances by the Clash, the Stranglers, and the Sex Pistols, among others. "There was a very-well known venue called the Rainbow [Theatre]," Ronnie said. "That was the one I used to go to the most." Despite this enthusiasm, he didn't adopt the scene's aesthetic. "Ronnie never embraced punk fashion and always wore his cap, tank top and plimsolls," Gary said. "I did manage to persuade him to shave off his beard, but that was as far as I got."

After his release from prison, Ronnie quickly returned to activism, forming a group of hunt saboteurs in North London. He didn't particularly worry this might endanger his parole. "My probation officer didn't care about that," Ronnie recalled. "He was very sympathetic to me. He said, I don't know why I'm having to see you; I don't consider you a criminal. Basically, it was just a formality that I went to see him." Ronnie also resumed his membership on the national committee of the Hunt Saboteurs Association. "I hadn't been thrown off the committee," Ronnie said, adding he didn't require reelection. "I kind of carried on where I left off."

The North London group decided they would fight back against those hunters who attacked them, a stance which was in opposition to the informal policy of the Hunt Saboteurs Association. "Hunt sabs would frequently be beaten up," Ronnie said. "They would kind of just curl up in a ball and be beaten by the hunt. We decided, we don't really like that; we're not going to go to a hunt and be attacked." The North London group resolved to meet any aggression on the hunters' part with immediate, significant force. "As soon as they laid the slightest finger on anyone, we'd attack," Ronnie said. "We wouldn't stand for any of it." He said his group's retaliation was proportional. "If somebody pushed someone, we wouldn't kill them," Ronnie said, noting their goal was self-defense. "But sometimes that would escalate." The North London activists got a reputation for violence, so other saboteur groups would refuse to work with them.

Beagle hunts were particularly prone to confrontation, since the hunters were on foot, amongst the saboteurs. Ronnie recalled one such hunt erupting in an unusual degree of violence. "One of the beagle hunters hit one of the hunt sabs," Ronnie said. "An all-out fight broke out, because we fought back against him. Then the others joined in." When it was over, the saboteurs defeated the hunters, having knocked over and bruised their opponents. "I remember walking along and there was a ditch at the side of the road," Ronnie said, laughing. "There were quite a number of these hunters just lying in the ditch, where they'd fell. We'd not quite knocked them out, but they'd been punched." The North London group left immediately after this, believing the hunters were no longer in a fit state to kill animals.

During this period, Ronnie and his fellow saboteurs disrupted a service held at Saint Andrew's Church, in Boscombe, by a reverend who, in his spare time, served as joint master of a Wiltshire otter hunt. "We went into church service and we had our own hymns," Ronnie said, noting one of the saboteurs had written variations of traditional Christian songs. "So we started singing these hymns, and they were all attacking the vicar for being involved in the hunt." According to a contemporary account in the *Montreal Gazette,* activists reimagined the lyrics of a popular hymn to read as follows: "All things bright and beautiful / All things great and small / All things wise and wonderful / Your preacher kills them all." Outraged, the reverend ended the service.

Ronnie and about 130 other saboteurs disrupted the Waterloo Cup, a large coursing event in Lancashire, held annually. "The police tried to form a cordon to keep us off the coursing field," Ronnie said. "We broke through the police line." Amongst the activists swarming the field, he spotted a police officer dragging a comrade by the hair. "I punched him to stop him from pulling her hair," Ronnie said. "She was screaming—it was really hurting her." Ronnie, who was arrested, was one of several dozen activists charged with causing a breach of the peace. This didn't effect his parole. "It really depends on your probation officer," Ronnie said. "One that was unsympathetic to me would have put pressure to get me taken back to jail. But my one wasn't like that."

Ronnie was also involved with a group, called Animal Activists, that staged occupations of fur stores and departments. Such protests became so frequent, the specialty businesses developed means to prevent them. "A lot of these shops had a system where you couldn't just walk in," Ronnie said. "You had to ring a bell on a shop door. Then the guy would look at you to see what you looked like." To circumvent this, one day, two activists dressed in expensive-looking clothes to ring the bell, while the rest of the group hid around the corner. When the door opened, Ronnie and the others burst inside. The proprietor fell to his knees, falsely believing the activists intended to harm him. "He started saying, please don't kill me; please don't kill me," Ronnie said. "I said, you deserve to be killed for what you do the animals, but we're not going to kill you; we're just going to wreck your shop."

Animal campaigners frequently expressed to Ronnie their interest in illegal action which went beyond this, more in the vein of Band of Mercy attacks. "I had loads of people come up to me and say, I want to get involved," Ronnie recalled. "I was amazed." In the years while he was incarcerated, the animal movement had grown significantly. "A lot more people had come into animal rights," Ronnie said. "It was like the feeling of the times. Peter Singer had written his book *Animal Liberation*. There were other philosophical books coming out—Richard Ryder's book for instance. There was this buzz in the air. It was something people, particularly young people, were getting interested in."

At first, Ronnie avoided direct involvement in covert attacks. Still, he participated in discussion about the subject, providing advice to those who were considering those tactics. But, in a series of informal conversations, with as many as 30 people, Ronnie got the impression new activists didn't particularly like the Band of Mercy's name. "It was just talking to people on hunt sabs, talking to people at demonstrations," Ronnie recalled. "They said, that's a funny name; what's it called that for? [They said], it doesn't mention animals; it sounds like a religious organization." Of course, Ronnie explained the history behind the name, but he began to think these activists had a point.

So, in June 1976, Ronnie came up with a new name, the Animal Liberation Front. "In Algeria, there had been the National Liberation Front, that fought against the French occupation," Ronnie said, adding he liked the associations implied by describing the group as a liberation front. "Liberation

front was associated with something more than a philosophy. It was associated with something active. It was associated with a militant struggle."
Those who expressed interest to Ronnie in illegal action were happy with
this new name. They were mostly under 25 years old, and divided roughly
equally between men and women. According to Ronnie, besides him and
Sue, there was no membership carryover between the Band of Mercy and
the rechristened organization.

That same month, one of the first actions claimed by the Animal Liberation Front took place, with activists rescuing three pregnant beagles
from a Pfizer laboratory in Sandwich. "There was a river directly behind
the compound," Ronnie said. "[The Animal Liberation Front] was going
to steal one of these boats, row across the river, break in the back, take the
dogs, and then row the dogs back across the river. And that's what they
did." Ronnie didn't participate directly in the raid, but, prior to the action,
he talked it over with those who did. "I had just come out of prison," Ronnie
said, laughing as he explained his absence. "I didn't really fancy being
arrested again immediately and going back. Of course, as someone just
advising people, I didn't stand the same chance of arrest as someone who
was actually there in the field." The rescued beagles had 13 puppies.

As more actions were claimed on behalf of the Animal Liberation
Front, Ronnie started to get itchy feet. The legal activism in which he participated, such as hunt sabotage, left him unsatisfied. "There was nothing
the same as going somewhere in the night and breaking in," Ronnie started.
"I thought that struck a harder blow at the animal abusers, to be honest....
These other things were good, but they weren't enough for me." So, in
August, Ronnie participated in an Animal Liberation Front raid that damaged four vehicles and a horse trailer associated with the Essex hunt. "We
pulled some electrical wires out from the engine, and we also poured water
into the fuel tank," Ronnie said, referring to the hound van.

Later that month, Ronnie and others attacked the Cambridgeshire
office of a man who bred pigs and sheep for vivisection. They painted slogans on the building, comparing the breeder's operation to Auschwitz concentration camp—which the man later took exception to, in the press, as
a former prisoner of Colditz Castle. "I had no sympathy for that," Ronnie
said. "I thought, if he'd been tortured, then surely that should teach him
not to send other creatures to be tortured." Despite destroying all of the
breeder's office equipment, the group saw Ronnie as having gone too far
when he stomped on the breeder's glasses. "I said, for me the only problem
was that he wasn't wearing them at the time," Ronnie recalled. "I said, when
he's running his business, to do with supplying these animals to laboratories,

Ronnie (second from left), photographed in June 1976, with a group of hunt saboteurs, about to disrupt the Border Counties Otter Hunt at Llandinam in Wales (photograph Mike Huskisson, courtesy Animal Welfare Information Service).

he wears those glasses." For Ronnie, this made them a fair target. However,
other members of the group saw breaking the breeder's glasses as too personal and refused to carry out future actions with Ronnie.

On another occasion, Ronnie served as driver for two activists vandalizing an Essex business that bred small animals for experimentation. After
dropping the pair off, Ronnie moved the vehicle to a housing estate a couple of miles away, where he waited for a prearranged time to pass, at which
point he planned to drive back to the establishment. "A police car pulled
up," Ronnie said, hypothesizing he looked suspicious sitting in his vehicle
in the early hours of the morning. "They said, what are you doing here? I
said, my car's broken down and I'm waiting for a friend to come and give
me a lift." The police accepted this explanation and drove off.

At the appointed time, Ronnie drove back to the business to pick up
his comrades, when he was spotted by the same police he'd just encountered.
"He said, what are you doing here?" Ronnie recalled an officer asking. "I
said, I've managed to get my car going; it appears to be okay now." When
the officer questioned him further, Ronnie said he was lost and trying to

work out where he was. "He obviously was suspicious," Ronnie recalled. "He said to me, are you a member of Friends of the Earth?" Ronnie believed the officer was warned the business might be targeted, but confused the threat—the Animal Liberation Front—with the environmental group. "He said, one of these places here is connected with experiments on animals, and Friends of the Earth has threatened to damage all these places," Ronnie recalled, adding the officer demanded his identification. "I had to give my proper details because he'd have found them out from the car registration anyway."

When the officer radioed police headquarters, he discovered Ronnie's entire legal history, including Ronnie's incarceration for Band of Mercy actions. "He said, right, I'm not happy about you at all, and I'm going to arrest you," Ronnie recalled, adding the officer took him to the nearest police station, where he refused to talk. Authorities searched his Nelson-Road squat and found what they initially believed to be explosive material, but merely turned out to be a barrel of engine oil. Ronnie worried about the activists he'd left behind at the breeding business—not so much because they'd need to make their own way home, but because any damage they inflicted could incriminate him. The police assured Ronnie they would check in with establishment to see if anything suspicious had occurred overnight.

Some hours later, Ronnie was released. "I drove back home and obviously the first thing I wanted to do was sleep," he recalled, adding he made contact, later in the day, with the activists he'd dropped off. The duo apparently witnessed Ronnie's stop by police and knew they had to escape on their own. "They said, we just walked for miles across the fields, made it to the nearest railway station, and eventually got the train and got back to London," Ronnie recalled, adding he asked whether they caused any damage to the facility before leaving. "They said, oh yeah, we sprayed slogans all over the place." Given this, Ronnie was mystified as to why the police released him. Thinking about it in retrospect, he didn't have further insight.

Ronnie wasn't chastened by this close call. "I thought, I'm just going to get back involved in it," Ronnie said, adding there were many minor incidents in which he broke windows of businesses connected to animal exploitation. "We were always trying to break fur-shop windows and butcher-shop [windows]." Ronnie and his comrades would keep bricks in their cars solely for this purpose. "Now, if you did that, you would be caught very, very quickly because of closed-circuit television," Ronnie said. "But in those days they didn't have it—or it was very rare." Meanwhile, the Animal Liberation Front was spreading. In October, activists released 1,500 foxes from a fur farm in Scotland, claiming the action on behalf of the group. "I was really pleased," Ronnie said, noting he had no prior knowledge of the action and didn't know who was behind it. "Obviously, if I had to be involved in everything that happened, that would severely limit how many things happened. I was delighted that other people were taking things into their own hands.... That's exactly what I wanted to see."

In November, Ronnie and a group of about four others targeted an Oxford Laboratory Animal Colonies breeding center in Capel Isaac, Wales. "This was, at the time, the biggest, beagle-breeding center in Europe," Ronnie said, adding he'd found homes for 13 puppies prior to the rescue. "That was only a fraction of the number there, but at least we'd save the lives of those dogs." The group sought to disable the facility's phone lines, so, if they were discovered, anyone working at the center wouldn't be able to call the police. "The idea was to throw a grappling hook over, on the end of a rope, catch the [telephone] wires and just pull them down," Ronnie said, noting that, when one of his comrades attempted to accomplish this, things didn't go exactly as planned. "He'd mistaken telephone wires for electricity cables. He threw the grappling hook up—it went over these cables—and all of a sudden all this electricity started shooting down."

After jumping out of the way, the group removed their grappling hook and proceeded without disabling the phone lines. They cut a hole in the facility's fence and removed 13 dogs from the kennels. "I think we put them in boxes," Ronnie said, adding the animals were only a few months old. "They were really, quite small." He and his comrades brought the beagles back to their rented van and drove to various sanctuaries, which previously had agreed to take the dogs. The rescue was covered in a number of the national papers, with reporters suggesting the Animal Liberation Front had climbed a wall blocking the entrance. "For some reason, in the newspaper stories, it was that commandos had scaled this huge wall," Ronnie said, laughing. "But we hadn't. We'd gone in the back and gone through the fence." Later that month, police came to question him about this action, and others he was involved in, but Ronnie refused to speak with authorities.

Ronnie and other activists frequently rescued hens from battery farms, which generally had no security. "They would be easy places to break in," he said. "We'd get in there and take maybe a couple of dozens hens." Ronnie would take the birds to rural sympathizers who owned barns or similar shelters. "They would take some time to recover," he said. "A lot of these hens would have most of their feathers missing.... They'd have to be nursed back to health so they began to—eventually—look like healthy hens." Not all of the rescues Ronnie participated in were so free of risk. As he had before, Ronnie believed he would ultimately be caught and accepted that possibility. "I knew I was on borrowed time, really," he said.

In early 1977, when the London and Quadrant Housing Trust began renovations on the squat, Ronnie and Cyril moved to live in Hounslow, West London, with Ronnie's friend Angie Wright and her partner. "They said that I could rent the upstairs of their house from them," Ronnie said, adding Angie ran a local vegetarian group, with members who Angie complained were too timid to get involved in activism, legal or otherwise. "So I came in the house from hunt sabbing one day, walked in through the entrance through the back, and she was sitting around in a circle with about eight of these people from the vegetarian group, having a discussion about recipes or something," Ronnie recalled. "I said, have you had the discussion about bombing the butcher's yet?" Ronnie's joke scared the group members, so Angie confronted him about it later. "She said, you could have destroyed the group saying that," Ronnie recalled, laughing. "She said, they might never come again."

Angie believed it was likely Ronnie, who she counted as a friend, was engaged in illegal action for animals, but didn't look into the matter. "I am not a naturally curious person," she said. "The police came to my place of work on one occasion—I was a teacher—asking questions about Ronnie. I denied knowing anything about him or his activities, and said that he was simply a lodger." Angie added that, while she wasn't sure about Ronnie's involvement in the Animal Liberation Front, she would have sanctioned it. "I would have supported Ronnie in any activities he undertook as he is an animal-rights vegan," Angie said, noting she shared his belief system.

On February 19, having received updated information on laboratory-animal suppliers, Ronnie and others targeted a London business which bred mice for testing. "There was a truck there that we damaged," Ronnie said. "We slashed the tires." Moving inside the facility, the group rescued 125 mice. "I think that was because the mice were probably in these trays, and we just took a whole tray of mice, which was 125," Ronnie said, adding he would have liked to have taken more, but was restricted by his ability to find homes for the animals. "The main aim was to cause damage. I think we painted slogans on the place." Believing the police didn't know his current address, Ronnie brought the rescued mice back to Angie's house.

But, unfortunately, the police knew he'd moved out of the Nelson-Road squat and would apprehend him later that day. "There was a knock on the door," Ronnie said, noting he believed this was Mick, having come to Angie's house to pick up the mice. "When I opened the door, it was the police. They said, we understand there's been a burglary at such-and-such place and we've got a warrant to search your house." The police found the mice, who were returned to the laboratory. The animals were gassed because—having left the controlled conditions of the facility—they were no longer suitable for experimentation. The police also found burglary equipment and spray paint at Angie's house. Ronnie was arrested, along with a number of his friends, including Mick. "They were released by the police, because there was nothing on them," Ronnie said. "I think it was just a fishing expedition."

He was initially taken to a police station in Wallington, where he refused to answer questions. Ronnie was charged with burglary and causing criminal damage. "There was nothing to connect me to anywhere else," Ronnie said. "It was just this one place." Refused bail on February 21, he was remanded in custody to Brixton Prison in London. Angie took care of Cyril. Patty would give birth to a daughter named Maxine shortly after, in March.

9

Second Prison Sentence

Every week or so, Ronnie was taken to the magistrates' court, where his solicitor would reapply for bail. "They kept refusing bail," Ronnie said. "On one occasion, I insulted the magistrate.... I realized the magistrate wasn't going to give me bail, so it didn't really matter what I said." But on March 24, 1977, a judge granted Ronnie bail. "If you've been refused bail continuously by a magistrate, you can apply to a judge," Ronnie said. "Of course, the prosecution can have someone arguing the other side. But it's in a closed-court situation. You just go and see the judge fairly informally." Dave stood surety for Ronnie for 2,000 pounds. "They imposed a 500-pound surety on me," Ronnie said, noting he would have to pay this amount himself if he failed to show up for court. "I don't know how they thought I had 500 pounds."

He and Cyril went to live with Mick and Adele Hugill, Mick's partner, in an apartment in Wood Green, North London. "I wasn't all that keen living out in Hounslow," Ronnie said, referring to the borough where Angie lived. "It was quite a long way from other people that I knew. I preferred the North London area." He rented a spare room from Mick and Adele, who lived on the top floor of an old house. The couple were karate enthusiasts and trained regularly in the apartment. "It used to be a terrifying experience for me, because in their living room—the one large room they had in the flat—they used to do their karate practice," Ronnie said, laughing. "I'd be pressed up against the wall, hoping that I wouldn't be caught by a flying foot or a flying fist."

Mick and Adele had a cat named Olive, who ate salad, in addition to her cat food. "I've never known a cat to eat salad, apart from Olive," Ronnie said, adding the animal also enjoyed going for rides in Mick and Adele's vehicle. "She would just sit on Mick's lap, or she'd sit on my lap, and just enjoy being in the car. She was a very strange cat." Initially, Olive and Cyril didn't get along. "She didn't like Cyril at first," Ronnie said, noting Olive was jealous of the new feline addition to the apartment. "But in the end, they got on okay."

A friend of Ronnie's, who lived elsewhere, had recently adopted a dog, who repeatedly jumped over this friend's garden fence. "People were complaining," Ronnie said. "She was very stressed out about this." So Ronnie, Mick and Adele told this woman they would locate some material to make her fence higher. "Near where we lived in Wood Green, there was a car park," Ronnie said. "They'd replaced the fencing in the car park and the old fencing had just been left lying on the ground." Ronnie, Mick and Adele drove to the property and were loading the fencing into Ronnie's van, when police showed up. "Mick and Adele ran away," Ronnie said, adding he bolted as well. "I was running along the road and I thought, well, that's silly; I've left my van." So he returned to his vehicle, at which point he was arrested.

When Ronnie was asked to identify himself at the police station, he provided false information. "I gave them my correct name, but I gave them a false date of birth and a false place of birth," Ronnie said, noting, as a result, the police were unable to locate him in their records. "So they weren't able to discover that I was already on bail." This was a risk on Ronnie's part, because, if the police chose to check his car registration, they would learn his correct information. "I took a chance that they wouldn't bother," Ronnie said. "It was such a minor charge. This fence was only worth a few pounds." Luckily, the police took him at his word. "They said to me, have you ever been in trouble with the law before?" Ronnie recalled. "I said, no, I haven't. So they thought this was a first offense." He declined to provide information about Mick and Adele, who the police had spotted running away.

Ronnie, charged with theft, was granted bail, but not before the police took his fingerprints. "When I had to appear at my next court appearance, they found out who I really was," Ronnie said, noting this was a result of matching his fingerprints. "But the police officer in charge of the case— he just joked with me. He said, you gave us the wrong information there, didn't you Ronnie?" The officer chose not to oppose bail, since Ronnie had shown up in court. "When the magistrate asked if there were any objections to renewing my bail, the police said no," Ronnie recalled, adding he was now on bail for two separate incidents, rescuing the laboratory mice and stealing the car park's fencing.

Some months later, Ronnie went on trial at the Crown Court for the latter offense. He contested the case. "I argued that I thought the fencing had been thrown away, so therefore it wasn't theft," Ronnie said, adding that, nevertheless, he was convicted. "The judge said he'd considered sending me back to jail, because he considered this animal related." The judge saw Ronnie taking the fencing on behalf of a friend's dog as of a piece with Ronnie targeting laboratory-animal suppliers. "I think I had a barrister then," Ronnie said. "He argued, this has nothing to do with Mr. Lee's previous conviction and what he's on bail for now." Ultimately, the judge relented and fined Ronnie 100 pounds, which he never paid.

Some of Ronnie's friends from the North London hunt saboteurs group lived in Muswell Hill, nearby Mick and Adele's apartment in Wood Green. "[They] had rented a big house and they all lived together," Ronnie said. "I used to frequently go there, to socialize with them and to plan hunt sabotage." Ronnie recalled one instance in which he and these friends stuffed a new saboteur in a closet until he promised to become vegan. "We tied him up in a sleeping bag and locked him in a cupboard," Ronnie said. "After about half an hour, he started shouting, let me out; I promise to go vegan." Surprisingly, such coercion worked and the new saboteur did, in fact, abstain from animal products. "We were all crazy, really—the people who lived there and myself," Ronnie said.

On another occasion, Ronnie was taking a nap at this house, having come down with the flu. As a practical joke, one of the residents, who owned a starting pistol, burst into the room in which Ronnie was sleeping. "I heard someone shouting, we've found you at last, Lee, you bastard," Ronnie said, adding he also heard the sound of gunshots. "I wasn't aware they had a starting pistol…. I genuinely thought that I'd been shot—that some animal abusers had found where I was and shot me." In his semi-conscious state, he felt his body for bullet holes. "I turned around and they were all rolling around on the floor laughing," Ronnie said, referring to the residents of the house.

Gary, who lived in the house, and Ronnie carried out similar pranks in the backyard for the sake of the neighbors. "I'd wander around the garden, and Gary would come out and go, oi, what's this about you and my wife?" Ronnie said. "And I'd go, yeah, I am having an affair with your wife; she doesn't want you anymore." This staged conflict would escalate until Gary pretended to shoot Ronnie with the starting pistol. "I'd fall down in the garden," Ronnie said. "What we were hoping was that one of the neighbors would call the police…. But they never did. We did this about three times and the police never got called."

During the Queen's Silver Jubilee, Ronnie and the residents placed anti-royalist posters in the windows of the house. One day, there was a knock on the door which Gary answered. "There was an elderly gentleman standing at the door," Ronnie recalled, adding Gary asked the man what he wanted. "This old guy said, I strongly object to those posters and I want you to take them down." Gary didn't know this man was the residents' landlord. "He thought he was a guy who had just been passing and knocked on the door," Ronnie said. "Gary told the guy, fuck off, you old bastard." The landlord promptly gave the hunt saboteurs an eviction notice.

Despite the uproarious atmosphere of the Muswell Hill house, the residents' commitment to animals was real and deep. "So much was happening, and at a very fast pace," Gary said. "It was a time when anything seemed possible. We really thought we were going to change the world as far as animal rights goes." This shared vision created strong bonds amongst the group. "I can honestly say it was the most exciting period of my life," Gary said. "I forged lifelong friends who—when we meet up—still talk fondly of the time."

During this period, Ronnie and others disrupted a film screening for bullfighting enthusiasts. "We had flour bombs," Ronnie said, explaining these consisted of thin paper bags filled with flour, which, after being thrown, would explode on impact. "We burst into this meeting. There was probably about 20 of these people there—the bullfighting supporters. They were all in their very best [clothes]. The guys had very smart suits on. The women were wearing very elegant dresses and skirts. They were all done up. We shouted abuse at them and we pelted them with these flour bombs." The activists quickly ran off, escaping on the subway.

On June 27, following rumors the seal hunt at the Wash might resume, the Animal Liberation Front damaged three vessels which belonged to those who previously organized the killing. Ronnie wasn't involved in the action, but, nevertheless, two days later, the police raided Mick and Adele's apartment and arrested him. "As the police were running up the stairs, Mick climbed out onto the roof," Ronnie said, adding Mick escaped. "They arrested Adele." Other known activists were arrested elsewhere. "We all got taken to the police station in Boston," Ronnie said, referring to a town on the east coast of England. "None of us said anything. In the end, they had to release us. They had no evidence against us. They were just hoping that one of us did it and somebody would talk."

Around this time, Ronnie rented a van for some members of the Animal Liberation Front who wanted to rescue hens from a battery farm. "I didn't go," Ronnie said, adding the activists were caught and arrested by the police. "Because the van was hired in my name, I got arrested as well. [The police] said to me, you've hired a van that's been used to commit an offense. I said I didn't know anything about it." Ronnie told the authorities that when he rented the vehicle, a friend asked to borrow the van to move furniture, which he agreed to. "I said, that's all I know about it," Ronnie recalled, noting that, since the police couldn't prove he knew the vehicle would be used on the raid, they had to let him go. "That was another scrape with the law."

On August 6, Ronnie was amongst approximately a dozen hunt saboteurs who rented a home in Looe, a seaside resort. "We had a friend who had a big house that she let out for people for holidays," Ronnie said. "Because she was sympathetic to hunt saboteurs, she'd let us rent this house really cheaply." Couples were allowed to take the rooms, while everyone else slept on the floor in sleeping bags. On their first day in Looe, the group rented some small boats with outboard motors. "We started off going near to the shore, where people were fishing, and we cut their fishing lines," Ronnie said, adding the group also destroyed fishing nets and lobster traps.

Later, the saboteurs in Ronnie's boat came across a fishing line with multiple hooks on it. "So we pulled this line into the boat, and there was a fish on one of the hooks that was very badly injured," Ronnie said. "The hook had gone through this fish's eye. This fish was obviously really suffering. So we actually killed the fish. We had to hit fish's head—to kill the

Ronnie (in sunglasses near left), with a group of hunt saboteur friends, on holiday in Looe in August 1977 (photograph Dave Wetton).

fish—to stop the fish from suffering." The owners of the fishing line, seeing all this from their own boat, chased the saboteurs. "They started gaining on us," Ronnie said. "So we beached our boat." The saboteurs ran away, before walking the long distance back to their rented house. "We phoned up the boat company and said that something had gone wrong with our boat and we had to leave it on the beach," Ronnie said. "They went to this beach and collected the boat."

After Ronnie and another saboteur briefly returned to London, they attacked a hunt kennel on the trip back to Looe. "We damaged one of their vehicles," Ronnie said. "We found the building where they kept the red coats that they wore, the hunting boots, and all of the hunting equipment." There was wire mesh covering the windows, since the kennel had been attacked previously. "I thought, if I can prise this wire mesh up, squeeze underneath, and get the window open, I can squeeze through," Ronnie said, adding his plan was then to open the door, allowing his comrade inside, where they could destroy hunting equipment. "[But] the belt of my trousers got caught on the latch of the window…. This mesh was pressing in my back, because I really had to force it to squeeze in."

Ronnie was stuck in a way that he couldn't go forward into the building or back outside. "We tried for ages—my friend and I—to free me," Ronnie said, noting they attempted this for about an hour, until Ronnie began to think hunters might arrive for an early-morning hunt. "I said to him, look, you're going to have to go, because there's no point in us both being caught. He said, I'm terrified to think what they'll do when they come along and see your backside hanging out of this window." Imagining the prospect, Ronnie made one last effort, managing to free himself and squirm inside the building. "I opened the door and my friend came in," Ronnie said. "We had sharp knives. We slashed all their hunting boots, their red jackets, and all the hunting stuff." Then they made their getaway, returning to Looe and finishing their vacation.

Later in August, Ronnie and other members of the Animal Liberation Front attacked the office of Gilbertson & Page, a company that supplied equipment to hunters and gamekeepers. In addition to trashing the facility, just north of London, the group stole beer, cash and office equipment they found at the location. "When we got back afterwards, we had a good drink," Ronnie said. "We toasted the raid with their own beer." The group took the cash and office equipment, which they sold, to finance future attacks. "At one time, that would have been frowned on," Ronnie said, recalling activists feared being seen as common thieves. "People had these foibles— oh, you're crossing a line now…. My lines were getting further and further away." Ronnie didn't have a problem with theft, so long as the Animal Liberation Front made it clear, in messages to the media, that stolen items would be used to further the cause. "If we'd taken money to spend on ourselves, it would have been different," Ronnie said.

After this burglary, the group still needed cash to pay for future attacks, which required expenditure on gas and other things. "When we did a raid, it wasn't just a question of going that one time to do the raid," Ronnie said. "Sometimes you would have to go three times beforehand to suss the place out. You would have to go in the day and case the place. There would be several journeys involved and some of these places would be some distance away." With this in mind, Ronnie remembered the well-stocked office in Cambridgeshire, owned by a former prisoner of war, who bred sheep and pigs for vivisection. "So we did another raid on that guy," Ronnie said. "But this time, instead of wrecking the office equipment, we took it. We sold it to get money."

Again in August, Ronnie and others targeted a business near London, which bred chicks for experiments. While there were no vehicles there, a common target for the Animal Liberation Front, the group found something else. "We found the storeroom where they kept all of the special boxes that they used for sending the chicks to laboratories," Ronnie said, adding the birds would often be delivered by train. "We spent about two hours getting all of these boxes out of the storeroom…. We made a great big pile of them in the middle of a neighboring field and we set fire to them." That same month, Ronnie and his comrades attacked the Essex breeding facility at which he had been previously arrested, essentially for loitering. "But this time, I actually took part in the raid," Ronnie said. "It was someone else who was driving the car." The group burned some empty buildings at the location, separate from where the animals were housed.

But Ronnie's luck soon ran out. Once a week, he had to go to the unemployment office to sign a form, indicating he was available for work, which would entitle him to benefits. On August 24, as he went to accomplish this, he noticed two men sitting in the back of the office, who appeared to be homeless. "I didn't pay much attention," Ronnie said. "There was a young guy behind the counter, who gave me the paper, and I saw him nod as I signed. I thought, he's obviously seen a friend of his." Of course, that wasn't the case. "He was nodding at these two guys that were dressed in scruffy clothes, because they were undercover police officers," Ronnie said. "He was nodding to say, this guy's Ronnie Lee." The two men arrested Ronnie before he left the unemployment office.

The police took him to a Southend-On-Sea police station, where they sought to question Ronnie about the arson he'd committed in Essex. "I said nothing," Ronnie recalled. "They had no evidence on me." But then the authorities raided Mick and Adele's apartment, where they took a number of Ronnie's belongings, including a notebook that other members of the Animal Liberation Front had stolen, among a variety of documents, from a Kent laboratory. "I was looking through these documents with [my comrades], and there was a notebook," Ronnie said, adding that because he needed paper, he took the notebook for himself. "I thought, what I'll do—first of all—is I'll tear out all of the pages that have writing from the laboratory. I thought, obviously when someone writes on a page, it leaves an impression, so I'll tear out a lot of the other pages as well." Having done this, Ronnie believed the notebook couldn't be traced back to the laboratory.

Unfortunately, the notebook's remaining pages had a faint impression, invisible to the naked eye, which the police detected with special equipment. "So they were able to prove that notebook, that they found in my room, had come from this raid," Ronnie said, adding he was moved to a police station in Ramsgate, before being remanded in custody to Canterbury Prison. "I was charged with burglary and receiving stolen property." Ronnie repeatedly applied for bail, but was refused. "I wasn't really surprised," he said, laughing. In the beginning of October, Ronnie was moved to Wandsworth Prison, where he met Jake Prescott of the Angry Brigade. "He and his colleagues had been very much an influence on me," Ronnie said. "I had a chat with him. He was obviously very sympathetic to the ALF."

On October 10, Ronnie went on trial for his attempted liberation of 125 mice from a London breeder. His defense amounted to this: he broke into the breeding facility because he believed the mice were being held in criminally inhumane conditions; therefore he should be acquitted. "But it didn't work," Ronnie said, adding he was declared guilty two days later. "I was convicted of taking the mice and also causing damage to the property. I received a prison sentence of 12 months." Cyril stayed with Mick, while Ronnie was sent back to Canterbury Prison, where he awaited his trial related to the notebook.

"For the six weeks that I was in Canterbury as a convicted prisoner, I got exactly the same dinner every day," Ronnie said, reiterating convicted prisoners couldn't consume meals made outside the prison. "It was very nice, but I got a little bit fed up." Ronnie was ultimately given a suspended sentence in the case involving the notebook. "I remember the judge saying, you're very luck I've only given you a suspended sentence, because if everyone behaved like you, we'd have anarchy," Ronnie said. "I shouted out, well, that wouldn't be a bad idea."

Following this, Ronnie was moved to Standford Hill, a semi-open prison on the Isle of Sheppey, where he shared a room with three other men. "I got a job on the gardens at Standford Hill," Ronnie said, adding there was a tradition amongst the gardeners that, the day before someone was released, his fellow prisoners would throw him in a pond. So when Ronnie was set for release on April 26, 1978—due to good behavior and time on remand counting toward his sentence—he tried to keep this information from spreading. However, the news got out, and on the day before his release, Ronnie's fellow gardeners tried to grab him. "But I ran and jumped in the pond," Ronnie said. "Because I thought, it's better to jump in the pond than to be thrown in the pond."

10

Continued Involvement

After his release from prison, Ronnie, then 27, moved in with a couple he knew from the Vegan Society, Rose King and Ray Barnes, in Palmers Green, North London. Adele had returned to her home country of New Zealand. Though Mick hadn't followed her yet, he planned to do so after selling the Wood Green apartment. "I thought there was no point in me going back [to Mick's apartment], because I may not be there very long," Ronnie said, adding that Cyril had been adopted by John Hicks, who operated Foal Farm Animal Rescue Centre in Kent. "At one time, [Mick] wanted to go to New Zealand as soon as possible. So he thought, what's going to happen with Cyril? I agreed with him—for John to take Cyril to Foal Farm." Shortly after his release from prison, Ronnie went to visit the sanctuary, where he was impressed with Cyril's new living conditions. "He had a much better life there than I could have ever given him in a flat," Ronnie said. "He had the run of the grounds. He lived in the house with the people who ran the Rescue Centre. He ended up living out his life there."

Despite not being involved in much activism themselves, legal or otherwise, Rose and Ray were not put off by Ronnie's criminal history. "I think they used to go on some animal-rights demonstrations," Ronnie said, adding he thought Ray was involved in the Hunt Saboteurs Association to a limited extent. "They were very sympathetic [to the Animal Liberation Front]. I don't think it was the sort of thing they would do, but they were very sympathetic." Though Ronnie initially lived on the pair's couch, soon Rose and Ray bought a larger apartment nearby, in which Ronnie paid to rent a bedroom.

Near to where Ronnie lived, there was a fur store. "As often as I could, I used to sneak out and throw a stone through the window of the fur shop," Ronnie said. "It was too much of a temptation." He would even break the store's window during the day. "I often had to walk past, because it was on

101

the way to the local underground station," Ronnie said. "If no one was around, I'd pick up a stone." Eventually, the store's owner put mesh in front of the window. "It just meant that I had to throw smaller stones," Ronnie said. "The mesh was wide enough for a small stone to go through it. So if you were lucky, you could still break the window."

Not long after his release from prison, Ronnie visited his parents—who he hadn't seen in more than two years—in Malahide, Ireland. "I got along okay with them," Ronnie said. "It was good to see them." While he was there, Ronnie and his parents decided to visit Margaret's childhood home. "Once we crossed the border from Southern Ireland to Northern Ireland, we were in what's called Bandit Country, which was an area more or less controlled by the IRA," Ronnie said, chuckling as he added his father wanted to pee during the drive, but refused to stop the car for fear of being shot by Republican militants. "It was totally ridiculous. They'd shoot soldiers, but they weren't going to shoot a guy just because he has an English number plate on his car."

Despite living with the Rose and Ray, Ronnie still spent a great deal of time with Mick, who wanted to start a business with him, providing household repairs. "He was in the process of selling the flat," Ronnie said. "But I think he realized he'd need even more money than that." Though Ronnie and Mick were on unemployment at the time, they were allowed to make a limited amount of money without jeopardizing their benefits. "I wasn't too bad at doing odd jobs," Ronnie said. "He was very, very skilled at repair work and everything. But he needed me to work with him, because he needed me to drive." Mick didn't have a license at that point. So he and Ronnie went into business together. "We put a small ad in the local newspaper," Ronnie said, noting a landlord who owned about a dozen properties answered their advertisement. "He said he would take us on to do all of his repair work."

They soon learned the landlord sexually harassed both his male and female tenants. "He enjoyed being spanked," Ronnie said. "He was always trying to create scenarios with his tenants whereby they would spank him." For instance, the landlord would tell his tenants he was putting on a play. "It was all a ploy," Ronnie said. "This play would involve someone being spanked, and he was the one who had to be spanked." The landlord enticed tenants to participate in these performances by offering reduced rents. "Invariably, when we got into conversations with the tenants, they would say, has he asked you to do any kinky stuff?" Ronnie said. "He didn't—he never said anything like that to us at all."

In addition, the landlord turned out to be quite stingy. "The money he was prepared to pay us wasn't that great," Ronnie said, adding they accepted the offer. "We thought, well, the thing is, at least with him we have regular employment." The landlord's stinginess extended to paying for repairs his tenants needed. "One of the tenants would complain about something that was wrong in their flat," Ronnie said. "He'd send us to see what needed to be done. We'd come back and say to him, well look, this is the work that needs to be done. He'd say to us, no, no—that's far too expensive—find another solution that's much cheaper." On one occasion, the landlord only allowed Ronnie and Mick to fill the cracks in a roof which needed much more serious repairs.

Despite earning a significant amount from his rental properties, the landlord was claiming unemployment benefits. "One day we were doing some work in his garden," Ronnie recalled. "He said, oh boys, can you come back and work tomorrow?" Mick answered they couldn't, as they had to go to the unemployment office the next day. Saying he understood, the landlord pulled out his own unemployment card. "We were absolutely shocked," Ronnie said. "We thought, it's one thing for us—we're doing a little bit of work; but you're making thousands and thousands of pounds from renting all these flats, and you've still got the cheek to claim unemployment benefits. We absolutely hated him even more after that."

So with no fond feelings for their employer, Ronnie and Mick set out to supplement their income by stealing from the landlord. "We started going on building sites and talking to the builders," Ronnie said. "They would sell us stuff from the building site. I suppose they weren't supposed to, but they did. So we'd get the stuff cheap." The landlord reimbursed them for the cost of materials. So Ronnie and Mick forged receipts, indicating the materials they purchased were not cheap items from a building site—but expensive ones from a hardware store, which was, of course, fictional. "We invented a company called TTN Supplies," Ronnie said, adding they didn't reveal the acronym stood for Through The Nose. The pair also stole items from the landlord's storeroom, such as lamps and heaters, making it appear as if unaffiliated intruders had burglarized the property. "[We] took a load of the stuff out, went to a second-hand store, sold it all, and got the money," Ronnie said.

Ronnie and Mick were supposed to monitor their income for the sake of their own unemployment benefits, but they didn't. "I used to say to [Mick], we really need to do that," Ronnie recalled. "He said, don't worry; they'll never find out about us." One day, the pair were in the Wood Green apartment when someone rang the door bell, who Mick believed was a representative from the unemployment office. "Mick immediately said, oh dear, there's a bloke with a clipboard," Ronnie recalled. "He said, I think they might have rumbled us." So, moving quickly, Mick gathered all of the receipts and records related to their work, piled them in a cardboard box, and set them on fire. "This was in the middle of the living room," Ronnie said, adding he tried to persuade Mick against the course of action. "We basically had to lie on the floor, because, of course, the smoke rises.... I thought I was going to choke to death." They never discovered if the person at the door was actually from the unemployment office.

During this period, Adele sent Mick letters indicating she didn't want to be with him or return to England. But Mick still planned to travel to New Zealand, hoping to win back her heart. "I said, what are you going to do if Adele doesn't want you back?" Ronnie recalled. "He said, oh, I'll kill myself." However, it was clear to Ronnie, after Mick read him Adele's letters, that Adele would never reunite with Mick. "I said, you're just crazy—there might be another woman in this country who you can feel the same about," Ronnie recalled. "You need to give it a try." Mick reluctantly agreed and started attending various social events.

Eventually, Mick met a young woman at a Vegetarian Society dance, who he wanted to bring to Rose and Ray's apartment. Mick, having told his date he was an airline pilot, asked Ronnie to play along. "I said, why have you said that?" Ronnie recalled. "He said, well, I wanted to impress her; I didn't want to say I was unemployed or doing odd jobs for a dodgy landlord." So Ronnie kept up the pretense when the woman came over. "I immediately said to him, well how did the flight go today?" Ronnie recalled, noting he added to the fiction. "I said, you're piloting the Concorde now, aren't you?" But this wasn't enough for Ronnie, so when Mick asked how his day went, he pretended to be a racecar driver. "[I said,] I broke the lap record again in practice down in Silverstone today and I'm very confident about the Grand Prix at the weekend," Ronnie recalled, laughing as he added Mick's date believed all of this. "She was sitting there with her mouth open." Perhaps it's needless to say, but things didn't work out between Mick and this woman.

Around this time, Ronnie began dating a hunt saboteur named Iyesha Khan, whose parents had separated. Her mother warned Ronnie that Iyesha's father might violently disapprove of Ronnie dating his daughter. "She said, he carries a big knife with him all the time, and he'll kill you," Ronnie recalled. "I said, why? She said, because you're not Muslim." Iyesha confirmed to Ronnie that her father was fanatical. "I was shitting myself," Ronnie said. "When I was on the underground, I'd be watching all around, in case I saw this guy coming up. But it didn't put me off seeing her." Ronnie recalled one incident in which he and Iyesha visited a department store.

"They were selling these giant teddy bears," Ronnie said, adding he picked one up. "I held the bear's face to my throat. I started staggering around the store—shouting, help me; help me; get it off me…. Iyesha was so embarrassed."

Frequently, when Ronnie visited Iyesha, a neighbor watched him as he knocked on his girlfriend's door. "So, one time, I went there and I turned around—and there she was spying on me again," Ronnie said, laughing as he described exposing his butt to the neighbor in response. "When I turned around, she disappeared from the window. She never spied on me again after that." Iyesha was, understandably, not thrilled to hear what Ronnie had done. "I think she was slightly annoyed, but she was amused as well," Ronnie said of his girlfriend. "She knew what I was like."

By the summer, Ronnie was sick of working for the landlord and began a car-repair course in Enfield, North London. "It would be a useful skill to be able to repair vehicles when they went wrong," Ronnie said, adding he was able to keep his unemployment benefits while taking the eight-week course. With his new qualifications, Ronnie got a job at an engineering company called William Press. "They did a lot of roadwork," he said of his employer. "I had a job servicing their vehicles." Ronnie was struck by his coworkers blasé attitude toward their own safety. "For instance, if you're meant to jack up a vehicle, and you're meant to put axel stands under it—they didn't used to do that," he said, adding his coworkers also never wore masks when cleaning brake liners containing asbestos. "I think they found it amusing that I used to do these things, which you were really supposed to do."

On June 24, Ronnie attended the Hunt Saboteurs Association's annual general meeting in Newcastle. There the organization voted to expel a member of the National Front—a fascist, white supremacist party—whose presence on the saboteurs' national committee was attracting attention in the press. This man was David McCalden. He will be referred to as David, while Dave Wetton will continue to be called Dave. Ronnie abstained from voting on David's expulsion. When the issue was debated, however, Ronnie pointed out what he saw as the saboteurs' hypocrisy. "My argument was really trying to get people to go vegan," Ronnie recalled. "[I said,] I understand why you're wanting to throw this guy out, because obviously he stands for some pretty nasty things; but, also, a lot of you that are voting to throw him out—you still eat meat; so you need to look at yourselves."

Dave opposed David's expulsion and recalled Ronnie feeling the same way. For his part, Ronnie said he was sympathetic to both sides of the debate at the time. "All these organizations that campaign for people, they'll allow meat eaters to be members—they'll even allow vivisectors to be members—and they don't throw those people out," Ronnie said, adding that this argument for retaining fascists became less convincing to him over the years. In retrospect, he wished he'd voted for David's expulsion, believing there were other factors to consider besides the man's stance on hunting. "I look at things more strategically now." According to Ronnie, any benefit David provided the saboteurs was overridden by his extreme racism, which represented an obstacle to the organization's growth.

On July 9, Ronnie and approximately 30 activists protested a battery farm run by a convent of nuns in Daventry. "We occupied the grounds," Ronnie said, adding they were holding an Animal Liberation Front banner, which was intended as a threat. "When the police came, there were negotiations." The nuns wanted the group to leave the grounds, which the activists refused to do. "There was an agreement that two of us would be allowed to go in the convent and talk with the nuns," Ronnie said, adding he was one of the activists chosen for this. The other was someone named Susan Roberts, then Susan Hough, who will be referred to as Susan—as opposed to Sue Smith, who has been called Sue.

"I had a real go at the mother superior," Ronnie said, adding he asked whether Jesus—if he existed—would condone the convent's treatment of animals. "She said, I'm sure he would approve; they're only hens. I said, these are creatures that have feelings and it's disgraceful that you're treating them like this." Susan remembered the debate with the nuns becoming theological as well. "We could not get them to understand our point of view," she said, noting this episode inspired her to rescue birds from the farm later. "One of their arguments was that chickens had no souls." Finally, Ronnie asked the convent authority whether she thought she would go to heaven. "She said, yes, I do think I'll go to heaven," Ronnie said, laughing. "I said, if you're in heaven, I hope I go to hell. So we didn't leave on very good terms." There were no arrests, but the protest gained a fair amount of publicity.

When Ronnie went to visit his sister at her new home in Stevenage, he noticed a battery farm on the edge of town. "I'd been able to have a walk around and take a look at it," Ronnie said. "So I got together with some other people and planned a raid." In August, Ronnie and about five other members of the Animal Liberation Front snuck onto the property and saved 70 hens, who were adopted by animal rescuers. "We found homes for them," Ronnie said. "They wouldn't have gone one by one. They'd have been put somewhere in quite large numbers." This was Ronnie's first major raid since he was released from prison.

Ronnie was operating on the belief he would be acquitted if caught—as previously apprehended members of the Animal Liberation Front, for whom he rented a van the year prior, were found not guilty. Those activists successfully, though untruthfully, argued they intended to borrow the animals to show the ministry of agriculture their dire condition. "I thought, aha, if I get done for these battery hens, I'll just use the same defense," Ronnie said. "So I felt a little bit braver doing that than maybe doing something that involved damage. I didn't fancy going back to jail, really—not quite at this point. With breaking the fur shop window, I thought, no one was going to see me. With this, I thought, there's a defense that's already worked."

That same month, when Ronnie and other saboteurs disrupted driven-grouse shooting in the East Midlands, one of the hunters pointed a gun at him and threatened to fire. "I said, well, go ahead," Ronnie said, adding he reminded the man he would receive life in prison for doing so. "All of his mates were saying to him, no, no, don't be a fool; put your gun down." Ultimately, the hunter lowered his weapon. Ronnie wasn't scared by the confrontation. "I suppose I didn't believe he would shoot me," Ronnie said, before noting he wasn't so sure in retrospect. "He might have had a rush of blood to the head and shot me—it was a possibility. My adrenaline was high and it probably overcame any fear I had."

Towards the end of September, while disrupting another grouse shoot, Ronnie and other activists discovered a hunter's hut stocked with beer. So they broke in and started drinking the alcohol. "We could see, down in the valley, the shooters coming towards us," Ronnie said, adding the hunters could see saboteurs drinking their beer. "We were holding up the beer cans—taunting them." The activists poured out all of the alcohol they couldn't finish inside the hut. "As they got closer, we just ran down the other side of the hill and got away," Ronnie said. "We were aiming to save the grouse from being killed. But we were also aiming to give [the hunters] maximum aggravation to deter them from going again."

Afterwards, the saboteurs went to a Derby pub, where they got in an argument with owner, who disapproved of their activism. "During the evening, he had to go down in the cellar to get some more beer," Ronnie said. "I closed the hatch and locked him in the cellar." So as to avoid blame, the saboteurs moved to another section of the bar. "I said, we need to go somewhere else now," Ronnie recalled. "He was banging underneath the floor. Then someone obviously unlocked it and let him out. But he didn't know who did it."

Ronnie had only worked at William Press for a few months when the company experienced financial difficulty and started laying off employees, including him. So Ronnie began working with Ray, who was a freelance computer programmer. "The company my dad had worked for, which was International Computers Limited, had some offices in North London," Ronnie said. "They had arrangement with [Ray]—that he could go there, after their own staff had gone, and use their computers to do his programming." Ronnie accompanied Ray on these night shifts. "He taught me some basic programming," Ronnie said. "I used to do the less complicated stuff that was time consuming."

Ray and his girlfriend frequently argued about his work schedule, which Rose didn't like. "One day, I heard Ray shouting, I've had enough of this Rose; I'm going to kill you," Ronnie said, adding this didn't worry him. "He wouldn't have hurt her. They used to just shout." After hearing this threat and the couple race out of the apartment, Ronnie went to a window to watch. "I saw Rose running down the garden path," Ronnie said, adding Ray, having jumped out of bed completely nude, was chasing after her, and actually ran partway down the road. "I think he realized— shit, I'm naked—and came back indoors. He was so angry, I don't think it struck him he was naked."

The master of a North London hunt, Raymond Brooks-Ward, a show-jumping commentator on television, hired a group of thugs—who called themselves the Hunt Protection Squad—to keep saboteurs away. In November, after these men beat up saboteurs, Ronnie's group brought some friends to the next disruption who were experts in karate. "All these members of this Hunt Protection Squad came running down the hill, and they were holding sticks," Ronnie said. "They'd obviously recognized us as hunt saboteurs." Ronnie was inside one of three vehicles filled with activists. When these thugs yanked open the doors of the foremost car, they were met with quite a surprise. "A boot came flying out and just kicked them in the face," Ronnie said, adding the karate experts made quick work of the Hunt Protection Squad. "They were so brilliant. As soon as they started on one guy, well, of course, all the others ran away. Because, they said, shit, these guys are going to kill us." Ronnie's group never had trouble with those thugs again.

That autumn, Mick left for New Zealand, where he quickly found a job. "He was trying to contact Adele," Ronnie said. "Her mother would answer the phone. When it was him, she would just put the phone down. He tried calling around the house and they would tell him to go away." One day, Mick parked his car outside of Adele's home and tried to kill himself with vehicle exhaust, before Adele and her mother alerted the police.

"He was taken to hospital," Ronnie said. "He kind of recovered. I think he wrote to me from the hospital, telling me what had happened." Mick sent Ronnie his driver's license, telling him he didn't need it anymore, and that it could be used as a fake license for Animal Liberation Front activities. "I felt quite helpless," Ronnie said. On January 15, 1979, he received news that Mick had successfully committed suicide. Ronnie—who Mick named an executor of his will—was upset, but not surprised. "I'd tried everything I could," Ronnie said. "He'd been a good friend." Apart from a few hundred pounds for his parents, Mick left everything to Adele, for whom Ronnie felt sorry. "She couldn't have feelings she didn't have," he said. "To put that kind of guilt on her is not a fair thing to do."

On March 20, Ronnie was amongst a group of demonstrators who attempted to storm the Canadian embassy in protest of the country's seal cull. "Certainly that day, it would be heavily guarded by police," Ronnie said. "We didn't have much of a chance." The activists rushed the facility, but were contained by authorities. A little over a week later, Ronnie and about 250 other activists protested the Savoy Hotel, which was hosting a fur traders' dinner. "There was a cordon of police holding us back," Ronnie said, adding the invited guests wore tuxedos. "These fur traders were going into the hotel. We were shouting and waving banners. As they were going into the entrance, we threw a volley of stink bombs." Only one activist was arrested.

Later that spring, Gary—recently released from prison for desecrating a famed hunter's grave and breaking into the offices of the British Field Sports Society—worked at Ferne Animal Sanctuary, in Somerset, which was run by John Bryant and Sue. "Gary got in touch with me and said, look, there's a job here," Ronnie recalled, adding it was a handyman position. "I got on wonderfully with Gary. So it was an opportunity to be with him again, and also to work on an animal sanctuary." Ronnie accepted the job. On the drive to Somerset, he briefly stopped in Huntley to visit his parents, who had moved back to England. According to John Bryant, getting Ronnie the job was a struggle. "I persuaded the sanctuary's trustees to allow me to offer Ronnie employment at the sanctuary as a handyman and gardener," he said. "I considered that getting him down to Ferne would enable him to help animals without getting into further trouble with the law."

Ronnie and Gary lived in a bungalow on the sanctuary grounds. "I did the repairs—things like putting in gate posts," Ronnie said. "When something went wrong with the tractor, I'd repair it." Still, John Bryant recalled him as an unproductive employee. "I gave Ronnie the task of creating a vegetable garden which would produce food for the staff and some of the sanctuary's animals," he said. "After several weeks it became clear that Ronnie spent much of his time talking animal-rights issues with other staff and that the garden project was virtually stalled."

During his free time, Ronnie wrote and sang punk songs. "Gary had a guitar," Ronnie said. "He'd say, what do you think of this one? And he'd play a tune. Sometimes I'd write additional lyrics. So we thought, wouldn't it be great to get a band together?" They wanted to call the group Total Attack and perform political music. While still in Somerset, they wrote a song, called 'Most People are Morons,' bemoaning the recent election of Prime Minister Margaret Thatcher. Ronnie remembered some of the lyrics as follows: "I hear the news / It's pretty grim / The bastards voted Thatcher in."

Despite Ronnie's initial enthusiasm for work at the sanctuary, he quickly found himself bored. "At heart, I was a campaigner," Ronnie said, adding he didn't enjoy living in a comparatively isolated part of the country. "Although I was interested in being a handyman and I liked looking after animals, the thing I was most of all into was campaigning." Beyond this preference, Ronnie felt protesting did more to help animals than caretaking. "I thought it went more to the root cause of things," he said, arguing sanctuaries would exist only so long as protesting was unsuccessful. Gary was starting to feel restless as well, so around June the pair moved back to London, living with Rose—who, by this point, had separated from Ray.

According to Ronnie, John Bryant and Sue were frustrated by their employees' decision. "They were more annoyed by Gary leaving," Ronnie said. "You can easily get someone to be a handyman. But Gary had been so good with the wildlife. They used to take in injured wild animals—like foxes, badgers and birds of prey. Gary would look after them, nurse them back to health, and rehabilitate them back to the wild. So it was quite an important job. It was harder to replace Gary than me." John Bryant confirmed this assessment to some degree. "Sue and I were I not annoyed with the loss of Ronnie, but Gary was a huge loss," he said. "After Gary left, we never found anyone as good."

Ronnie believed John Bryant and Sue blamed him for persuading Gary to leave. "Gary had been quite happy working away there and then I arrived," Ronnie said. "It was the chemistry of the two of us together. We wanted to get back into action." Besides wanting to campaign, their desire to make music affected their choice. "We knew we couldn't do the band there, right in the middle of nowhere," Ronnie said. "We'd have to come back to London to get people together."

11

Kym and Total Attack

In the period lasting from the summer of 1979 to early 1983, Ronnie lived with a girlfriend for the first time, sang in a band which performed before hundreds of people, and was involved in the planning and execution of numerous illegal actions for nonhumans. He also created a position for himself—that of Animal Liberation Front press officer—which would be carried on by others going forward. In addition to all of this, Ronnie continued to participate in more conventional forms of activism.

In the latter half of 1979, Ronnie and Gary enjoyed teasing Rose, who they lived with initially. "Rose was a very gullible person," Ronnie said. "You could more or less get Rose to believe anything." On one occasion, he and Gary convinced her beetroot was a remedy for dry skin, so for a week she went to work with a purple-stained face. Similarly, according to Ronnie, one day he managed to persuade Rose that extraterrestrials had come to Earth. "When Rose came in from work, I deliberately made a play of rushing around the flat, throwing clothes into the holdall," Ronnie recalled. "Rose said, what's happening, Ronnie—what's happening?" He claimed the media was reporting aliens had landed in London, and, since no one knew if the creatures were hostile or not, evacuation was required. "She actually believed this," Ronnie said, laughing. "She started running around, packing a suitcase." In the end, he lost his composure and revealed the ruse. "She wasn't really cross," Ronnie recalled. "She just said, oh, you are awful, Ronnie."

Ronnie, Gary, and Rose took turns cooking. "Rose's cooking was terrible," Ronnie said, amused. "She never used to cook anything enough. She thought it was unhealthy to cook stuff too much. So we'd sit down to a dinner and the potatoes would only be half-cooked. You'd be crunching on these half-cooked potatoes." On one occasion, their toilet became clogged. When the plumber came to fix it, he found raw chickpeas blocking the pipe. "He said, has one of you poured a can of peas down the toilet?" Ronnie recalled, adding they didn't tell the plumber what really happened. "We'd shat them—because they hadn't been cooked properly. We were there, trying not to laugh. Then afterwards, we said, Rose, you have to cook stuff more, because it's blocking up the toilet." Before long, however, Rose moved out of the apartment, having found a new boyfriend. She and Ray still owned the dwelling, which Ronnie and Gary rented until it was sold.

Gary briefly dated a hunt saboteur named Kym Reynolds. "They didn't really get along," Ronnie said. "Gary and her mutually agreed they didn't want to go out together anymore. Then—because I got on so well with Kym—I started going out with her." This didn't cause any bitterness between the two friends. "Gary didn't mind," Ronnie said. "It wasn't as if I'd stolen her from him or anything. They'd already finished their relationship. He was quite happy. He said, you're welcome to go out with her. He said, she's not really for me."

Once, while waiting to meet Kym, Ronnie was nearly crushed by a crowd of people entering a rummage sale. "I couldn't breathe," he said, adding he actually began to lose consciousness, before fighting his way through the mob. "I staggered out of this place and I sat on this wall outside, with my head in my hands because I was feeling very, very faint." In retrospect, Ronnie found the incident quite amusing. "To be quite honest, that is the closest I've come to death," Ronnie said, laughing. "That would have been a very ignominious end to me, wouldn't it—to be killed at a jumble sale?"

Kym quickly moved in with Ronnie and Gary. "Kym and I had what had been Rose's bedroom," Ronnie said. "Gary moved into my room." One of the things Ronnie found most attractive about his girlfriend was her strong nature. "When there was an election, I used to hate going anywhere with Kym," Ronnie said. "If she saw someone with a Conservative-Party poster in their window, she'd stand outside the house and shout, you Tory bastards." Embarrassed and worried they'd be arrested, Ronnie would pull her away. For Ronnie, this was a bit of a role-reversal. Generally, he was being told by others to moderate his political passions. "I liked that she wasn't a shrinking violet," Ronnie said. "She was someone who stood up for herself. She was outspoken."

Around this time, a friend dared Ronnie to purchase a pair of crotchless women's underwear, on display in a store window they passed, promising him 5 pounds to do so. Ronnie accepted the offer and, hoping to amuse his friend, even asked the clerk if he could try the garment on prior to buying it. "She became enraged," Ronnie said of the clerk. "She either thought I was some kind of kinky guy who wanted to try on crotchless knickers or she might have thought I was taking the mickey in some way." After purchasing the underwear, Ronnie frequently hung them on the apartment clothesline, hoping people would mistake them for Kym's. "She'd be angry with me for doing this," Ronnie said, laughing. "But I used to think this was a great joke."

Eventually, Rose and Ray sold their apartment, so Ronnie and Kym rented the upstairs of a house in Finsbury Park, London, owned by an elderly couple. Ronnie liked the wife—who doted on him—but Kym couldn't stand her, feeling the woman constantly intruded on their relationship and space. "She used to always bring me food," Ronnie said of the wife. "She'd always be accusing Kym of not feeding me properly." In addition, this woman often cleaned the younger couple's quarters, against Kym's wishes, and used Kym's stuffed animals to prop open their windows. "Kym just said she couldn't live there anymore," Ronnie said, adding the wife's behavior simply annoyed Kym too much.

So the younger couple moved to a studio apartment in New Southgate, London. They hated their new landlord. "He was involved somehow in pornographic filmmaking," Ronnie said. "He was always trying to get Kym to take part in these films." The landlord frequently did this when Ronnie wasn't home, offering Kym large amounts of money. "She'd tell him where to go, basically," Ronnie said. Further, the landlord acted in a racist manner toward a black tenant, who, one day, threw the landlord down the staircase. "He came rolling down the stairs," Ronnie said. "I don't think anything was broken, but he was injured. I had opened the door and he said to me, did you see that? I said, no, I didn't see anything actually." Ronnie refused to serve as a witness to the incident.

One day, while Ronnie and Kym lived in New Southgate, a handyman repaired their apartment window. "He saw a cat down in the courtyard," Ronnie recalled. "He said, I hate bloody cats. He said, when I'm driving my car, if I see a cat, I'll always do my best to run the cat over. He said, I'll even go up on the pavement to run them over." Ronnie was immediately furious with this man, so much so he wanted to push him out of the window. In fact, he made a move to do this. "But then something stopped me," Ronnie said. "I thought, hang on a minute; it's only three stories; what if he's not killed?" Ronnie didn't want to go to prison, so he held back. But the handyman was alarmed by Ronnie's lunge forward. "He said, what are you doing that for?" Ronnie recalled. "I said, I thought you were going to slip. He said, no, no—I'm all right." Ultimately Ronnie had to settle with giving the man's information to his friends in the Animal Liberation Front.

Around this time, Ronnie got a vasectomy. "Kym didn't want children,"

Ronnie said. "She didn't want the burden." Terrified of becoming pregnant, Kym wanted to be sterilized. "They refused her," Ronnie said. "They said, oh no, you're too young." This inspired Ronnie, some years older than his girlfriend, to get a vasectomy. "With me it was political," Ronnie said. "First of all, even in those days, I believed the human species was overpopulated—I didn't want to add to it. Secondly, I wanted to devote my time to campaigning for animal liberation." For Ronnie, it wasn't a hard decision. "I don't dislike children," Ronnie said, noting he got along well with Patty's kids. "I didn't want children of my own. That wasn't how I wanted my life to go."

During this period, Ronnie and Gary also formed their politicized band, Total Attack, which had been hypothetical up until that point. Ronnie, who didn't know how to play any instruments, was the singer, while Gary played guitar. They recruited three hunt saboteurs—Aubrey Thomas and Rick Ferry, as additional guitarists, and Steve McGeary, to play drums. Rick, who moved into Rose's apartment, was far more skilled than the others. "You just had to know two chords and you could be a punk musician, which was ideal for us," Ronnie said, noting, in contrast, Rick knew a great deal. "He could even play the Himalayan nose flute. He could play everything.... He had more talent in his little finger than the rest of us had in the whole of our bodies put together." Rick's addition to the band allowed Ronnie to write music, in addition to lyrics, as Rick could play back any tune Ronnie hummed to him. "Ronnie would either sing his tunes or play them on his stylophone," Rick said. "I would get his key on my guitar and try some chords and find the ones that sounded best. He knew instinctively the right key that suited his voice and the best tempo [or] feel for the song."

Gary soon left the band and returned to Ferne Animal Sanctuary, where he sold his guitar and took up photography in his free time. "He went back and did the same thing as he did before, looking after the wildlife at Ferne," Ronnie said. "I was sad, really. In a lot of ways, he was my best mate. But that's just how he felt. He was the sort of guy who used to get itchy feet with things." In Gary's absence, Iyesha, with whom Ronnie had separated on good terms, joined the band as a new bass guitarist. "We were all very friendly," Ronnie said, adding Kym and one of her friends, Georgie Stagg, provided backup vocals for Total Attack. Later, Mike August took over for Iyesha, when she tired of the band.

Total Attack performed in and helped organize Rock Against Bloodsports, a concert series benefiting the Hunt Saboteurs Association. "We'd play and we'd get other bands to play as well," Ronnie said. "They'd come along and play for nothing. The money would go to the hunt saboteurs."

Ronnie (center) performing with Total Attack in Slough in early 1980. Mike August on bass guitar (left) and Rick Ferry (right) on lead (photograph Dave Wetton).

Total Attack played before audiences ranging in size between 50–200 people. At one such gig, held in a Palmers Green pub, Ronnie's band had a minor mishap. "Aubrey was one of these guys that jumped around a lot," Ronnie said. "He'd jump around onstage. He'd jump in the audience with his guitar and walk amongst the audience playing his guitar. He was quite a show-off type of guy. It was funny though." At this performance, however, Aubrey jumped so much he broke through the floor of the stage. "All you could see was the top half of his body, still playing the guitar," Ronnie said, laughing. "He just carried on playing."

At another such gig, held in Finsbury Library Hall, Aubrey wanted to deploy a smoke bomb—which saboteurs typically used to disrupt hare-coursing events—at the end of Total Attack's set. "He said to Georgie, when we finish our last number, I want you to let off this smoke bomb, so it looks really spectacular," Ronnie recalled, adding Georgie wanted to know when to deploy the firework. "Aubrey said, don't worry; I'll nod to you." Per usual, during the set, Aubrey was jumping around. "We'd done about two or three numbers, and Georgie thought she saw Aubrey nod," Ronnie said, noting Georgie then set off the firework. "So much smoke came out of it, that it set all of the fire alarms off. The hall had to be evacuated—about 200 people." When the firefighters came, Total Attack had to explain what they'd done. This, of course, infuriated the other bands scheduled to perform. "The whole thing got held up for about an hour," Ronnie said.

For Ronnie, besides raising money for the hunt saboteurs, performing the band's music was itself a form of activism. So he was frustrated when his voice—and the political message he was trying to communicate—couldn't be heard over Total Attack's instrumentation. "I even wrote a song called 'Turn It Down,' which was about how they played too loud," Ronnie said, adding the band produced lyric sheets for the audience as a solution to the problem. "To me, the words were really important."

Total Attack hoped they might get a record deal, according to Ronnie, who—in retrospect—laughed at the unlikely possibility. "We decided we'd like to go in a recording studio and lay down some tracks," Ronnie said, noting the studio they chose was located in Notting Hill, London. "We had to pay for the recording session, but it was fairly rudimentary." The songs they recorded included "Strike A Blow" and "Total Attack," about the Animal Liberation Front, "Most People Are Morons," about Margaret Thatcher's election, "Suicide Attack," about an animal activist who vows to commit suicide if captured by police, and "Refugee," about homelessness. Ronnie couldn't remember if the latter track was inspired by an eye-opening experience he had around this time.

One day, while traveling to the band's rehearsal in Camden Town, Ronnie came upon a dead homeless man. "He was cold and he wasn't responding," Ronnie said, adding he called the ambulance and police. "That disturbed me quite a bit." It was particularly unsettling as he often passed and gave money to the homeless people in that location, who lived under the railway arches. Ultimately, the man's death reinforced Ronnie's left-wing views. "He wasn't a young guy, but he wasn't an old guy either," Ronnie said. "I just felt tremendously sorry that this guy had been killed by the system. He'd been forced to live in that situation that had—no doubt—led to his death. I thought it was appalling there were no homes for people and they had to sleep rough."

After Total Attack finished recording, the band members set out to promote their finished product. They wanted to get their cassette tape into the hands of John Peel, a disk jockey famous for playing music by unknown artists on the radio. "A lot of those bands got well known through John

Peel," Ronnie said. "He was the guy you wanted to play your stuff." Of course, many bands had the same idea as Total Attack. But Steve had a friend who worked at the BBC, who could place their tape directly on John Peel's desk—perhaps giving them an edge. "This guy goes and puts it on John Peel's desk," Ronnie said, laughing. "John Peel comes in his office, sees a strange parcel on his desk—these are the days of the IRA and the bombs—and they put the thing in a bucket of water and destroy it." Needless to say, the disk jockey never played Total Attack's tape.

The band also sent their tape to a number of record companies, including Rough Trade Records, a left-wing label that took issue with "Most People Are Morons"—perhaps viewing it as condescending towards the working class. "We sent them a copy of the tape," Ronnie said. "A couple of weeks later, we got this five-page letter from Rough Trade, all going into why it was wrong to call most people morons." Ronnie suggested the analysis was somewhat over his head. "It was quite complicated stuff," he said, noting Marxist dialectic was mentioned. "We went to sleep halfway through reading it." Total Attack didn't receive a deal from Rough Trade Records or any other label. "The closest we came was having an offer from [International Fund for Animal Welfare] to record a few anti-fur numbers on an LP they were making, with well known bands," Rick said. "It was to be recorded in Canada, with Narada Michael Walden as the producer. He worked with guitarist John McLaughlin, a top man. [But] Ronnie was too busy at the time."

When the band performed at Lee Festival, in London, they performed a song, which Ronnie had written, called "Donegal Bay." It was about a second cousin of Queen Elizabeth II, named Lord Louis Mountbatten, who was assassinated while fishing by the Provisional Irish Republican Army in 1979. Ronnie remembered some of the lyrics as follows: "He murdered wild creatures with rod and with lead / Don't ask me to weep now the bastard is dead." The audience at Lee Festival did not take kindly to this, and threw eggs at Total Attack. "I just made a joke," Ronnie recalled. "I started saying, I hope those are free-range." Steve did not take it quite so well when eggs hit his drum set. "We had to stop because he just walked off," Ronnie recalled, adding Steve quit the band. "We got another drummer, but it was never the same. I don't think we ever gigged again."

Also during this period, Ronnie started getting contacted by the media to comment on Animal Liberation Front actions. "I was being treated as a press officer," Ronnie said, adding that, as a result, he started referring to himself as such. "It became a very, very busy job. There was a lot of ALF stuff happening." In addition to answering mainstream-media enquiries,

Ronnie worked to promote the Animal Liberation Front, trying to convince left-wing publications to run stories on the group, while producing his own newsletter centered on illegal action for nonhumans. He'd launched this zine following his release from prison in 1978, but, as his audience grew over the intervening years, a sympathizer allowed him to work on the newsletter in the downstairs of her house in Winchmore Hill, London. "I got this copying machine," Ronnie said. "I had a filing cabinet and stuff like that. I think I had a typewriter. So it was too much, really, to have in our little flat."

There was a campaign around this time, led by a group called Coordinating Animal Welfare, to radicalize the British Union for the Abolition of Vivisection. Ronnie supported the campaigners' goals, but loathed their tactics. "It was quite dirty," he said, adding the president of the union, Betty Earp, committed suicide as a result of this campaign, which accused her of financial impropriety with the organization's funds, among other things. "I thought it was wrong.... Although it may not have been something the organizers of CAW did themselves, or that they desired to happen, it came from people who were supporting CAW." Ronnie believed the union could be radicalized with debate, rather than smears.

Angela Walder, founding member of Coordinating Animal Welfare, suggested the campaign did become vicious. "I simply do not know if it was responsible for the sad demise of Betty Earp—though I suspect it may have been a contributing factor," she said. Ultimately, when leaders of the insurgent group took over the British Union for the Abolition of Vivisection, they provided Ronnie access to the union's headquarters, where he did his work as Animal Liberation Front press officer. The facility had telephones, which Ronnie's office in Winchmore Hill didn't have.

This period also saw the emergence of activists unwilling to abide the Animal Liberation Front's credo of avoiding harm to humans. "They formed an organization called the Animal Rights Militia," Ronnie said, adding he knew some of the group's members. "I was really relieved they didn't do it as the ALF." The Animal Rights Militia sent incendiary devices to numerous government locations, including a device that ignited inside 10 Downing Street, headquarters of Britain's executive branch. According to Ronnie, the devices were sent due to the government's intention to veto a ban on seal-skin imports from Canada. Ronnie, whose commitment to the Animal Liberation Front's credo was more strategic than philosophical, disapproved of the Animal Rights Militia's tactics. "I was worried that, if you just send a device through the post, innocent people could be hurt," Ronnie said. "It's out of your control. If you go up to a vivisector and just punch the vivisector—or even kill a vivisector—at least you know that's a guilty person that you're attacking."

Despite the attacks being claimed by the Animal Rights Militia, Ronnie was still contacted by the media to provide his perspective as Animal Liberation Front press officer. "I was always being asked, would you condemn these people?" Ronnie said, adding he refused, trying to change the press' focus. "I'd say, if you want me to condemn someone, I condemn the politicians that are going to allow the slaughter of baby seals; whatever people think about these incendiary devices, it's nothing compared to what's happening to the seals." Further, Ronnie would suggest the government had brought the attacks on itself. "I said, if you stop the slaughter of baby seals, you won't get these incendiary devices," Ronnie recalled. "I had misgivings about it, but I wasn't going to tell the media that."

Later, the Animal Rights Militia sent letter bombs to the Canadian embassy, the British minister of agriculture, a Bristol University laboratory, a Cambridge University researcher, and two furriers. "None of these devices went off, but they were explosive devices of some description," Ronnie said. "Probably what people were doing was getting stuff out of fireworks. I don't think we're talking about plastic explosives or anything."

Similarly, during this period, activists injected weed killer into turkey flesh sold in supermarkets. "They would do it to maybe one or two," Ronnie said. "They'd tell the media where these were and then claim they'd done it at loads of other places. So just to be on the safe side, [the authorities] had to check all of the other places as well." To add to the hysteria, the activists would make puncture marks in flesh in other locations, without injecting chemicals. "I wasn't involved in that, but I had to deal with the media saying, you're going to kill people," Ronnie recalled, adding that, once again, he refused to condemn those responsible. "I'd always turn it to talk about what the animals go through." Despite the unease Ronnie felt about the action, he did nothing to diminish fears it stoked. "I thought, well, this is probably a hoax," Ronnie said. "But I couldn't say that, because that would spoil the reason for doing it."

Ronnie believed that—as press officer—he should provide explanations for illegal actions on behalf of non-humans, even if they fell outside the guidelines of the Animal Liberation Front. "Otherwise, all you'd get was these lunatics had poisoned turkeys," Ronnie said. "You had to have someone there to say, well look, no, there is a reason why people are driven to do this; this is what happens to the animals and this is what ordinary people can do about it. That was my job."

Throughout the years, Ronnie provided his comrades in the Animal

Liberation Front with potential targets by combing through publications at the library. "I would look through the scientific journals, get the names of these people, and work out—from the establishment they worked at—where they were likely to be living," Ronnie said, adding he would find out researchers' addresses from telephone books. "Then I would get the electoral register for that area." From this, he would find out the names of the experimenter's neighbors, whose phone numbers he would also look up. "I'd phone one of the neighbors and say, is that Mr. So-And-So who works at the university?" Ronnie recalled. "They would say, oh no, he lives next door. I'd say, I'm ever so sorry; there must be some problem with the lines." This is how Ronnie verified targets without tipping them off.

One researcher, after his home was vandalized by the Animal Liberation Front, denied to the media that he was a vivisector. But, of course, Ronnie knew he was—having supplied the attackers with the man's address. Incensed, Ronnie wrote a letter to a local newspaper, in which, posing as another scientist, he said the vivisector was lying and referenced a publication to prove this. "I didn't want to say who I was because then they would have sussed out that I might have had something to do with it," Ronnie said, adding he used his two middle names, Anthony Denis, to create a pseudonym. Despite this precaution, he was interested enough in the newspaper's response to attach his real return address to the letter. In the end, Ronnie received a reply. However, his penmanship was not very good, and the newspaper editors misread the "D" in Denis as a "P." "I received a letter back from them—Dear Mr. Penis," Ronnie said, adding he believed

the editors didn't take him seriously because of the miscommunication. "They probably thought it was a joke."

Perhaps most remarkably, Ronnie coordinated attacks on three-dozen vivisectors in a single night. "I spent ages in telephone boxes, phoning up ALF activists that I knew," Ronnie said. "I didn't know everyone in the ALF, but I knew key

Kym Reynolds (right) with Ronnie's mother and father, circa 1982 (photograph Ron Lee, courtesy Patricia Lee).

people. In a particular town, I might know one person. I didn't know the other people they worked with." In addition to spray-painting slogans on researchers' homes, activists targeted the researchers' cars—slashing their tires, breaking their windows, and covering them with paint stripper. Ronnie didn't participate in the attacks directly, wanting to serve a more organizational role. That said, he still engaged in some Animal Liberation Front actions during this period.

For instance, Ronnie and others raided a slaughterhouse and burnt two trucks on the premises. By this point, he had stopped using gasoline for arson. "We worked out that it was better to use something that wasn't so volatile, but was more slow-burning," Ronnie said, adding he used paraffin or methylated spirits instead. "We'd get the cabs open, pour the paraffin on the seats, light it, and then just go." Paraffin was physically safer for activists, as it didn't explode like gasoline did. Further, paraffin allowed activists more time to escape before a fire reached noticeable size.

Ronnie also participated in more traditional activism for animals, including a World Day for Animals in Laboratories march—which about 5,000 people attended—to Porton Down, a military research facility. "Two thousand of us broke off and tried to storm the laboratory," Ronnie said. "They had these various rings of fences. They didn't have just one fence around it." The marchers managed to destroy the first barrier, which was topped with barbed wire. "We tore down the outer fence and got through that," Ronnie said. "But, of course, loads of police came and drove us back. I can't remember anyone being arrested. I think the police were just happy to be able to chase people away."

In early 1983, someone broke into Ronnie and Kym's apartment in New Southgate. "It was really strange," Ronnie said. "Some of the more valuable items in the flat hadn't been taken." But the intruder had taken all of Kym's soft toys. "She was very distressed," Ronnie said, adding he and his girlfriend suspected their landlord had something to do with the break-in. "Basically, Kym couldn't live there anymore." Feeling violated, Kym moved back in with her parents, having lived with Ronnie for about four years. The couple continued to date. Ronnie left the apartment soon after, moving into the downstairs of the Winchmore Hill house, which he'd used as an office. He paid rent to the sympathizer who owned the property.

12

Press Officer

Spring of 1983 to early 1986 was the period in which Ronnie engaged in illegal action for animals most frequently. Including impromptu vandalism—such as smashing windows—Ronnie sometimes participated in multiple attacks every week. But, also during this time, Ronnie broke up with his long-term girlfriend, lost his work space in internecine struggle, and was ultimately arrested on charges which led to his third prison sentence.

In the spring of 1983, a broker working on the London Stock Exchange arranged to meet Ronnie, then 32, to provide a donation for Animal Liberation Front. "He supported the ALF," Ronnie said. "I thought, oh great, a stock broker. We're going to get thousands of thousands of pounds." But when the meeting came to pass, the man only gave him 100 pounds. "In some ways, I was disappointed," Ronnie said. "Although he was a stock broker, he wasn't particularly wealthy." Still, the broker donated funds on a regular basis, which Ronnie distributed to other activists to buy equipment and fuel. The broker also bought cigars and vodka for activists to enjoy following raids. One day, Kym and a friend drank a whole bottle of this vodka between them. "They were staggering all around," Ronnie recalled, laughing. "I said, do you realize how many ALF raids you've got to go on now to make up for all that vodka you drank?"

One night, Ronnie and Kym came across a pair of drunken men vandalizing an ambulance. After threatening to call the police, Ronnie was attacked by the men, who cut his face with what Ronnie thought must have been a broken bottle. "I got taken to hospital," he said. "I had to have 32 stitches in my face." Ronnie applied for and received funds from the Criminal Injuries Compensation Board—totaling 2,000 pounds—which he put toward the Animal Liberation Front. "I've still got a very slight scar from where I was cut," Ronnie said. "That kind of turned out well, I suppose."

Slowly, Ronnie and Kym—who were still dating, despite not living together—started drifting apart on an emotional level. Ronnie was spending a lot of time at the British Union for the Abolition of Vivisection headquarters and visited his parents frequently, as his father developed bowel cancer. Further, Kym was losing her interest in activism. "She was still a vegan," Ronnie said. "She still cared about animals…. But she ceased to be an activist. That had an effect on my feelings for her." The couple parted amicably and by summer they began seeing other people. "It was a gradual separation," Ronnie said. "There wasn't that sudden, traumatic moment that some people have when relationships come to an end." Following his breakup with Kym, Ronnie had a number of brief, relatively inconsequential relationships during this period.

That summer, the British Union for the Abolition of Vivisection moved its London headquarters from Charing Cross Road to Crane Grove. "They wanted to get bigger premises," Ronnie said. "It was also cheaper because it was not so much in the center of London." In the new location, Ronnie was provided with dedicated space for the Animal Liberation Front Press Office. "There was a sense of privacy," Ronnie said, adding he received a dedicated phone line as well. "Activists used to come and visit me in the office. Just coming into the general BUAV, they would be worried about being overheard with their conversations and that kind of thing."

Ronnie's office was adjoined by another, which the British Union for the Abolition of Vivisection provided to groups such as the Sea Shepherd Conservation Society and Artists for Animals. "In these two offices, where we had activists, we had a policy that no animal products were to be consumed," Ronnie said, adding that, one day, the boyfriend of a visitor to Sea Shepherd was eating flesh in the nearby space and refusing to leave when asked. "So I immediately got up, went out and said, oi, what's your game eating meat in our office?" Ronnie said, adding the man ignored him. "I said, right, out you go. And I just grabbed him and threw him out." When the man's girlfriend started crying, Ronnie offered her little comfort. "I said, well listen, what are you doing, going out with a meat eater, if you care about animals?" Ronnie recalled. "I said, don't be upset about him being thrown out; he should be thrown out. I said, you need to throw him out of your life as well."

Ronnie enjoyed playing practical jokes on visitors to his office. Some of these gags relied on the Animal Liberation Front's violent reputation. For instance, when visitors came to visit his office, Ronnie frequently pretended to be in the midst of a call. "I'd have the phone in my hand and say, look, we can't put up with anymore of this nonsense; you're going to have to have him killed," Ronnie said, laughing. "I'd put the phone down and say, can I help you?" He quickly let visitors know it was all a prank. "If it was somebody who wanted to be a potential activist, I didn't want them to think, oh my God, I've been involved in an organization that's being run by a gangster," Ronnie said. "After I'd amused myself with the shock and horror on their face, I'd say, don't worry; I was only joking; that was just a pretend phone call."

Ronnie enjoyed similar jokes carried out by others. For instance, the union's leadership believed the founder of the Animal Liberation Front Supporters Group—which raised funds for illegal action and produced a newsletter—had an overly-militaristic attitude. So, one day, while working in the press office, this man wore a military uniform, which his mother purchased from a rummage sale. "He made a sign to put on the desk that said: Supreme Commander, All the Animal-Rights Armed Forces." Ronnie said, laughing. "He put this on the desk and sat there in the uniform, precisely to take the mickey out of them. He thought, if they think I'm militaristic, I'll really show them." Ronnie found this to be a great source of amusement.

In his role as Animal Liberation Front press officer, Ronnie frequently found himself speaking to the media about actions in which he directly participated. "I found it quite amusing in a way—commenting as an outsider on something that I'd actually been involved in," Ronnie said, adding this wasn't difficult for him. "It's a case of wearing different hats, isn't it?" He also arranged meetings between journalists and other underground activists. For instance, on one occasion, he drove a reporter from the Yorkshire Post to interview members of the Animal Liberation Front in their home. Ronnie insisted the journalist wear a Margaret-Thatcher mask, with the eyeholes taped shut, so he wouldn't know where he was. "Unfortunately, I wasn't able to park the van right outside of the house," Ronnie said. "So I had to park it down the road. I then proceeded to walk [the reporter] up the road to this house." Laughing, Ronnie recalled the strange scene and his fear a neighbor would report it to police.

Besides reporters, with a dedicated phone line, Ronnie was also contacted by those attacked by the Animal Liberation Front. For instance, someone called whose business had recently been struck with arson. "He said, did you burn my offices?" Ronnie recalled. "It was me—but I said it wasn't." After denying his involvement, Ronnie pivoted to declaiming the caller's company. "He phoned me up to abuse me, but it ended up the other way around," he said. Similarly, a man, whose business Ronnie had personally vandalized, called the press office to say he would find Ronnie and attack him. "I said, no need to bother looking for me," Ronnie recalled. "[I said] you name a place; I'll meet you there; and we'll fight; but when I fight you, I'll fight you to the death." The man hung up, perhaps not seeing though Ronnie's bluster. "I just wanted to show him that I wasn't afraid of him," Ronnie said.

On August 1, Ronnie and other members of the Animal Liberation Front attacked a chicken-processing plant in Bedfordshire. "When we got there, there was a fence that we had to climb over," Ronnie said, adding an Alsatian guard dog ran towards them as they scaled the barrier. "I thought, I'm going to be savaged by this dog. But he just started sniffing me and then he was really friendly." So Ronnie stroked the animal. "Then I said, well, off you go," Ronnie recalled. "He went where I told him." After sending the dog away, Ronnie torched multiple vehicles—including a bus—on the plant's grounds.

Some months later, on December 14, Ronnie took part in a raid on a South Mimms laboratory, inflicting 100,000 pounds worth of damage. To avoid alerting those nearby, activists probably didn't batter the equipment. "Sometimes you had to do damage that was more to do with bending things—you know, putting crowbars into things," Ronnie said, noting this was most often the case. "You had to do damage quietly. You couldn't just go smashing and make a big noise. But if you've got sophisticated, calibrating equipment and stuff like that in a laboratory, it doesn't take a lot to do a great deal of damage."

Shortly after, on Christmas morning, Ronnie and others burned five vehicles at a frozen-poultry factory in Luton. On January 21, 1984, Ronnie torched two trucks in London which belonged to a meat company. The damage was later assessed at 100,000 pounds. "I think these were quite new lorries they had there," Ronnie said. "That was the second time I'd attacked that place." That same month, while driving on the highway, Ronnie spotted a poultry truck, which he followed to a farm—the offices of which he set on fire. On February 1, he returned to the Colney Heath offices of Gilbertson & Page, a company that made snares and traps, which he'd struck in 1977. "This time we burnt their offices," Ronnie said. "We also damaged a vehicle."

The Animal Liberation Front engaged in more property destruction than non-human rescues, because the latter was more expensive. "Causing damage didn't cost any money," Ronnie said. "It was very simple. You didn't need many vehicles. It was where animals were rescued that you needed the money. Because you would sometimes have to hire a vehicle. You'd need more people. There would be a lot of fuel involved in taking the animals around to where they were going to go." Still, Ronnie engaged in a number of rescues during this period. For instance, on February 28, he and others raided the Institute of Psychiatry in London, rescuing 40 rats and causing 50,00 pounds worth of damage.

During this period the British Union for the Abolition of Vivisection was involved in a campaign called Putting Animals Into Politics, which sought to advance animal welfare through the Labour Party. Ronnie disagreed with this approach, because he was fundamentally opposed to electoral politics and saw little difference between the Labour and Conservative parties. Instead, Ronnie wanted the union to offer greater support for illegal action on behalf of animals.

On April 10, the Animal Liberation Front Press Office was evicted from the Crane Grove facility. Ronnie believed this was because he sought to replace members of the union's ruling body. "We had a meeting about how we could put forward and promote candidates to the BUAV committee—they're the policy makers—who were more radical," Ronnie said, noting that when he left the meeting, held in the press office prior to its eviction, he spotted one of the union's leaders. "I saw him come out of a room, where he wouldn't normally be, where he could have put his ear against the wall and heard what we were saying."

The rationale the union's leadership gave for evicting the press office was different. "The reason they gave at the committee meeting was that the ALF supports violence," Ronnie said, noting the ruling body disapproved of illegal action involving property damage—as opposed to animal rescue—and his refusal to condemn the Animal Rights Militia. "I thought, well, this is ridiculous. Because, a), it's not true we support violence, and, b), all the things you're using to justify that you've known about for months and months and months." Ronnie found the leadership's timing suspicious.

Eventually, he rented a new space for the press office in Putney, London. "Everything had to be done under a pretext," Ronnie said, arguing landlords wouldn't rent to those associated with illegal action. "We said that we were a tax-advisory service." Ronnie and the founder of the Animal Liberation Front Supporters Group chose this facade because the latter man had previously worked as a tax officer. "He was able to talk the talk," Ronnie said. "We called ourselves the Independent Tax Advisory Service, and we rented [the space] under that name."

Around this time, the sympathizer, whose house he lived in, demanded he move. "She said, you've not done the decorating you said you'd do," Ronnie recalled. "I said to her, well, you know the reason; you know that it's because my father's been ill." This made no difference. According to Ronnie, over a brief period, this woman changed dramatically—a change he believed was the result of thyroid medication she started taking. "She turned against all of her friends," Ronnie said. "I immediately blamed these new tablets for it." He wanted to fight the eviction, but ultimately he decided to rent a studio apartment in Hammersmith, London.

Ronnie regularly visited Patty and her family. One day, Anthony, by then 13, told him he found animal traps and snares in the woods. "He took me to this place," Ronnie recalled, noting he destroyed the devices while Anthony watched. "I showed him how to do it. I said, oh, this is what you do." When they returned to Patty's house, Anthony explained what happened to his mother—who was, of course, furious. "She really had a go at me," Ronnie recalled. "She said, you're trying to get my son involved in stuff. She said, I'm not having him go to prison like you." In retrospect, Ronnie acknowledged he was trying to interest Anthony in the Animal Liberation Front. "I wasn't expecting Anthony to do anything illegal at the age of 13," Ronnie said. "But I was hoping that, when he got older and became an adult, he would then make the decision to become an activist."

When Ronnie visited his parents, he sometimes had to restrain his mother when the Rev. Ian Paisley, a loyalist politician from Northern Ireland, appeared on television. "My mum absolutely hated him," Ronnie said. "She would be sitting there knitting and the news would come on the television. My mum wouldn't really take any notice." This changed when the loyalist spoke on screen. "My mum would immediately become totally transformed," Ronnie said, laughing. "She'd leap up from her seat and actually attack the television—start shouting and swearing.... I'd say, mum, mum, he's on the telly; you can't get him. I'd have to calm her down and sit her back down in her seat."

On June 30, Ronnie and others attacked a cancer-research charity in Burnt Oak, which supported vivisection. "We daubed slogans on the shop and threw a brick through the window," Ronnie said. "That's very similar to lots of different things I was doing, but I mention that because it was a different kind of target." Ronnie was unconcerned about negative publicity the attack might generate. "I don't think we were bothered about that," Ronnie said. "We'd try and give a reason. When I called the press, I'd say, look, we're not opposed to cancer research; just don't do it on animals."

On July 7, Ronnie broke into the Windsor office of *Shooting Times*, a hunting magazine. "This was, more or less, across the road from the grounds of Windsor Castle, so we were a bit wary of security," Ronnie said. "Because you do get more and police and that around there because it's a royal residence." After quietly removing a window, he and others entered the office's basement. "We blocked the sinks up and we turned all the taps on," Ronnie said, adding they flooded the building. "There were was some office equipment there, that we found, that we just damaged. We weren't really in a position to take anything away with us because of where we were parked."

Later that month, on July 21, anonymous activists declared they had inserted bleach in containers of Sunsilk shampoo, which was made by a company engaged in animal testing. The hoax was carried out in what was now a familiar pattern. However, in this case, the action was claimed on behalf of the Animal Liberation Front, which, as press officer, Ronnie didn't repudiate. "I didn't think it really breached the guidelines of ALF actions," Ronnie said. "No one really was at risk, not in reality." Once again, he didn't tell the media he assumed this to be a hoax. Ronnie publicly maintained the action—as it was presented—fell within Animal Liberation Front guidelines, because activists provided warning about the supposed contamination.

By autumn, Ronnie had moved the press office to Hammersmith, and Vivien Smith, who previously ran Artists for Animals, had taken over the Animal Liberation Front Supporters Group from its founder, who resigned because of health problems. Ronnie and Vivien worked together in the new location. While her predecessor wrote most of the supporters-group newsletter himself, Vivien had a different style. "She solicited contributions from other people," Ronnie said. "She compiled the diary of actions and laid the whole thing out. Of course, in those days, we didn't have computers. So basically you had to paste it onto sheets of paper and use something called Letraset to make the headlines. It was really quite a work of art." Vivien would make hundreds of copies of each issue on the office photocopier.

Ronnie wrote a great deal for the newsletter. Sometimes he used his own name and sometimes he used pseudonyms—like Captain Kirk and Luke Skywalker. "I was a big fan of *Star Trek*," Ronnie said. "I was never particularly into *Star Wars*. But *Star Wars* was very popular at time time, and there was obviously the film called *The Empire Strikes Back*. I thought *The Empire Strikes Back* was a good headline for an article that described how the state was attacking activists and striking back against the ALF." For consistency's sake, he used the Skywalker nom de plume.

In November, the Animal Liberation Front claimed to have spiked Mars Bars with poison, in protest of the Mars company's animal research. "This was a huge thing—because Mars Bars, first of all, was such a popular confectionary," Ronnie said. "Secondly, because it cost this company millions." Ronnie was interviewed about the hoax on national news by presenter Frank Bough. "He was trying to really screw me down," Ronnie recalled. "He was saying, it's out of control, Mr. Lee, isn't it?" But Ronnie refused to be knocked off message. "I said the usual thing," Ronnie recalled. "I didn't want to really talk about the Mars Bars. I wanted to be talked about the experiments on chimpanzees and how's the Mars company was disgraceful."

Unbeknownst to Ronnie—at that very moment—in the West Midlands, a 12-year-old girl with cerebral palsy watched his interview on television. Her name was Louise Ryan and she was instantly struck by Ronnie. "He was a little kind of guy, with round, Lennon-type glasses," Louise recalled. "I said, mum, mum, this man on telly—he thinks like I do." If anything, she felt the Animal Liberation Front didn't go far enough. Out of concern for animals, Louise had become a vegetarian earlier that year. "I went very, very quiet," Louise recalled, adding her mother asked if anything was wrong. "I said, you know that man there? I said, I'm going to be with that man." In fact, many years later, Louise would date and ultimately marry Ronnie.

On March 5, 1985, Ronnie and about three other activists drove around the London area, using an air rifle to shoot out the windows of businesses associated with animal exploitation. "This was in an evening, when these places were closed," Ronnie said. "I think there were six butcher shops, a fishmonger's ... the [administrative section] of a vivisection laboratory, [and] the offices of *Shooting Times*.... There was a halal-meat shop and a meat factory, where we also shot out the windows of a lorry and a car." On a similar trip, around this time, Ronnie and a companion used a slingshot to break the windows of more the 80 establishments, while travelling to and from the North London home of a chicken-slaughterhouse owner, where they caused extensive damage to the owner's car.

Later that month, on March 20, the press office was searched by police, while Ronnie and Vivien were arrested. "The police were looking for documents that had come from a South East Animal Liberation League raid on a laboratory in Kent," Ronnie said, adding the police also searched the offices of the British Union for the Abolition of Vivisection. "We were taken to the local police station in Hammersmith. It was on suspicion of receiving stolen property." While Ronnie and Vivien didn't have the stolen documents for which the police were searching, they had others. "They were still in the envelope they came in," Ronnie said of the material. "So the police couldn't prove that we deliberately received this stolen property." Ronnie and Vivien were released the same day and faced no charges.

Also during this period, in the aftermath of an Animal Liberation Front attack in Leicester, where Ronnie had given a talk promoting illegal action, Ronnie was arrested for incitement. "This car pulled up and I thought it was the taxi," he said. "Then these guys jumped out and it was the police. They got me in this police car and took me to the police station." But Ronnie refused to talk. "In the end—because they had no evidence against me—they had to let me go," Ronnie said.

On March 21, in Scotland, the Animal Liberation Front claimed to have urinated in Lucozade bottles, in response to the Beecham Group's animal research. Shortly after, activists claimed to have entered stores and poisoned chicken carcasses in the south of England. Ronnie spoke to the media about both of these incidents. "It's ever such an easy thing to do," Ronnie said, referring to contamination scares. "It kind of caught on and became something that quite a lot of people did claim." On March 30, he participated in the rescue of 22 hens from a battery farm in Welwyn Garden City.

Sometimes during this period, Ronnie went to visit Sue, who was living in Somerset, having broken up with John Bryant and left Ferne Animal Sanctuary. "I was still very friendly with Sue," Ronnie said. "She was doing up an old house that had quite a lot of land around it. She was, once again, wanting to set up some sort of animal sanctuary. She was living in a caravan." During his visits, Ronnie and Sue would engage in Animal Liberation Front attacks with other activists in the area. For instance, on May 20, they damaged six trucks at a meat factory in Totnes. "Sue was still an activist," Ronnie said. "She was very good company."

In August, Ronnie and others caused approximately 40,000 pounds worth of damage to a car dealership in Thames Ditton, which was renting cars to the police, who were using the unmarked vehicles to follow animal activists. "We went to their premises in the middle of the night," Ronnie said. "All of these very, very expensive cars were parked outside in the forecourt of their business." The raiders doused a significant number of vehicles with paint stripper. "We claimed responsibility for it," Ronnie said. "We wanted them to pay the price."

On August 24, Ronnie attended Mike's bachelor party. The revelers, made up of animal activists, intended to spend a day in Boulogne-sur-Mer, France. But when the group arrived at the French border, Gary and another man announced they hadn't brought their passports. "We thought, how are we going to get these guys in through the customs?" Ronnie said, adding they settled on creating a diversion. "So what we did was a load of us just fell on the floor and started kicking our legs up in the air and shouting. All of the customs guys looked at us and thought, what the hell is going on? As their attention was distracted, these two guys without the passports snuck through the barrier."

The bars were too expensive in Boulogne-sur-Mer, so the group bought beer at a supermarket. "It wasn't much of a visit to France," Ronnie said, amused. "Basically, all we did was sit on a bench at the side of the road, just drinking all of this beer. Then one of the guys went off, came back and said, I found a butcher shop." The drunken activists decided to attack the business right there and then. "We all charged down the hill, about ten of us, towards the butcher shop," Ronnie said. "There were one or two guys that knew French and they were shouting stuff." This, of course, alerted the proprietor. "He came out with a meat cleaver and we ran back up the other way," Ronnie said, laughing.

In late autumn, a group of Animal Liberation Front activists in Sheffield showed Ronnie a timed-incendiary device disguised as a packet of cigarettes. "[It] involved a watch, some wiring—I think match heads—and firelighters," Ronnie said, adding the group didn't want him to be taken off guard as press officer by their action. These activists planned to hide the device in a department store, where it would set off the sprinkler system and cause a great deal of damage. Ronnie made sure he understood the plan, and a couple of weeks later, a member of the group planted the device in the Sheffield Rackhams. "It worked exactly to plan," Ronnie said, adding the sprinklers caused 150,000 pounds worth of damage to Rackhams overnight. "The same sort of thing started happening elsewhere, in other stores."

But in early 1986, the Sheffield group was apprehended by police. "Where they made a huge mistake—the people in Sheffield—was that they did it in their own town," Ronnie said. "Like the saying [goes], never shit on your own doorstep, basically." To make matters worse, police had secretly recorded one of the group's meetings, in which activists referred to Ronnie in the context of a planned attack. "They mentioned my name in a kind of jokey fashion," Ronnie said. "They said, oh, Ronnie Lee will be pleased when he hears about this." The recording would soon help justify his arrest.

In January, Ronnie participated in an arson attack on the Kimpton offices of a company which supplied equipment to the poultry industry. "There was 100,000 pounds worth of damage done," Ronnie said. That same month, the Animal Rights Militia placed bombs—which didn't detonate—under the cars of four vivisectors. "They weren't on a mercury tilt or anything, so they would go off when the guy was driving the car," Ronnie said, referring to the bombs, which he believed were simply meant to destroy vehicles. "But it was so cold it actually stopped the timers from working properly." Following this action, a special police squad was formed to investigate animal-rights militants.

When discussing the attempted car bombings in the media, per usual,

Ronnie tried to shift attention to the animal abuse to which activists were responding. But, in private, Ronnie had serious misgivings about the Animal Rights Militia action—unrelated to danger posed to vivisectors. "It's out of control, as Frank Bough said," Ronnie stated. "If you're watching and can press a button and detonate [the bomb], that's different. But you're not. It's on a timer. So you don't know what the situation will be when that goes off. That bomb could go off when there's a cat on the car. That bomb could go off as a child is walking past. That bomb could go off as the postperson is coming to deliver a letter. There's too much of a risk there to innocent life."

On March 12, Ronnie was arrested for conspiracy to commit arson and criminal damage, as well as conspiracy to incite others to commit arson and criminal damage. "I didn't know what evidence they had," Ronnie said. "I thought, well, how are they going to make this stick?" Vivien faced the same charges. Other activists associated with the Animal Liberation Front—Roger Yates, Brendan McNally, and Neil McIvor—were arrested too. "One thing that worried me was that we had a number of young, male rats in the [press] office," Ronnie said, noting these were animals rescued from laboratories, or the offspring of such creatures. "But, thankfully, the police allowed a friend of ours to take these rats away and look after them. So they were okay." Ronnie was remanded in custody to Hull Prison, East Yorkshire.

13

Third Prison Sentence

In 1986, while Ronnie was on remand, his barrister tried multiple times for bail, but was refused. "I remember one court appearance, where the prosecution lawyer was arguing against me getting bail," Ronnie said, amused. "He was performing in a very theatrical way. He gave all the reasons why I shouldn't get bail. Then he said to the magistrate.... Mr. Lee is a very dangerous man. As he said that, he swung around to look straight at me. I put my one finger up right in his face." After using up all of his options, Ronnie was forced to reconcile himself to the fact he would be in prison at least until his trial.

The authorities were putting together a case against Ronnie—using documents they'd found in another raid on the press office, appearances Ronnie had made in the media, and copies of the Animal Liberation Front Supporters Group newsletter. "They were alleging I was the publisher of that newsletter, because I was handling the ALF bank accounts," Ronnie said, adding some of these funds were used to finance the publication. "Therefore, as the publisher, I'd be responsible for everything that was in that newsletter." Further, the police were able to identify Ronnie by one of his pseudonyms, Captain Kirk, after finding a draft of an article, written under that name, in Ronnie's handwriting. "A lot of the stuff in the newsletters was blatantly inciting people to carry out ALF actions," Ronnie said, adding his barrister, after initially telling him he could face a life sentence, ultimately thought he would receive 15 years in prison. "At least I would have had a release date. So that was some, small relief."

By this point, it was much easier to receive vegan provisions in prison. As a result of negotiations between the prison service and the Vegan Society, any members of the latter group could receive food without animal products. "It still wasn't really fair," Ronnie said. "If somebody was a vegetarian, or a Muslim, or a Jew, all they had to do was say they were that. They didn't have to have a membership card for any organization or a letter from the Rabbi or anything to prove what they were. They just said they were that and they got their diet. With the vegan diet it was more difficult. You had to join the Vegan Society." Still, Ronnie was happy with the food he was provided. In fact, according to him, many prisoners—unmoved by animal suffering—joined the Vegan Society in order to eat what were widely regarded as more delectable meals.

Ronnie, who was a smoker, found it easier to quit tobacco in prison than outside. "You're only allowed to go to the prison shop once a week," Ronnie said, noting if he could resist the urge to purchase cigarettes in that moment, he would be forced to go without for a week. "You can't really scrounge [tobacco] off other people, because it's a very precious commodity and they wouldn't be too keen to lend that to anyone." Around this time, one of Ronnie's friends sent him a booklet, printed by the Canadian military, about keeping fit in a confined space. "I'm not quite sure under what circumstances the Canadian army would need to know this, but it was published by them," Ronnie said. "It was stuff like doing exercises using a chair, push-ups, sit-ups and all of that kind of thing." He diligently followed the recommended regime.

While in Hull Prison, Ronnie shared a cell for some time with Roger, who had been a regional press officer for the Animal Liberation Front. "We rescued a pigeon who was injured in the exercise yard and kept her in the cell in a cardboard box," Roger said, adding prison officials eventually discovered and removed the pigeon. "Ronnie insisted that they take the bird to a bird sanctuary or else he would go to the press. [I'm] not sure how the story ends though. I think they agreed." According to Roger, the pair also kept in their cell a number of copies of an anti-vivisection book—*Slaughter of the Innocent*, by Hans Reusch—to give to other prisoners. Eventually, Roger was granted bail.

That autumn, Ronnie was transferred to Armley Prison, in Leeds, to stand trial. "I remember looking at this place with horror, because it was like a big, black castle," Ronnie said, noting the prison walls were made of sandstone. "Over the years, the sandstone had absorbed all of the dirt and turned it black." The conditions inside were worse than those of Hull Prison as well. "It was an older prison," Ronnie said of the Armley facility. "It was dirtier. I was in a cell all of the time with three other guys." His trial began on January 12, 1987, at Sheffield Crown Court. "The prosecution outlined their case," Ronnie said, adding they assigned military ranks to those involved in the Animal Liberation Front. "I suppose they thought it would probably help the jury understand." Ronnie was described as a general—

making him General Lee. Enjoying the historical allusion, while finding the rankings ludicrous, Ronnie embraced the designation going forward as a joke.

Ronnie pleaded not guilty. Though, of course, he'd committed the crimes for which he was accused, Ronnie hoped the prosecution wouldn't be able to prove it. His comrades watched the case from the public gallery. On one occasion, when Ronnie turned to see them, a friend made him laugh. "He got a black handkerchief out of his pocket and put it on his head, which is what judges used to do when they were sentencing people to death," Ronnie said. "It was a kind of sick humor." In early February, Ronnie was found guilty and sentenced to a decade in prison. "I kind of punched the air with delight," Ronnie said. "I know it sounds rather bizarre that someone could be pleased to get a 10-year sentence. But I was actually very relieved, because I was thinking I would get more than that."

When he was returned to Armley Prison, Ronnie was treated as a top-security prisoner. He believed this decision was the result of financial considerations, as it provided further employment to guards. "Wherever you go, you have to have three prison officers with you if you're a Category-A prisoner," Ronnie said, noting this included trips to the bathroom. "It was in the interests of the prison officers to have all these [Category-A] cells filled." In the facility, there were about a half a dozen of these cells, which were especially secure. "They had extra thick walls," Ronnie said. "They had extra bars at the window. The furniture in these cells was made of cardboard." Ronnie's bed, chair and desk were all made out of the compressed material. "That's so it couldn't be used as a weapon," he said, noting the furniture was still quite strong. "I was doing my exercise regime and I used to do step-ups on this chair." After about six weeks, Ronnie's classification was lowered. "The reason was that a guy had been done for rape," Ronnie said. "They had found someone else who could take my place."

In Armley Prison, Ronnie had a number of cellmates, including a former member of a fascist gang. "I remember one day the door opened and this young, tall guy came into the cell," Ronnie said. "When I looked at him, I was shocked, because he had a swastika tattooed in the middle of his forehead." Eventually, Ronnie was surprised to find himself on friendly terms with the man, who had rejected his far-right past and planned to remove the tattoo. "I actually ended up getting on very well with him," Ronnie said. "Through talking to me, he became a vegetarian." At the time, the prison dentist, who was known for his harsh methods, was a staunch supporter of Israel, with Zionist posters covering his office walls. "This guy, [the ex-fascist]—he developed a toothache," Ronnie recalled, laughing. "I said, well, before you go to see the dentist, I think there's something I have to tell you. He was devastated." Ultimately, the ex-fascist was in so much pain, he went to see the dentist despite his fear. The meeting resulted in nothing more than awkward conversation about the swastika tattoo. "[The ex-fascist] came back very, very relieved from that experience," Ronnie said, amused.

Both Ronnie and the ex-fascist disliked a third man who was briefly their cellmate. "He had a 28-day sentence," Ronnie said, adding the newcomer frequently complained about his incarceration. "Obviously, this did our head in—that this guy was moaning about being in prison, when he had such a short sentence." So Ronnie and the ex-fascist started playing practical jokes on their cellmate. For instance, the pair gave him false information about prison rules. "I think it was quite warm weather at the time," Ronnie said. "[The newcomer] was just wearing his underpants." Ronnie and the ex-fascist told the man that, when leaving the cell to go to use the toilet, he needn't be fully dressed. This, of course, wasn't true. "We said, oh no, you can just go like that; they don't mind," Ronnie recalled, laughing as he described the newcomer exiting in his underwear. "You just heard the prison officer bellowing his name and shouting at him." According to Ronnie, these pranks never got the man in serious trouble.

For Ronnie, an enduring result of his time in prison was a hatred for talk radio. "There was an appalling program that [my succession of cellmates] loved," Ronnie said, referring to *Our Tune*, a sentimental program hosted by broadcaster Simon Bates. "It was about really sad things that had happened to people." For instance, Ronnie recalled one episode in which a man crashed his car on the way to visit his wife in the hospital. "I used to think, why the hell would you want to listen to that for?" Ronnie recalled. "Is it because you're pleased that some other bugger is worse off than you are? I just couldn't understand it…. And, yet, *Our Tune* was the favorite program of so many prisoners. I was kind of forced to listen to it." As a result, Ronnie said, decades later he still loathed talk radio.

In December, he was moved to a prison called Long Lartin, in South Littleton, near Evesham. "I should have been moved to a prison in the north of the country," Ronnie said, adding, however, a special allowance was made for him because his father was fighting bowel cancer, and not able to travel great distances. "If I was in prison in the north of the country, he wouldn't have been able to visit me. But Long Lartin isn't far from Gloucester, where my parents were living." The facility offered better conditions than the one Ronnie would have been moved to otherwise. "It was a more modern prison," he said, noting he had a degree of privacy there. "I had a cell of my own." Ronnie resolved to add a new decorations—such as photographs and postcards, which were mailed to him—to the walls of his cell every day. "My cell became renowned," Ronnie said, noting other prisoners visited just to admire his decorations. "It was so nice." Additionally, Ronnie had his own curtains and rug.

During this period, the French actress and animal activist Brigitte Bardot sent him a letter, but it never reached him. "I think what had happened is one of the prison officers had intercepted the letter and and sold it to a national newspaper," Ronnie said, adding he believed it was printed in the *News of the World*. "I was incensed. I made inquiries about where was this letter and came up against a brick wall." Ronnie, who was learning a number of languages while in prison, sent the actress a letter in French. "I thought it was polite, because Brigitte Bardot was French," Ronnie said. "Also, it was good practice for me." He received no response.

Ronnie continued his efforts to stay in physically good shape. "They've stolen these years from my life," Ronnie said, referring to the justice system. "One way of fighting back against that is to keep fit—to try and live longer to make up for the time they've taken away from me." During his exercise period, Ronnie ran around the prison field. "When I first started running, I could only run a very small amount before I was out of breath," he said. "But gradually I built this up. After a few weeks, I was able to spend the whole of the hour running around this field." Ronnie estimated he ran about five miles a day.

At Long Lartin, Ronnie became friends with Alan Heyl, a South African bank robber and the last surviving member of the Stander Gang. "He was a vegetarian," Ronnie said. "I got on really well with him." Ronnie met again with John Walker, who remembered him from their shared time at Wormwood Scrubs. Ronnie also spoke with Gerry Conlon, who, like John Walker, was falsely accused of involvement in Provisional Irish Republican Army bombings. "He actually came to see me," Ronnie said. "We had a chat in my cell." For the most part, Ronnie's fellow prisoners were respectful of his dietary choices. "There used to be a bit of banter about me being vegan," Ronnie said, laughing as he described teasing omnivores back. "I cut this cross out of some cardboard and put it on [a prisoner's] tray in front of the chicken carcass. It was just a way of trying to get a point across without getting too argumentative with people."

Officials in the South Littleton facility allowed prisoners to keep birds as companion animals, a policy which Ronnie opposed. "It's bound to be the case that some of these creatures will be ill-treated," he said. "They wouldn't all be. Some of [the prisoners] were very, very loving and very, very kind [to their birds]." The policy being what it was, Ronnie helped rehabilitate injured birds, as he'd attempted to do in Hull Prison. "These birds would be allowed to fly around the cell," Ronnie said, adding sometimes they were hurt as a result of flying in confined space. "I would always have these animals brought to me." Ronnie recalled the unusual manner in which he splinted a bird's wing. "I got some sock material, or cut a sock up, and wrapped this sock around the bird—to keep the wing still," Ronnie said. "You left it for a couple of weeks and the bird was okay."

One day, perhaps in 1988, Patty and Kyall came to visit. Ronnie did his best to entertain his nephew, who was about 12 years old at the time. "All the visit, he was going—Uncle Ronnie, Uncle Ronnie—is there a murderer in this room?" Ronnie recalled. "Other prisoners were having visits at the other tables, you see. I had to point out to him who was a murderer." But the man Ronnie motioned toward had only killed one person, which didn't impress the boy. "Kyall went, no, no, no—I mean a real murderer," Ronnie said, laughing. "He probably meant one of these mass killers." Similarly, Kyall asked Ronnie to point out a gangster in the room. "I had to look and see if I could see anyone who was a gangster, trying not to catch their eye," Ronnie said, amused. "I didn't want them to think I was staring at them."

In the summer of 1989, Ronnie was moved to a semi-open prison called Channings Wood, in Denbury, near Newton Abbot. "There was a lot of freedom to walk about," Ronnie said. "We were only locked in our cells at nighttime." Once again, Ronnie had his own living space, which he decorated. He was even eligible for home leave. "It was once every six months," Ronnie said. "I'd go and spend a weekend with my parents." That winter, he helped launch an animal-rights magazine called *Arkangel*, as production of the Animal Liberation Front Supporters Group newsletter had stopped. The magazine's title—which evoked the term archangel—referred to Noah's Ark, which, of course, sheltered animals in the Old Testament. "So Arkangel was like the angel of the ark, the angel that looks after all of the animals," Ronnie said. "That was the thinking behind it. It was a kind of play on words." Vivien, who was by then out of prison, edited the magazine. Ronnie's visitors sent his contributions to her. "I was only allowed to write extensively for the first two issues," Ronnie said. "After that, the prison authorities barred me from handing contributions to the magazine out to my visitors."

In the evenings, Ronnie watched television in one of the prison's common rooms. "There were a few of us there who were *Star Trek* fans," Ronnie said, noting they watched both the original *Star Trek* and *Star Trek: Next Generation*. "We would all gather to watch." He also viewed wildlife

Ronnie on Gloucester railway station in autumn 1989, with Vivien Smith (left) and his mother and father. He had spent the weekend on home leave from Channings Wood prison and was about to catch a train back (photograph Patricia Lee).

programs and the occasional film. But Ronnie—having given up tobacco—hated that prisoners were allowed to smoke in these common rooms. "I couldn't stand it," he said. "It used to, more or less, cause me to have problems with my throat." When he was named a representative on a prison committee, Ronnie had an opportunity to change this. "We wanted smoking banned in the television rooms," he said. "But the prison authorities wouldn't agree to it. They said they would have trouble on their hands, that the smokers would be up in arms."

Also while Ronnie was in Channings Wood, Robin Webb, a former member of the executive council of the Royal Society for the Prevention of Cruelty to Animals, asked if he would support him as a new press officer for the Animal Liberation Front. Since Ronnie's imprisonment, one man had tried to fill the position but was quickly arrested for his work. "The job of the press officer became a very dangerous one to do," Ronnie said, referring to legal consequences. "Nobody wanted to do it. The press officer job—at least temporarily—came to an end." So when Robin Webb offered his services, Ronnie approved. "He was concerned that people wouldn't take kindly to him being the press officer, because he had no known history of activism," Ronnie said. "I thought, it's better for him to do it than not to have anyone doing it."

Ronnie's fellow prisoners were aware of his involvement with the Animal Liberation Front, though some ludicrously overestimated the group's power and reach. After Ronnie joked he would sic activists on a prisoner who had stepped on a frog, the man came to Ronnie and asked for clemency. "He said, I didn't deliberately try to stamp on a frog," Ronnie recalled. "[He said], it was an accident; the frog jumped out in front of me." The man pleaded with Ronnie to call the activists off. "I said—I tell you what—I'll give you this one chance," Ronnie recalled, describing how he played along. "I said, I'll put the word out to the boys.... But, I said, if I hear of you doing anything again, then I'll be back in touch with them about you." The man was most grateful. "He went, no, no, I'll never do anything like that," Ronnie said, laughing. "He was really apologetic."

False rumors even spread about the reason for Ronnie's imprisonment. One day he overhead a pair of prisoners talking about him. "They obviously didn't think I could hear them," Ronnie recalled. "One of them said to the other, see that little guy there with glasses—what do you think he's in prison for? The other guy said, oh, by the look of him, I'd say he's probably in for some sort of fraud. And [the first speaker] said, no, no, he's fucking dangerous; he cut a butcher to pieces; he slashed a butcher right up." Ronnie was dumbfounded. "I thought, where did that come from?" Ronnie said. "I just laughed to myself. I thought, this is the madness of prison rumors." And so the small, bespectacled vegan developed an intimidating reputation. More realistically, prison officials worried Ronnie might confront Princess Anne, a hunt supporter who toured the facility. But Ronnie remained in his cell during the visit.

Around 1990—by which time she was 18 years old and a vegan, animal-rights campaigner herself—Louise began corresponding with Ronnie. She was reluctant at first, but a friend encouraged her, believing she would get along well with the prisoner. "I didn't really want to be a Ronnie hag [or] fan," Louise said. "There were a lot of people writing and I didn't want to fall into that bracket." Her correspondence with Ronnie covered a broad range of subjects. "From campaigning, what we were doing, how busy we were at this end with animals—obviously, you couldn't put anything in there that you were actually going to be doing illegally," Louise said. "They were very warm letters." According to Ronnie, Louise's correspondence immediately stood out, as her penmanship was affected by her disorder, which she explained. "But reading what she said, I thought, well, this is really interesting," he said. "I began to correspond quite regularly with

Louise." As he did with all of his friends, family, and pen pals, he asked for photographs of Louise and her companion animals, which he put up on his cell wall.

Ronnie diligently continued his study of foreign languages, maintaining a relentlessly positive attitude. "The belief of most guys in prison was that if you sleep as much as you can, then you're actually in prison for a shorter time," Ronnie recalled. "I used to say, no, I don't agree with that. Because it's still your life. You're actually sleeping your life away." Ronnie couldn't understand how his fellow prisoners were bored during their sentence. "I used to say, how can you be bored?" Ronnie recalled. "There's a whole library of books in this prison with interesting things you can read about." Ronnie would stay awake until the early hours of the morning—practicing German, French, Spanish, Polish and Italian.

At Channings Wood, there was a mentally ill prisoner, who was a former naval officer. "He was very proud of the fact that he'd been a captain," Ronnie said. "Guys would use me to wind him up. They'd go, well you're not the highest-ranking officer on this landing. He'd say, yes I am; I'm a

Ronnie (fourth from left) with friends at Sue Smith's home in Somerset, while on home leave from prison in October 1991 (photograph Dave Wetton).

captain. They'd say, no you're not; there's a general on this landing." This was in reference to Ronnie's nickname. "He'd go, he's not a general; he's a tea boy," Ronnie said, laughing, before adding a friend forged a letter from the Queen, that appeared to validate the generalship, which only angered the captain further. "In the end, they moved him to a closed prison. Really, he shouldn't have been in prison, to be honest. He wasn't right in the head."

Top: **Ronnie on home leave in April 1991, pictured with a campaign poster calling for his release (photograph Dave Wetton).** *Bottom:* **Ronnie at his parents' house in Gloucester, on the day of his release from prison in November 1992 (photograph Patricia Lee).**

During his time at the Denbury facility, prison officials installed a telephone for inmates' use. "This was a new thing for prisons," Ronnie said, noting that, as a result, many people on the outside didn't know prisoners could make calls. "I thought, I'll use this for a bit of fun." So he called up one of his comrades and pretended to be in the midst of the 1991 Gulf War. "I said, listen, I can't speak for long," Ronnie recalled. "I said, they let some of us out of prison, provided that we go and help the troops out in Kuwait." Ronnie's comrade, without another explanation for Ronnie's ability to call, believed this. "She was really worried," Ronnie recalled, laughing. "I said—hang on a minute—there's a big missile coming over." Ronnie played similar pranks on others. After making plans to rent an apartment in Crouch Hill, London, from a friend, Ronnie was released from prison early, due to good behavior, on November 13, 1992.

14

Louise

Shortly after his release from prison, on November 27, 1992, Ronnie, by then 41 years old, met Louise at Kidderminster railway station, while on a trip to an animal-rights gathering in Blackpool. "I just hugged him," Louise said. "I put my hand up to his face and said, all right then, mate, how are you doing? I said, it's great to meet you; it's great to see you. I said, after all the conversation we've had on the phone and the letters—you dirty, old bugger. I just thought he was ace."

Before continuing on his journey the next day, Ronnie stayed the night at Louise's home in Blakedown, where she lived with her parents. The pair spoke openly for the first time, as his communication had been monitored in prison. Their conversation made Ronnie's fondness for Louise grow. "I felt deep admiration for her," he said, adding Louise told him about the traditional and underground activism in which she was involved. "Despite her disability, she still took part in these things. I thought that was absolutely brilliant."

Ronnie was especially protective of Louise because of her disorder. "I used to say she was like an angel who had fallen from heaven but landed badly," Ronnie recalled. "[So] I think there was that element." Louise agreed. "I just felt that he saw me like how he's always seen lots of things," she said. "There was a potential for me to be treated unfairly. I think that made him feel protective. He could see the vulnerability—but he could also see the strength." This didn't feel condescending. "Sometimes I'd play up to it," Louise said.

They visited each other frequently. One day, Ronnie was cooking for Louise, intent on showing her some of the recipes he'd developed in prison. "We were so busy talking, while the cooking was going on, that the food got burnt," Ronnie said, laughing. "It was absolutely horrible. She always insisted that these prison recipes were no good.... It was actually just that one occasion, but I'm not sure she really believes me on that." The pair also went for walks near his Crouch Hill apartment. "There was a path where the railway track had been," Ronnie said. "It was lovely there. Because it was down in a cutting, and there were high banks, it was almost like you weren't in London. It was like a piece of countryside."

Additionally, they visited Vivien, who was incarcerated again. "She'd gotten six years for various ALF actions," Ronnie said, noting Vivien was held in Holloway Prison, North London. "She was actually caught in a raid on a chicken farm. The police pulled in front of her to stop her and she crashed into the police car." Their trips to see Vivien were generally pleasant. "You would be in a noisy visiting room at a small table," Ronnie said. "But they were enjoyable visits. We used to have a good laugh with Viv." They also visited a friend of Louise's, Angie Hamp, who was in prison as well for Animal Liberation Front activity.

For some time, Ronnie—who, following his break-up with Kym, had resolved not to enter a serious relationship—struggled with his growing love for Louise. "I was starting to have feelings for Louise that I never really had for anyone else before," Ronnie said. "I kind of fought against that. I didn't want that. I thought, what's happening to me?" He described himself as in a state of turmoil. "I'd already decided on a certain way forward in my life, but my feelings were challenging that," Ronnie said. "It even resulted in me feeling quite ill at times. I developed quite a bad skin condition on my face and around my eyes." He never felt such stress during his previous activism, legal or otherwise. "This was completely different," Ronnie said. "It was a much more emotional thing. When I prepared for a raid, it was like being a soldier."

Louise confirmed their relationship was initially difficult. "It was a very unhappy time," she said, adding their unhappiness lasted for about two years. "I'm not going to lie. It was not good." Some of this resulted from Ronnie's wariness of romantic commitment. "He had lots and lots of irons in the fire, shall we say," Louise recalled. "He had a massive struggle with settling down." Beyond this, according to Louise, their unhappiness was also the result of Ronnie's prison experience. For instance, he was jumpy and cried frequently, behavior which she saw as a negative effects of his incarceration. "He could laugh things off with humor," she said. "But I definitely think it left its mark. I wasn't the only person to say that." On the other hand, Louise felt incarceration had become a valued part of Ronnie's self-identity, which he'd lost. "It defined him as an ALF person in prison and he drew great strength from that," she said.

When Ronnie introduced Louise to his parents, his father didn't approve of the young woman. "Louise had very short hair," Ronnie said. "My dad took a dislike to her because of that. He didn't think women should have short hair. He wasn't very polite to her. He called her 'it,' instead of calling her 'she,' which I took extreme objection to." Similarly, when Louise brought an avocado-based meal for the Lees, Ron was less than pleasant. "As soon as my dad saw that, he said, what's this green muck?" Ronnie recalled. "My dad would have never eaten avocado. He was very traditional in the food he ate."

During this period, Ronnie discovered his father was deeply in debt. Ron had even spent his son's savings—which he managed while Ronnie was incarcerated—and sold Ronnie's coin collection. "It's still a kind of mystery, whether he was a secret gambler or something," Ronnie said. "But this money went somewhere." Since Ron wasn't getting along with Margaret, he decided to separate from her, sell their house to pay off his debt, and move back to Ireland. "My dad put the house up for sale, but he was having difficulty selling it," Ronnie said. "So [Patty] said that she would buy it." After his daughter purchased the property, so Margaret could remain there, Ron decided to stay in the house with his wife. "I just thought

Ronnie with Louise on trip to Paris in spring 1993 (photograph Eric Moreau).

my dad had pulled quite a clever stroke, really," Ronnie said, with what sounded like amused resignation. "He'd been able to pay off all of his debts and still remain living in the same house."

In the summer of 1993, when Sue went on vacation for about 10 days, Ronnie and Louise took charge of the animal sanctuary she'd established in Somerset. One morning, they found an elderly goat dead. "I phoned Sue up," Ronnie recalled. "Sue thought that it had probably been heart failure, just to do with his age. So I said, what do I do with the goat? Sue said, well, chop him up and feed him to the dogs; that's what we would do." Ronnie deliberated over this for some time, eventually following Sue's advice, as the dogs were fed meat anyway. "The goat's dead," Ronnie said. "If I chop the goat up and feed the goat to the dogs, then that's less money going to the butcher. So, therefore, the most ethical thing to do is actually to feed the goat to the dogs." This was a deeply unpleasant experience for Ronnie and Louise. "When I told other people in the animal-rights movement about chopping this goat up, they were horrified," Ronnie recalled. "They said, I can't believe that you did that."

By early autumn, Ronnie's friend, who owned the Crouch Hill apartment, needed to raise his rent in order to pay off her mortgage. "She said, well, haven't you got anymore money?" Ronnie recalled. "I said, I haven't; I just can't afford it." So Ronnie talked the matter over with Louise. "Louise said, why don't you come back and live with me and my parents?" Ronnie recalled. "In the end, that's what I decided to do." He got along well with Louise's parents, Celia and John Ryan, who, by this point, were vegan and vegetarian, respectively, due to their daughter's influence. "They were very supportive of animal rights," Ronnie said, noting, however, he still found it difficult to live with them. "I'd been used to living a semi-solitary existence." Louise agreed the transition was hard for him. "[Ronnie] couldn't really cope with that," she said, referring to the hustle and bustle of the Ryan home. "He would spend a lot of time up in my bedroom, with me, because it was quite separate to the rest of the house."

The Ryans had several dogs, including a German Sheprador who had to be separated from the others because of her aggressive nature. Louise had named the animal Demo, in reference to political demonstrations. "I felt sorry for her, because she was kind of on her own," Ronnie said of the dog. "So I used to enjoy taking her for walks. I got very close with her." Demo wasn't very well behaved. "There was some kind of banquet going on in this hall," Ronnie said, laughing as he described how, while on a walk, the dog ran inside. "I was desperately calling her back. I think she must have jumped up on the table, because loads of shouting and screaming came from this place." When Demo exited the building, Ronnie quickly skulked away with the dog.

Around this time, Ronnie became Louise's official caregiver. "Because she had a disability and received disability benefits, she was entitled to have somebody who would look after her and help her," Ronnie said. "She found difficulty in carrying things and stuff like that." As Louise's caregiver, Ronnie received additional benefits and was no longer put under pressure by the authorities to seek work. "This was something I was already doing," he said. "This meant that I would receive a bit of extra money for doing that, which Louise and I would really have jointly, because we had decided to pool our money. Also, it meant I no longer had to go and sign on every week at the unemployment office."

Following his release from Channings Wood, Ronnie didn't participate in Animal Liberation Front actions for a number of reasons. One of these, of course, was his fear of being sent back to prison. "I knew the police were watching me very closely, so I wouldn't be able to get away with anything," Ronnie said. "[And] I knew that if I went to prison again it would be for a very, very long time." This fear was exacerbated by his commitment to Louise. "I felt, I've got this responsibility now," Ronnie said. "When I'd been doing ALF stuff before, I had no responsibilities." Although he defended illegal action in the future—and even provided aid to Animal Liberation Front fugitives—his decision was also the result of an ideological shift. "I started to think, if we can educate enough people about stuff, then results will come," Ronnie said. "There won't be the immediate gratification of seeing a butcher-shop window break or a truck destroyed, but nevertheless that's still important." Even at the time, he knew his decision was a permanent one. "I don't think it was bittersweet, really," Ronnie said. "I was very practical."

According to Louise, many people in the animal-rights movement blamed her for Ronnie's choice. "I'm not so sure everybody thought that it was Ronnie that was stopping Ronnie," Louise said. "You just kind of knew that they were thinking it's because he's got in with this person." But she rejected the notion. "I wouldn't have cared if he'd done two or three or four sentences after meeting me," Louise said. "I would have been quite happy to be a prisoner's wife and support him. It wouldn't have mattered." In fact, Ronnie's choice puzzled her to some degree. "You had these two different people almost," Louise said. "You had the old Ronnie who would be doing stuff and then this new person who wouldn't be so in your face. I think people—certainly around the time of the early '90s—thought he would go on to still do ALF stuff. But, of course, you're not going to go on forever doing that."

She agreed Ronnie's choice was motivated by a desire to avoid further prison time. "I don't think he wanted to face doing years and years and years again inside—and certainly not after meeting me, having a home, and all of the comforts that meant," Louise. "Remember, he had a very austere lifestyle to begin with, that fitted in with going to prison. I'm sure I'm not the only person to say, for people who have been in prison, that's how you have to live your life when you're doing those [illegal] things. But when you take on a house, animals, and somebody that you want to be with, it's not conducive to going back to jail. You just don't."

While he didn't return to illegal action, Ronnie did, however, speak before local animal-rights groups about his incarceration and prior activism.

"People wanted me to go along to their meetings and give a talk about my experience," he said. "Also, they wanted to know a bit about the history of the ALF and the Band of Mercy—because, of course, this is quite a few years later. We're now in the early '90s. So it had been almost 20 years. A lot of these people were a new generation of activists." His audiences ranged in size from about 30 to 100 people. "Obviously, I'd served a long prison sentence for incitement, [so] I had to be careful about what I said," Ronnie recalled. "More or less, I was speaking about what people had done in the past. It wasn't about what I thought people should do now."

While Ronnie lived with Louise's family, Celia introduced him to a new form of activism. "At the time, she did lots of street stalls," Ronnie said, noting Celia frequently advocated anti-vivisectionism from these booths. "I thought, that's a good way you can spread the message and educate people—but you're not breaking the law." However, despite his experience as Animal Liberation Front press officer, Ronnie was still nervous about dealing with the public. "I never really wanted [to have] anything to do with ordinary people, because to me they were meat-eaters," he said. "But by doing a street stall, you have to mix amongst them. You have to talk to people. That's what it's about. That's the purpose of it. This was totally alien to me."

So, anxious as he was, Ronnie managed street stalls alongside Celia and Louise at first. Eventually, he gained enough confidence to manage stalls with just Louise. "I used to think, God, you can speak to the media; you can go on telly; you've done loads of shit," Louise said, noting she was befuddled by Ronnie's fear of leafleting. "That's who he was. To create damage and to do things ... you don't have to formulate relationships. It was ideal for Ronnie. In fact, I think the ALF was built around Ronnie—because that was Ronnie. It's like an autism almost."

On one occasion, while the couple were handing out anti-vivisectionist leaflets at a booth in Tamworth, Ronnie and Louise were confronted by an argumentative, self-declared animal researcher. "I grabbed hold of him by his collar," Ronnie said, adding he walked the man away from the stall, threatening him as they went. "We'd gone quite some distance. This guy was cowering and trembling. When we got to the other side of the crowd, I thought, well, what am I going to do with this guy?" Unsure of himself, Ronnie punched the man in the stomach. "I said to him, if I ever see you again, I'll kill you where you stand," Ronnie recalled, adding the melodramatic line became an inside joke amongst his friends. "I went back to Louise and said, listen, the police are probably going to be here any minute." Ronnie and Louise remained at the stall, expecting authorities to show up, but they never did. "Having the anti-vivisection boards did occasionally cause problems with people that supported animal experiments," Ronnie said, noting this wasn't the only physical confrontation he had during this period while managing booths. "[But] most people were very sympathetic."

In the spring of 1994, Ronnie received news that Vivien had gone on the run, while on a brief furlough to attend a college class. "I was really surprised," Ronnie said. "Because, I thought, she's only got a year left of her prison sentence. It just seems a bit daft to me. But she was a bit impulsive like that." According to Ronnie, Vivien didn't turn herself in for approximately another 20 years. "It's a very long time to not be able to operate properly," he said.

That May, Ronnie and Louise moved to a terraced house on Talbot Street, Kidderminster. "It was through a housing association," Ronnie said, adding he and Louise became partial owners of the property. "There wasn't really any way that we would get a mortgage to actually buy a house." While the property itself left things to be desired, it was in a beautiful location, opposite of a park, which the couple appreciated. Since Demo didn't get along with the Ryan's other dogs, Ronnie and Louise brought the German Sheprador with them. "We felt sorry for her," Ronnie said. "She came to live with us." Louise believed it was the move out of her parents' house that finally raised Ronnie's spirits. "We needed room to grow as a couple," she said. Over time, they slowly made improvements to the Talbot Street property, beginning with the garden. "Louise was the one who had the plans for everything in her head," Ronnie said. "She'd tell me how she wanted it. She'd do a bit of work in the garden, but I'd obviously have to do the heavy work. We created flower beds. We planted trees, shrubs and climbers."

In the summer, the couple adopted a greyhound, who they renamed Billy. "He seemed very docile and very placid," Ronnie said, "We thought, that's an ideal dog to go with Demo…. He's going to let her be the boss." But they had Billy for only few months before he died tragically. "Just a few miles away from us, there was a forest," Ronnie said. "We used to take Billy and Demo there for a walk. We'd let them off the leads and they'd run in the forest and have a great time. But on this one occasion, Billy caught sight of a deer." The greyhound chased after the wild creature. "The deer ran quite some distance and ran across a road," Ronnie said. "Billy ran after the deer and got hit by a car and killed." Of course, the couple was devastated by this. "I remember taking him home and burying him in the garden," Ronnie said. "It took a hell of a lot to bury him because, of course, he was such a big dog. I dug a huge hole."

In the wake of Billy's death, Ronnie and Louise wanted to adopt

Ronnie with Billy and Demo in the Wyre Forest in August 1995 (photograph Louise Ryan).

another animal as soon as possible. Later in this period, they would get a number of rats, mice and hamsters—some of whom had been rescued in Animal Liberation Front raids. But in that moment, they adopted a second greyhound named Bernie, who got along well with Demo. But quickly after bringing him home, the couple learned Bernie, who they believed was the victim of abuse, was terrified of humans. As a result, no one else could watch the dogs. Either Ronnie or Louise had to remain at the house when the other left for any length of time. "That was the reason we never went on holiday," Ronnie said, laughing. "So I started to do the stalls on my own, which I was quite confident about now." In the hopes of attracting more people to his booth, Ronnie refocused his leafleting on whale and dolphin conservation, which he saw as less contentious than anti-vivisectionism. "I always gave them some sort of a go-vegan leaflet as well," Ronnie said. "I'd be doing these stalls two or three times a week."

While Ronnie didn't participate in many demonstrations during this period, Louise was very active in this respect. "It could have been me going on these things and Louise staying home [to care for Bernie]," Ronnie said. "But I'd kind of think, well, I'd had this life of activism. I'd done all of this stuff earlier in my life. So it was only fair, really, for Louise to be allowed to do stuff." He managed the street stalls as Louise—who couldn't drive or carry all the necessary items—was unable to manage them on her own. "[Participating in demonstrations] was something she enjoyed doing and was able to do," Ronnie said.

On February 1, 1995, an activist named Jill Phipps—who Louise knew—was crushed to death by a truck while protesting the live export of veal calves at Coventry Airport, in Baginton. "She was a very quiet, kind of unassuming girl," Louise said. "She was very, very pretty. She seemed like such a nice person." In the immediate aftermath of Jill's death, many people believed Louise was the victim. "We started getting phone calls because it had been on the news that a female protester had been killed," Ronnie said. "Louise's brother phoned up in a terrible state because he thought it might have been Louise that had been killed, because the name of the woman hadn't been released." About two weeks later, Ronnie and Louise attended Jill's funeral in Coventry Cathedral, in Coventry. "The cathedral was packed," Ronnie said. "Hundreds of people went to her funeral." Shortly after, Louise was arrested for disrupting the live export at Coventry Airport.

In 1996, Louise organized an anti-vivisection campaign targeting a laboratory in Ledbury owned by a company called Quintiles. "There were demonstrations being held against this laboratory every so often," Ronnie said. "But then Louise decided that she wanted to make this a really properly organized campaign." Ronnie assisted her, doing behind-the-scenes work and dealing with the media. The campaign was called Stop Quintiles Animal Testing. "They used to have demonstrations outside of this place twice a week," Ronnie said, adding the protests coincided with workers leaving the laboratory. "[Workers] would have their cars kicked and their cars rocked."

That spring, Ronnie and Louise adopted a third dog—a healthy lurcher they renamed Moss—whose previous caretaker brought him to the veterinary office to be euthanized. "He was a dog with a very good temperament," Ronnie said. "He was great with people. He was great with other dogs." By this point, Ronnie and Louise volunteered for Greyhound Rescue West of England, transporting and fostering dogs, as well as evaluating potential homes for them. "Louise always found [fostering] very difficult, because she always wanted to keep the dogs," Ronnie said. "I think if they had been all right with our dogs we would have. But quite often we had to keep them in a separate room, because Demo would go for another dog if the other dog wasn't totally submissive to her. And some of these dogs were themselves not the easiest of dogs."

According to Louise, she was unconcerned by Ronnie's vasectomy, because of animals like these. "I had committed myself to being a mother to all living things," she said. "I could care, look after, and be maternal with the creatures that needed my help." She agreed with many of Ronnie's objections to procreation. "If the world population was smaller, everything was greener, and the world was a happier place, you probably could do that," Louise said, referring to ethically reproducing. "I knew that bringing babies into this world takes a lot of time and energy." They wouldn't discuss getting married for a number of years.

15

Greyhound Action

In 1997, Ronnie and Louise founded Greyhound Action, which began primarily as a leafleting campaign targeting the racing industry. "It was more Louise's idea, to be fair," Ronnie said, noting his wife also coined the slogan "you bet, they die," which became popular in anti-racing literature. "She said, we need to do something about this; it's not good enough just rescuing these dogs, having some of them in our home and finding [other] homes for them; we need to do something more fundamental to stop this from happening." Ronnie agreed, and set out to help Louise by managing press relations and any written communication the group required. "Louise is dyslexic," Ronnie said. "So if any letters needed doing—which, of course, there would be—I would need to do it." He published a newsletter for the organization that quickly boasted hundreds of subscribers, a number which would grow significantly in the coming years.

Many members of rescue organizations, including Greyhound Rescue West of England, looked upon the founding of Greyhound Action unfavorably. "These rescue organizations were on friendly terms with greyhound trainers, so that—when some of these dogs had come to the end of their racing career—the trainer would hand the greyhounds over to the rescue, instead of having them put down," Ronnie said, adding members of these organizations worried the existence of Greyhound Action, which sought to end commercial greyhound racing altogether, would strain relationships with trainers. "We'd say to [those members], well, look, you're only rescuing a small fraction of these dogs; the vast majority of them are being put to death; that needs to be addressed."

Meanwhile, many animal-rights activists were apathetic towards the issue. "People didn't realize what the situation was with greyhound racing," Ronnie said. "Most people thought, all it is is dogs running around the track and they probably enjoy running around the track—so why are you campaigning against it?" But, of course, there was more to greyhound racing than this. "It's a bit like the dairy industry and the egg industry, where people think, oh, these cows need to be milked and these hens are all happy," Ronnie said. "The appearance of it is very different to the actual reality." He and Louise struggled to educate fellow activists about the true costs of greyhound racing. "We'd have to explain to people, this is the situation and here are the facts and figures," Ronnie said.

By this point, the racing industry was on the decline. Greyhound Action merely hoped to hasten its demise. "The heyday of dog racing had probably been in the 1950s," Ronnie said, noting the introduction of on-street betting shops in the 1960s had hit the industry hard. "It took a lot of people away from the tracks." Also, he argued, there were simply more entertainment opportunities than there had been previously. "At one time, there wasn't a lot of things that people would go out to," Ronnie said, adding changing gender roles effected racing attendance as well. "It used to the be the case that the woman would stay at home and the man would go out to the pub and the dog racing." But, increasingly, these standards began to shift. "Dog racing didn't really fit into that," Ronnie said. "These places were often very rough places, where guys would be okay. But if a guy wanted to take his wife or his family, it wasn't a suitable environment."

When communicating with the media on behalf of Greyhound Action—and Stop Quintiles Animal Testing, for that matter—Ronnie used a false name. "I was worried that attention would be focused on my past, rather than on the issue," Ronnie said. "So I adopted a pseudonym of Tony Peters." Anthony, of course, was his middle name, while Peter was his confirmation name. "It didn't involve any television appearances," Ronnie said, referring to his early duties for Greyhound Action. "It just involved letters [and] possibly the odd radio interview. But it wasn't anything where people would see me and say, I know him; that's Ronnie Lee; why is he using a false name?" By the time Greyhound Action was influential enough to merit television coverage, no one recognized him as the founder of the Animal Liberation Front.

Interestingly, even some of the activists Ronnie worked alongside didn't know his real identity. "Some did and some didn't," he said. "It depended on who the people were. If they were people that had been involved in the animal-rights movement for some while, they knew who I was. But other people didn't. Other people knew me as Tony." Of course, word got around amongst the activists. "I was informed by someone I did an anti-vivisection protest with, who was a bit more knowledgable about people in the animal rights movement," said Steve Norman, a member of Greyhound Action.

"I didn't hold anything against [Ronnie]." But this wasn't a universal reaction. "Some of these people, when they found out, were quite concerned," Ronnie said, adding they worried that—if representatives of the racing industry discovered his criminal record—it could be used to do discredit Greyhound Action. "Surprisingly, they never did."

That year, Ronnie bought his first computer. "I was still in touch with the guy who had started the [Animal Liberation Front] Supporters Group," he said. "He kept nagging me to get a computer. He'd set up a small, mail-order business and he used a computer in connection with that. He said it really helped his business." Ronnie resisted the suggestion, arguing a typewriter suited his needs, but ultimately purchased a portable DOS computer. "It started not working properly," he said. "So I took it back to the company, because I'd only had it a very short while." The company offered either to replace his device or replace it with a more-powerful, desktop computer. Ronnie chose the latter option. He used the desktop to keep a database of Greyhound Action supporters, write snail mail, and design leaflets, among other things.

On November 9, Ron died of bowel cancer. "It wasn't unexpected," Ronnie said. "It was sad, but, in a way, it was a relief he was no longer suffering. When someone's suffered for a long time and you expect them to die—although you're sad, there's an element of relief as well about it. I think that's how we all felt." Shortly before his father passed, Ronnie received a call advising him to hurry home. "I dashed down to Gloucester," he said. "But I actually got there too late. He'd already died. My sister was there and my mum." About a week later, the Lees held a funeral service for Ron in a Catholic church. "I spoke at his funeral and basically told some funny stories about him," Ronnie recalled. "My sister sang."

In the spring of 1998, Ronnie started doing administrative work for the Animal Liberation Front Supporters Group. To complete his responsibilities, the organization provided him with a laptop. "This had Windows 95 on it, so it was an icon system—which I wasn't used to," Ronnie recalled. "I hated it. I said, I can't work this bloody Windows; can I change it back? But I did get used to it in the end." This was the first computer from which he sent email.

The supporters group had changed significantly since his imprisonment. By the late 1990s, the organization no longer raised funds for underground attacks, focusing solely on support for incarcerated activists. "What they did now was that before they got the newsletter published, they had it looked over by a lawyer," Ronnie said. "On that basis, I thought, I'm safe doing it." The risk of being charged with incitement was reduced by allowing a lawyer to proofread the publication. "If you accidentally incite someone, you can't be convicted," Ronnie said. "Of course, you were having it checked by a lawyer because you didn't want it to be inciting. So, even if the lawyer made a mistake, and it looked like it was inciting, the fact that you had taken it to a lawyer in the first place meant you had a defense." Ronnie did administrative work for the supporters group.

Around this time, the Stop Quintiles Animal Testing campaign expanded, targeting the company as a whole, rather than just those facilities associated with animal testing. "Quintiles had a laboratory in Scotland, in Edinburgh," Ronnie said, adding he was in touch with activists protesting the location. "But, also, Quintiles had a lot of other outlets throughout [England] that dealt with other aspects of their business.... So we decided, we'll put pressure on their other outlets as well." The demonstrations continued to be quite raucous. On one occasion, Louise scuffled with a laboratory worker. "He actually hit Louise around the face," Ronnie said. "So Louise just grabbed his hair and repeatedly punched him. He was screaming for mercy." During the autumn of 1999, as a result of a separate incident, she was found guilty of engaging in threatening behavior, but was given no punishment. Louise was arrested later during this period and unsuccessfully attempted to sue the police for use of excessive force.

In June of 2000, a company called Sequani took over the Quintiles laboratory in Ledbury, and so Louise and Ronnie changed the name of the opposition campaign to Stop Sequani Animal Testing. But Louise was growing exhausted by her leadership role. "With all the stuff that she'd done with the Quintiles campaign, it was proving very tiring for her," Ronnie said, adding that, as a result, she allowed others to manage the rechristened group. "Although Louise occasionally went on the demonstrations there, she no longer was involved in running the campaign." Ronnie continued to manage media relations for the new leaders. On August 11, John Ryan died of cancer, which had spread throughout his body. "In some ways, I was probably more fond of Louise's dad than my own dad," Ronnie said. "It was obviously a very upsetting time." Though Louise's father had been ill for many years, he was only in his 50s when he passed away.

On November 5, 2001, Barry Horne, a well-known Animal Liberation Front prisoner, died while on a hunger strike, demanding the Labour government keep its pledge to hold a public inquiry into animal testing. "I only met Barry once, very briefly," Ronnie said. "And he didn't leave a very good impression on me, because when I greeted him in a friendly manner, he just grunted. However, there is no doubting his courage and commitment to the cause of animal liberation." As Ronnie interacted with the public more while running street stalls, his opposition to electoral politics began to fade. Barry's death only furthered this. "A lot of people would have thought, there you go—that's more evidence that all governments are rubbish," Ronnie said. "Whereas, I thought, hang on a minute, are we really going to have a situation where there is no leadership? We're not really. We have to get good leaders. The reason why this happened is because the people who are in power are corrupt."

During this period, though the racing industry as a whole was on the decline, Greyhound Action was engaged in frequent battles with people seeking to open new tracks. "It would often involve lobbying of the local authority," Ronnie said. "I'd send emails from Greyhound Action to them, but we'd also encourage lots of other people to write to them as well." He spoke at public meetings and helped organize demonstrations against the tracks as well. "The decisions on planning applications can't be made on moral grounds," Ronnie said. "It's to do with stuff like noise pollution, disturbance to the neighborhood, and all of that kind of thing. But what we found was that—[if] you put the moral case to the councillors—they'll bear that in mind, and then they try to find a legal reason to stop it." Perhaps surprisingly, Ronnie's often-successful dealings with local authorities on the issue didn't play a role in his broader reconsideration of political involvement.

While it's hard to measure the degree to which Greyhound Action influenced the closure of existing tracks, Ronnie believed the organization had a significant effect. "I think the people leafleting outside played a considerable part," he said, in reference to the shuttering of a particular location. "You have an industry that's on the edge anyway, because you have declining attendance that's been caused by other factors. They're operating on a very small profit margin. So you only have to reduce the attendance by a bit more to push them over the edge." Louise struck a similar note, arguing Greyhound Action picketers dissuaded members of the public from watching races. "The fact that we were there as a visual presence—with big, beautiful boards and big, beautiful banners—made people feel very awkward," she said.

On June 29, 2002, Ronnie and Louise were married in the Kidderminster register office. "Our wedding was the cheapest we've ever come across," Ronnie said, noting it was a joyful event nonetheless. "I think the whole thing only cost us about 300 pounds." He joked with Louise's brother following the ceremony. "I said, the last time someone called me Ronald Anthony Denis Lee, I got 10 years," Ronnie recalled, laughing. "I said, this time I got life." Ronnie and Louise had decided to get married for practical reasons. "It kind of arose out of the death of Louise's dad," Ronnie said. "We realized the fact that Louise's mum and dad were married actually made it a lot easier for [Celia]. Had they not been married, it would have been more of a problem for her afterwards—with receiving what benefits she should receive." Despite the practicality of his initial intentions, and having lived with Louise for nearly a decade, Ronnie said it felt different being

Ronnie and Louise after their wedding in Kidderminster in June 2002 (photograph Patricia Lee).

married. "You've made a commitment to that person in front of other people," he said. "It felt good."

A couple of days later, Ronnie learned that Sue died on the day of his wedding, following a mysterious, months-long decline in health. "I was really upset," Ronnie said. "She'd been a good friend. We'd been on ALF raids together. She was one of the founders of the Band of Mercy. She was one of the first people I met when I was involved in hunt saboteurs. So we'd gone back a long way." While Sue's reported cause of death was pneumonia, Ronnie believed it was somehow connected to her breakup with a long-term partner. "I wondered if possibly she didn't want to live anymore and she'd taken something," Ronnie said, before floating another theory. "They say people can die of a broken heart, don't they? I don't think they actually die of a broken heart, but it could have been that so effected her immune system—through grief, I suppose." Ronnie attended Sue's funeral about a week after her death.

That summer, Ronnie and Louise set up an international branch of their anti-racing organization, which they called Greyhound Action International, that supported like-minded groups in Ireland and Australia. "It was communicating with people in those other countries [and] raising funds for them," Ronnie said. "We designed leaflets for them as well." A friend of the couple, named Raven Haze, ran the international branch. Not long after, Greyhound Action launched a website with the help of a sympathetic designer. "This guy had a greyhound himself," Ronnie recalled.

"He said, look, I'll do your website; I'll do it for nothing and run it for nothing. So that's what he did. He set it up and it became very popular."

In November, Ronnie and Louise adopted another abused greyhound, who they renamed Tom. "After a few days, we allowed our dogs into the room where he was, so they could sniff him and get used to him," Ronnie said. "They got on fine with him, because he was such a placid dog." While the other animals were on vegan diets, Tom didn't take to the new food. "The only way that we could get him to eat was to put ... meat in with his food," Ronnie said, laughing. "Of course, when the other dogs found this out, they wouldn't eat their food. They wanted meat in their food as well." In the end, Ronnie gave all of the animals a small amount of flesh.

During this period, Bernie grew comfortable enough with Celia that she was able to care for him—allowing Ronnie and Louise to leave the house together. In August of 2004, Moss, who was about 9 years old, collapsed and died. "It was never known what was wrong with him, what the cause of this was," Ronnie said, adding the animal's death was particularly heartrending as it was so sudden. "We buried him in the back garden of Celia's home." That December, Ronnie and Louise put Demo to sleep, after she suffered a stroke, and scattered her ashes in Wyre Forest, where she used to play with Billy.

In March of 2006—following numerous demonstrations by Greyhound Action, and property damage inflicted by the Animal Liberation Front—the beleaguered owner of a race track met with Ronnie in the hopes of ending the conflict. "This guy who came out of the offices almost looked like someone who someone lived on the street," Ronnie said. "He had several days' growth of beard. His clothes were all scruffy." It took Ronnie a moment to realize this was the owner, as the man had been meticulously dressed and groomed prior to Greyhound Action's campaign. "He said, I've decided to close the greyhound track," Ronnie recalled. "He said, I've had enough enough of it all now." Before halting the protests, Ronnie demanded the owner sign a statement to this effect, which the owner did. "He closed the track," Ronnie said.

That May, following years in which Celia was in poor health, Ronnie and Louise moved in with her in Blakedown, after selling their stake in the Kidderminster property. "It really made more sense to have them back," Celia said. "My husband had passed away. I was here on my own in a three-bedroom house." Of course, the couple brought along their dogs and various rodents, who lived with Celia's approximately six cats and five dogs. Louise collapsed twice over the summer, for reasons medical professionals were unable to fully explain—which, of course, worried Ronnie a great deal. "They

Ronnie and Louise with their van outside her mother's home near Kidderminster in April 2004 (photograph Celia Ryan, courtesy Ronnie Lee).

couldn't determine what was the matter with Louise," Ronnie said. "They thought maybe she hadn't had enough to eat and she was suffering from low-blood pressure or something like that." But, finally, a doctor tested her for thyroid disease. "Readings for her thyroid hormones were absolutely through the roof," Ronnie said, noting Louise's condition was almost life-threatening. "So she was put on special medication." As a result, her hormone levels were slowly reduced.

Ronnie with Greyhound Action stall at London Vegan Festival in September 2006 (courtesy Ronnie Lee).

Around this time, Ronnie was threatened with legal action by betting company William Hill, after he said the bookmaker was responsible for the work of David Smith, who—it recently had been discovered—was paid by trainers to kill and bury thousands of unwanted greyhounds. "They sent me a letter," Ronnie said. "They sent it to my pseudonym." While speaking before a couple of hundred people at a rally in August, he tore the message to pieces. In addition to this political theater, Ronnie had actually written back to William Hill, declaring his intention to continue making such claims. "I said, there's no way you're going to shut me up," he recalled. "I said, I've got no money anyway, so go ahead [and sue me]. I said, I'll use it to create even more publicity against you."

In May of 2007, dozens of organizers for a grassroots, anti-vivisection campaign—Stop Huntingdon Animal Cruelty—were arrested in coordinated raids. While Ronnie hadn't been involved in the campaign, the mass arrest of its leadership made him consider electoral action further. "That was another thing that got me thinking about the political side of things," he said, adding some of the apprehended organizers eventually received long prison sentences. "At the end of the day, the government holds the trump card." Ronnie started to believe his indifference to the political process, and the indifference of like-minded activists, was harmful. "We'd ended up with a government that not only propped up [Huntingdon Life and Sciences, a company engaged in animal testing], but brought in repressive measures against anti-vivisection activists," he said. "I thought, unless we make an effort to get a decent government into power, we can hardly complain when we get a bad government." Ronnie and Louise visited imprisoned leaders of the Stop Huntingdon Animal Cruelty Campaign frequently.

In September, Ronnie and Louise put Bernie to sleep, as the aging dog—whose troubles largely inspired the founding of Greyhound Action—was immobile, incontinent and suffering. "I think we scattered his ashes in the garden," Ronnie said. "We did a piece about Bernie in the [Greyhound Action] newsletter." In 2008, the couple euthanized three kittens they adopted, all of whom had contracted leukemia. "Of all the animals we've had that have died, for me that was the worst," Ronnie said. "They were so young." Around this time, he and Louise took in five new cats. "We did continue to adopt," Ronnie said. "I won't go into every single one." Tom was euthanized during this period as well, after developing cancer.

In the spring of 2009, Ronnie joined the Green Party of England and Wales. "I'd looked into what the Green Party stood for and what their values were, and thought, yeah, that's very close to what I believe," he said.

"I thought, if there is going to be one of the parties in government eventually, I'd prefer it to be the Green Party." His decision not to join an organization like the Animal Welfare Party or the Animal Protection Party was pragmatic. "In order to be elected, you have to have a wide range of policies on everything," Ronnie said. "The Green Party is still very far from being

Ronnie dressed as a rock star at a costume party in Birmingham, July 2010 (photograph Louise Ryan, courtesy Ronnie Lee).

able to form a government, but something like the Animal Welfare Party would never be able to—because people see them as [focused on a] single issue."

While he had joined the Green Party, Ronnie didn't yet involve himself deeply. His attention was still elsewhere. "I was probably working about an 80-hour week on Greyhound Action," Ronnie said. "It was getting more popular. We were setting up local groups and there was just loads of [administrative work] and stuff to do—you know, doing newsletters and designing leaflets." Occasionally, he and Louise attended unrelated events, but not very often. "I didn't really have time for anything else," Ronnie said. "I didn't really do anything within the Green Party."

By 2011, Ronnie started developing problems with his eyes, which included pain and poor vision. "Two of my friends had suffered really-bad eye problems," he said. "It frightened me." An eye specialist advised Ronnie to drastically reduce the time he spent in front of a computer screen, working on behalf of Greyhound Action. "I decided that I could no longer run the campaign—that I had to try to find other people to do it," Ronnie said, adding that, in May, his and Louise's organization merged with Action for Greyhounds. "They took the campaign over." Louise found this result somewhat bittersweet. "There was a kind of sadness in letting it go," she said. "But we felt it was the right time."

16

Vegan Outreach
and the Green Party

In the spring of 2011, by then 60 years old, Ronnie found giving up his involvement in Greyhound Action to be something of a blessing in disguise. "For quite some while, I'd felt a need to do something more wide-ranging," he said, noting the non-human victims of the racing industry were significantly fewer than that of the food industry. "I very much wanted to get involved in vegan outreach. Obviously, that goes right to the root of why animals are abused and slaughtered." Ronnie started attending the meetings of a nearby group called Wolverhampton Vegans and Veggies—which, despite its name, focused primarily on promoting veganism. "They weren't a hugely-active group," he said. "They probably did about a half-dozen events a year."

Ronnie and Tony Harris, another member of the group, sought to change this. "When he and I teamed up together, we started organizing loads of stuff," Ronnie said. "I became the communications officer for the group and dealt with media—dealt with sending out messages to supporters of the group to let them know about events." By this point, he used his real name, as Ronnie believed his criminal history was so long in the past it wouldn't become an issue. He and Tony organized everything from street stalls to film screenings for Wolverhampton Vegans and Veggies. "The group became a lot more active," Ronnie said. "We'd often combine a social element with a campaigning element." Though this and other activism required him to do some work on the computer, it was still much less than that required to run Greyhound Action.

"As attendance at the [Wolverhampton Vegans and Veggies] meetings grew, Ronnie suggested we might get more done if we kept social [or] open meetings separate from organizers' meetings," Tony said. "Some people were not enthusiastic about this at first but it did make things easier and more productive. It seemed pointless to have people at organizers' meetings who did not really wish to organize things." Ronnie also helped divide responsibilities amongst the organizers. "Ronnie believes that structure is really important and, indeed, it did improve the group," Tony said.

In July, Ronnie began volunteering with the Wyre Forest Green Party, which was working to elect a man named Steve Brown to the local authority. "We delivered newsletters promoting Steve," Ronnie said. "We'd have meetings every month. Sometimes we'd have a meeting just of our own party and sometimes we'd meet together with a couple of other local parties." According to Mart Layton, press officer for the Wyre Forest Green Party, Ronnie was quite an asset. "His skills were invaluable to us, and his experience meant that we could mobilize a campaign very efficiently," Mart said. "You could always count on him to be aware of the live issues we needed to be addressing, to have the leaflets and placards designed and printed, the street stall organized, and the petition ready to go. I think his energy and commitment were a real motivating force for everyone in the party."

The local organization valued Ronnie for other reasons as well. "He still greets us all with a hug and always asks after our partners and companion creatures with genuine affection," Mart said. "His involvement with us goes beyond common cause and many of us count him amongst our personal friends." As a result of his involvement in the Green Party, where he met a local leader of Friends of the Earth, Ronnie also worked with the environmental group during this period. "Damage to the environment—it's bad enough how it impacts on humans," he said. "But, of course, it impacts on animals, particularly wild animals, far more than it impacts on humans. So I saw campaigning for environmental protection as an animal-liberation issue."

During the next month, Ronnie spoke before an animal-rights conference in Northamptonshire about the need for local activism. "I think my talk went down well," he said. "I spoke about what we'd done with the Wolverhampton

Ronnie with rescue rat Dennis Pickles in the back garden of their home near Kidderminster, August 2011 (photograph Louise Ryan, courtesy Ronnie Lee).

group—how we'd gotten more people involved and how we'd gone about promoting the group—even though I'd only been doing that a few months." Attending the event felt like something of a homecoming for Ronnie. "I'd been out of touch with the rest of the movement, really, because I was so involved in Greyhound Action," he said. "I was getting my links back with the rest of the movement. It was great."

In April of 2012, Ronnie assisted in organizing that month's World Day for Animals in Laboratories march in Birmingham. "I designed all of the leaflets and the literature," Ronnie said, adding that—through these— he hoped to introduce a broader perspective to the public, that recognized a variety of forms of animal exploitation. "Although the march was against animal experiments, I wanted to use that leaflet to make people think more widely and to think about veganism." Defying the wishes of local politicians and police to hold the procession on back streets, organizers led approximately 700 supporters through the city center. "These days, that's quite big for a World Day march," Ronnie said, noting he spoke at the event. "[But] I remember going on a march, in the early '80s, where there was about 10,000 people. Louise remembers one in the late '80s, when I was in prison, where there was almost 20,000. So the numbers had gone down."

That spring, Ronnie and others founded Worcestershire Vegans and Veggies, which was modeled on the Wolverhampton group. "There wasn't a lot of campaigning for animals in Worcestershire," he said. "There had been in Worcester, which is the county town about 15 miles south of us. There had been an animal-rights group some years ago, but that had folded." To celebrate the launch of the new organization, members held a vegan-food fair at Cafe Bliss, in Worcester. "For that day, the cafe would sell only vegan food," Ronnie said. "There would be a marquee outside, where we would have vegan food samples and give away vegan literature." The event was a success for both the business and his group. "They sold the most food that they had ever sold—before or since then," Ronnie said of the cafe. "We signed up 80 people who were interested in either becoming involved in the group or hearing about future activities."

He and Louise marked the summer solstice at the Stonehenge monument in Wiltshire. "Obviously, I'm not into religion," Ronnie said. "But we thought that this would be a little bit of a spiritual experience … that it would be a pleasant and probably quite-gentle event to watch the sunrise over the stones." The couple couldn't have been more wrong. "We went in this field and it was packed with cars," Ronnie said. "People were very rowdy—drinking and taking drugs. When night fell, it was just noise, loud music, people off their heads, staggering [and] falling around." He and

Louise tried unsuccessfully to get some sleep, before rising at dawn to make their way to the monument, located beyond passed-out revelers. "It wasn't a very good sunrise, because it was quite cloudy," Ronnie said, laughing. "It was just a nightmare."

That autumn, Ronnie helped launch an organization called Birmingham Animal Action, sharing lessons he'd learned from running vegan-advocacy groups in Wolverhampton and Worcestershire. While there was an existing organization in Birmingham, it wasn't very active. Founding members of Birmingham Animal Action sought to engage in more campaigning. "For a while I did go along to their meetings," Ronnie said. "I did help with some of their actions and some of their street stalls that they held, because it's only a half-hour train journey to Birmingham."

Around this time, Ronnie began working with the Green Party's animal-policy group, which primarily communicated over email. The group nominally sought to improve positions of the broader organization on non-human issues, but wasn't very focused on doing this. Instead, the group shared petitions and publicized demonstrations unrelated to reforming the party. "After I was involved with it a little, I said—hang on a minute—this group isn't doing what it's supposed to," Ronnie recalled. "I kind of pulled it back to what it really was supposed to be."

Ronnie with Louise at a rally in Bristol against the badger cull, September 2012 (courtesy Ronnie Lee).

He argued in favor of pushing a total opposition to commercial animal racing. "But not everyone on the policy group were animal liberationists," Ronnie said. "There were some people on there who were welfarists and some people who were more hesitant than me." Ultimately, the group agreed to a compromise, in which they advocated stricter measures related to horse racing and the abolition of greyhound racing on non-linear tracks, which caused frequent injuries. "Effectively, that would mean the end of the dog-racing industry," Ronnie said, noting the industry relied on stadium attendance. "A stadium can only operate if it's an oval track or possibly a circular track." These positions were put forward as a motion, which was passed, at the Green Party's September conference in Bristol. "People voted for that without realizing—in a lot of cases—that would actually outlaw the [greyhound] industry," Ronnie said, laughing.

That same month, Ronnie met with activists seeking to establish new vegan-outreach groups and formed an umbrella organization called Encouraging Vegan Education. This was used to help launch groups in various locations. Initially, members of Encouraging Vegan Education sought to establish a group in Northamptonshire using the method Ronnie had employed in Worcestershire—in which he held a food fair to garner interest. "We worked on setting up this fair, getting loads of leaflets done, [and] getting publicity," Ronnie said, adding he was friends with the operator of a sanctuary called Animals In Need. "So we decided to hold the vegan festival at the animal sanctuary." Once again, the strategy was successful and a Northamptonshire group was formed.

In October, at a rally following the National March for Farmed Animals, Ronnie said in a speech that he preferred to be remembered as the founder of Encouraging Vegan Education, as opposed to the founder of the Animal Liberation Front. "Although I think direct action has achieved a lot, has saved a lot of animals, and isn't something I regret doing, I think if we can educate enough people to be vegan we will save a lot more animals," Ronnie said. "I don't think it's a question of good and bad. I think it's a question of good and better." Of course, during this period, Ronnie faced criticism for his new focus on vegan education and electoral politics, but it didn't bother him. "If I hold a particular view, and then I get presented with evidence—or I come across evidence—that view is mistaken, I feel the right thing to do is change that view," Ronnie said. "I want to do the best thing I can to achieve animal liberation."

But Ronnie wasn't just involved in animal-rights activism. For instance, also in October, Ronnie participated in a massive anti-austerity protest in London. "I think about a quarter of a million people took part in it," he

Ronnie with a stall for Friends of the Earth's campaign to protect the bees, Worcester, October 2012 (courtesy Ronnie Lee).

said. "Louise and I went down on a coach." Similarly, later, Ronnie demonstrated in Kidderminster against the regressive bedroom tax, along with other members of the Green Party. "There were people there from various different parties—though not the Conservatives, obviously," Ronnie said, laughing. "All over the country people did that. We did that locally." He was also involved in other human-centered activism. "We worked together on campaigns to save subsidies for local bus routes," Mart said as an example. "Although, at heart, I think he will always be an animal liberationist, the connecting theme with these seemingly unrelated issues is his concern for justice and his compassion for those in need."

In February of 2013, Ronnie established Greens for Animal Protection, which, unlike the Green Party's animal-policy group, would be a campaigning organization. "A lot of people became involved in it," Ronnie said, adding the organization managed stalls at both vegan fares and Green Party conferences. "At vegan events, we were educating people about the Green Party policies on animal protection, how good those polices were, and trying to encourage people to join the Green Party. At Green Party conferences, we were trying to encourage Green Party people to go vegan and Green Party people to stand up more for animal protection." Ronnie and his comrades also distributed leaflets about the organization at various marches and demonstrations.

In May, Ronnie and Louise launched Wyre Forest Vegans and Veggies, as a branch of the Worcestershire group. "We wanted a group that would focus on doing things locally," Ronnie said of the branch. "There were quite a lot of people living in this local area." The new group began by protesting an upcoming badger cull, which the British government announced after farmers claimed the creatures were spreading tuberculosis to their cows. "Really, this was counter to all of the scientific evidence," Ronnie said. "This wasn't the case—that badgers gave TB to cows. In fact, it was probably the other way around. The reason cows had TB was to do with a number of other factors, including the conditions they were kept in." At their stalls which focused on the issue, Ronnie and Louise stocked petitions, anti-cull postcards, and booklets about veganism.

By this point, Ronnie felt overwhelmed by the numerous groups he was involved in. "I thought, I can't do it all," he said, adding he resolved to continue his involvement in the Worcestershire and Wyre Forest Vegans and Veggies groups as these were closest to his home. "I resigned from the organizers' group of Wolverhampton Vegans and Veggies. I also left the organizers' group of Birmingham Animal Action." Tony left the Wolverhampton organizer's group around the same time, which ultimately led to

Ronnie (right) and Louise (foreground) with friends at a march against the badger cull, London, June 2013 (courtesy Ronnie Lee).

the collapse of the organization as a whole. Ronnie also temporarily halted operation of Encouraging Vegan Education, as the other leaders were involved in other projects, and he didn't have the time to manage it on his own.

Despite this, in July, Ronnie and Louise established a feline-welfare group which they called Kozykatz. "It was Louise's idea to do it," Ronnie said, adding the group was represented by stalls at vegan fairs. "We wanted to promote neutering and spaying. We also wanted to promote [the idea] that people should get cats from rescues, and not get them from breeders or pet shops." By selling used items and vegan sweets, Kozykatz also raised funds for the care of Ronnie and Louise's many rescue and foster cats. "Our policy was that after we'd had a cat for a certain period of time, and didn't find a home for the cat, then the cat would stay," Ronnie said. "We worked closely with larger cat-rescue organizations."

The animal-policy group, of which Ronnie was still a member, put forward another motion at the Green Party's September conference. "For the first time, we had a motion there that talked about the slaughter and suffering of fish," Ronnie recalled. "It also said the Green Party would seek

Top: Ronnie with Worcestershire Vegans & Veggies stall at Farm Animal Sanctuary Open Day, near Evesham, September 2013 (courtesy Ronnie Lee).

to move society towards a plant-based diet. It didn't say that meat-eating should be banned—but that the Green Party would discourage animal farming." The whole of the motion was passed aside from a line calling for a ban on slaughter of non-stunned animals, over fears this would prompt objections from Jewish and Muslim communities. "We were worried about running out of time," Ronnie said. "So we decided to withdraw that small section."

At the Green Party conference in February 2014, the animal-policy group put forward two motions. The first proposed banning the importation of foie gras. "It's something that needs to be done," Ronnie said. "Also, it's a good way of getting the Green Party popular with animal-protection campaigners." The second proposed strict control of fireworks and bonfires. "I bloody hate fireworks and how they terrify animals," Ronnie said, before explaining the other motion. "People make big bonfires. They'll make them days before. What happens is that animals like hedgehogs crawl in there. Then they set fire to the bonfire and the hedgehogs are burned. So the policy said that bonfires must only be constructed on the day they're going to be lit." Neither motion passed. "Both of them were so far down the agenda

Ronnie with Greens for Animal Protection stall at West Midlands Vegan Festival, Wolverhampton, October 2013 (courtesy Ronnie Lee).

that they didn't get reached," Ronnie said. "So—apart from having our stall at that conference in Liverpool—nothing else was achieved."

In March, the Wyre Forest Green Party faced a minor crisis, after Steve, the organization's perennial candidate, declined to run again. "Immediately, I thought what are we going to do now?" Ronnie said. "For a while, we didn't have anyone to promote as a candidate." But, finally, a woman named Natalie McVey—who was a member of the Wyre Forest Vegans and Veggies as well—agreed to fill the role, running for both the local authority and parliament. "We started producing newsletters, leaflets and

Ronnie (right) with fellow campaigner Phil Oliver holding Wyre Forest Green Party banner at anti-cuts protest outside Worcestershire County Council offices, February 2014 (courtesy Ronnie Lee).

everything to promote her, which we put through people's letterboxes," Ronnie said. "That was a process that happened throughout that year." Around the same time, he was named campaigns officer for the local party.

The Green Party had a policy that after a motion was debated and voted upon at a conference, another motion on the topic couldn't be put forward for another two years. So it wasn't until the September conference that Ronnie was able to revisit the organization's stance on animal racing. "We're talking about something very close to my heart," Ronnie said, noting his prior leadership of Greyhound Action. "I wasn't happy with this fudge of a policy." The animal-policy group put forward motions calling for bans on commercial racing and the importation of foie gras. But, like the group's February proposals, these motions were so low on the agenda they weren't reached. Finally, in February 2015, the Green Party voted to add banning the importation of foie gras to the organization's platform.

That year, the general and council elections—in which Natalie was running—were held. "She got a huge increase in the vote for the Green Party," Ronnie said, noting Natalie lost both races. "But I thought that standing in the general election took a lot out of her, because it's ever so different to being in a council election. A council election is primarily concerned with local issues and being community minded.... [In the general election], there's these things called hustings, where you have to debate with the other candidates, you get difficult questions thrown at you, and it's about national issues. She kind of found it difficult to cope with that, because it's more like gladiatorial combat than about whether or not a person will actually make a good member of parliament."

In August, Greens for Animal Protection sought formal recognition from the broader party. "It meant we would be promoted on official party literature and on the website," Ronnie said. "To do that, we had to adopt a constitution, have an annual general meeting and everything." The group held a gathering in Manchester, where they took steps to meet these requirements, in order to gain official status. At the Green Party's September conference, hoping to avoid religious objections, the animal-policy group put forward a vaguely-worded motion calling for the slaughter of non-humans to be completed in the manner which caused the least suffering. However, with Ronnie's reluctant agreement, members of the group withdrew the motion at the last moment—fearing that, without the support of Muslim and Jewish leaders, it might still be too controversial. "Someone believes

Ronnie and Louise with friends Steve Peters (left) and Rhian Owen (right), promoting veganism at the London Climate March, November 2015 (courtesy Steve Peters).

in hocus pocus and animals are going to suffer more because of that," Ronnie said. "To me, it's just appalling."

Following this—and an unsuccessful, grueling attempt to help Natalie win a special election—Ronnie reassessed his priorities. Louise, Celia, and Margaret were all suffering from poor health at the time. "I was once again in a situation where I had to let something go," Ronnie said. "I decided that it had to be the Green Party." He resigned his positions as Greens for Animal Protection coordinator and the Wyre Forest Green Party campaigns officer. However, Louise and Celia's condition eventually improved, and in December Margaret moved into a nursing home, allowing Ronnie to increase his activism once again.

Though other members of the Wyre Forest Green Party knew and accepted Ronnie's criminal history, his past was a liability in some respects. For instance, in May of 2016, a right-wing blogger attempted to discredit Natalie Bennet, leader of the Green Party of England and Wales, by linking her to Ronnie. "Although she barely knew him, there happened to be a photo of her sitting next to him at an event," Mart said. "We weren't too worried about this, although the regional party worked hard to limit the negative coverage. Within the local party, we joked about how ridiculous it all was. Tongues firmly in our cheeks, we threatened to photoshop the picture so that it would show Ronnie in stereotypical ALF balaclava and black combat fatigues."

Around this time, according to Mart, organizers of an animal-rights demonstration invited Ronnie to deliver a speech at their event, but the invitation was withdrawn after a local parliamentary candidate

Ronnie takes a break from his research for this biography to care for Misty, one of his and Louise's many rescued cats, April 2016 (photograph Louise Ryan, courtesy Ronnie Lee).

refused to share a platform with the founder of the Animal Liberation Front. "Ronnie graciously stepped down without causing a fuss," Mart said. "As long as he could distribute leaflets among the crowd, he was happy for someone else to take his place. After these two events, he decided to stand down from contesting a seat in the district-council elections because he did not want to cause problems for the party. We reluctantly allowed him to do so, admiring his integrity. I think Ronnie wasn't too bothered anyway, as he is much more the activist than the politician."

On April 23, Ronnie spoke at a World Day for Animals in Laboratories rally in Manchester, where approximately 300 activists placed flowers before an animal-research center in memory of its nonhuman victims. "[I said], you need to get back to your hometown, get involved in your local vegan group or animal-rights group, go out and spread the message," Ronnie recalled. "[I said], if there isn't one, then organize one; start a group and do a load of stuff locally."

Ronnie with Wyre Forest Vegans & Veggies stall at an animal sanctuary fundraising event in Stourbridge, May 2016 (courtesy Ronnie Lee).

Appendix One:
A Greenprint
for Animal Liberation

by Ronnie Lee
(originally published January 5, 2014)

What follows is my personal opinion formed after over 40 years in the animal liberation movement.

It is intended for those who wish to see animal liberation, i.e., an end to all persecution, exploitation and killing of other animals by human beings or for us to reach a situation that is as near to that as possible.

It is also focused on what we should be doing in England. In other countries the situation may be different, particularly with regard to the political aspect.

What has concerned me for a long time is that we have no overall strategy or masterplan for the achievement of animal liberation and that the lack of this causes disunity among us and inefficiency in the use of our resources.

In order to formulate such a masterplan or blueprint, or greenprint, as I prefer to call it, I think we first of all need to try to understand why it is that the human species persecutes, exploits and kills other animals in the first place.

Although there are many things that exacerbate the mistreatment of other animals by humans, there is one fundamental cause of it, which is speciesism or human supremacism, i.e., the arrogant, selfish and irrational belief that human beings are somehow more important than other sentient animals.

As a socialist I want to see an end to capitalism, but although the greed, wastefulness and desire for profit inherent in the capitalist system certainly increases the mistreatment and exploitation of other creatures, animal abuse would still exist in a socialist society if speciesism continued to hold sway.

All abuse of other animals flows fundamentally from speciesism, so if we are to achieve animal liberation we need to challenge the speciesist mindset in human beings and strive to create a situation where humans behave towards other animals in a non-speciesist way.

We tend to divide animal abuse into various areas—vivisection, the fur trade, zoos, hunting, farming etc.—but all these areas of animal abuse are really symptoms of an underlying disease, which is speciesism, and unless we treat and cure that underlying disease, we will be forever having to deal with its symptoms.

If we are to persuade human beings to live in a non-speciesist way, the most important thing we need to do is to educate them to end their consumption of animal products, because eating flesh, eggs and dairy is the most fundamental speciesist thing that most people do and also because, when we consider all the areas of animal abuse normally campaigned against by our movement, 99.5 percent of the persecution of other animals by humans occurs in the food industry (several billion animals slaughtered annually for consumption by humans in England, with the next highest area being the approx. 4 million victims of the UK vivisection industry).

Thus, the most important form of activism for other animals is vegan outreach and our main focus as a movement needs to be on educating members of the public to become vegan.

This doesn't mean we shouldn't also campaign against other forms of animal abuse, but that we should always seek to promote veganism at the same time.

So, on our stalls we should always have vegan information to give to the public and on any demos or protests we do, the leaflets we give out need to contain information that will lead people towards veganism, in addition to information about whatever form of animal abuse we are protesting against.

If we are to educate ordinary people to become vegan, we need to consider what are the best ways of doing this.

To educate the public, we need to be where the public are—and that means we have to do street stalls, stalls at community events, free food events to which the public are invited, etc., etc.

We also have to be in what the public read and listen to, which means articles and letters in local newspapers and interviews on local radio/TV.

So what is going to be the vehicle for these local outreach events and this local media presence? It has to be local vegan outreach groups.

Therefore, what we need to do is to try to set up a large network of such groups throughout the country, so that every town and city is covered, and to train and give confidence to the people within those groups to engage positively with the public and the local media.

Of course, educating people to go vegan is not an easy task and we need to try to understand how people operate in order to do this effectively.

People, in general, tend to be passive creatures of habit who don't like change and want to be the same as everybody else and not stand out from the crowd. Animal liberationists are not at all like that, but we need to take people for what they are and not presume that everybody is fundamentally the same as us.

Thus we need to make veganism seem as "normal" and easy as we possibly can and not get frustrated when there appears to be a slow uptake of the vegan message. That is bound to be the case at first, but as the number of vegans gradually increases, a level will be reached when veganism is no longer considered to be that unusual and that will then cause the amount of vegans to rapidly increase.

It isn't just a case though, of persuading ordinary members of the public to go vegan, but of persuading existing vegans to become involved in outreach.

The Vegan Society has estimated there are at least 150,000 vegans in the UK. Opinion polls have put this figure as high as 600,000, but, for the sake of argument, I'll stick to the lower estimate.

I've done many vegan outreach events just on my own or with the help of only one other person, but if, once again for the sake of argument, we say it would take 10 vegans to do one event, this would mean that if each of the estimated 150,000 vegans in this country just took part in one outreach event per month, that would equal 15,000 events per month, 3,000 events per week and about 500 every day. And just think how many more vegans could be created, if that were to happen!

The vast majority of vegans are vegan because they are opposed to the suffering and slaughter of animals and so they would, presumably, want that suffering and slaughter to end entirely (or, at least, as near as we can possibly get to that situation), but that won't happen unless we persuade lots of other people to go vegan and that, in turn, won't happen unless we get out there and interact with the public in order to do it.

Surely the difficult bit is actually becoming vegan, with all the initial trials and tribulations that involves, especially on a social level. So, having become vegan, it would only take a comparatively tiny step more to do a bit of outreach. So many vegans seem unable to take it, however, and this is a problem we have to try to solve, if we really want animal liberation to be achieved.

I've spoken above about the importance of vegan education in persuading people to change their attitudes and, hence, their behaviour towards other animals.

It would be naive in the extreme, however, to suppose that we can succeed in educating everybody and we need to accept that some people will remain unaffected by our educational efforts and will wish to continue their support for or involvement in animal abuse.

People change their behaviour for one of two reasons, either because they want to or because they fear the consequences of not doing so. Thus there are two ways of changing human behaviour, education and coercion, and with those who refuse to be educated, we are left with coercion.

I've talked about local vegan outreach groups being the vehicle for education, but what is to be the vehicle for the coercion we need in order to change the behaviour of those we are unable to educate?

Basically, there are two types of coercion that could be applied to enforce correct behaviour—coercion by the individual (or group of individuals) or coercion by the state.

Non-state coercion would need to take the form of illegal direct action and the problem with this is that it is highly unlikely that enough people could be persuaded to do this in order for it to be effective.

This leaves coercion by the state, in other words the passing and enforcement of laws to protect animals from abuse and in order to get such laws passed, we need an elected government that would be prepared to pass them.

Governments are formed by political parties, which means that all of us who want animal liberation need to support the political party which gives the best hope for strong animal protection legislation.

I think we can say immediately that isn't going to be the Tories or the Lib-Dems, so is it going to be Labour?

Sadly, there is nothing in the fundamental philosophy of the Labour Party or its record in relation to animal protection to indicate that this would be the case.

We must never forget how Labour reneged on their promise of a Royal Commission to investigate vivisection, how the number of cruel experiments increased under their administration and how they brought in new laws to persecute anti-vivisection activists.

Apart from a half-hearted "ban" on hunting with dogs and the abolition of fur farming (but not the fur trade) most forms of animal persecution continued to increase and prosper when Labour were last in power.

In my view, the best hope of a government for animal protection lies with the Green Party.

The Greens have policies that would end the badger cull, ban all animal experiments, abolish the fur trade, end the use of all animals in circuses, strengthen the law against hunting, abolish shooting and snaring, end live exports and factory farming and encourage veganism through the promotion of a diet free from animal products.

The strong environmental protection policies of the Green Party are also of great benefit to non-human animals in terms of preserving their habitats and reducing the risk of them being harmed by pollution, climate change etc.

A large number of Green Party politicians and activists are already involved at local, national or European level in fighting factory farming, live exports, animal experiments, the badger cull, bullfighting and many other forms of animal abuse.

We need to get the Green Party into power if we are ever to truly protect animals in this country and if we don't try our utmost to do so, we will be partly to blame for the continuing persecution of other creatures under Tory and Labour regimes.

A Green Party government is not an impossible dream. The Greens are not only the best party for animal protection, but also the best for social justice and the environment—and if everyone who cares about all or any of these issues were to support the Green Party, they could easily sweep to power at an election.

Let's not forget that only about 20 percent of the population would need to vote Green in order for that to happen.

As I mentioned above, it is a fundamental trait of humans in general to be passive and to not want to stand out from the crowd. However, in order for us to get a Green Party government, most people don't need to be outspoken activists. They just need to put a cross on a piece of paper in the right place!

Anarchists within the animal protection movement will object to my support for the Green Party, but it is my contention that those who support anarchism are harming the cause of animal liberation by advocating that members of the public should not vote at elections.

Most human beings are fundamentally leader-followers, so the problem is that if there is no good guy (or gal!) for people to follow, most of them will inevitably follow the bad guy. Therefore anarchists are playing straight into the hands of the bad guys by advocating that animal protectionists do not vote, because all that achieves is to make sure that animal abuse supporters will continue to get elected.

Likewise support for the Animal Welfare Party can also be harmful to the cause of animal liberation in that it takes the votes of animal protectionists away from the Green Party. Unlike the GP, the AWP has no chance of ever being able to form a government, because it can only ever appeal to that small minority of the population that is highly focused on animal protection above everything else. On the other hand, with its excellent policies on social justice and the environment, as well as on animal protection, the Green Party has the potential for mass appeal.

There is also an argument that if we just persuade enough people to go vegan, politics will change accordingly and we'll get animal protection legislation without supporting the Green Party.

However, just having a large number of people wanting animal protection doesn't mean that legislation will be passed to enforce their views. For decades a substantial majority of the public were opposed to hunting with dogs without it being abolished, for instance, and a large majority against the badger cull hasn't prevented that from going ahead. Similar failure to reflect the views of the majority in legislation can also be seen with regard to the fur trade, live exports and animal experimentation.

This means that hand in hand with educating people to go vegan, we have to build up the political force that will form a government for animal protection and reflect the views of vegans in its legislation.

Thus my Greenprint for Animal Liberation is a combination of vegan outreach and support for the Green Party and I would urge every single person who yearns for animal liberation to do the following in order to help achieve it:

(1) Join your local vegan outreach group (or, if there isn't one, form one) and start educating members of the public to go vegan.

(2) Join your local Green Party and help them with the process of getting people elected both at a local and a national level.

None of this will be easy, but I see no other way. What I am talking about is basically the creation of a new type of animal protection movement that focuses less on shouty demos and hero-worship of direct action and more on vegan education and political involvement.

We have to find a way of moving away from being brave losers, constantly trying to throw ourselves against an overwhelming force, and towards a situation where we ourselves become that overwhelming force that can make the world our own and carry all before us in the struggle for animal liberation.

The above is just my opinion and I welcome constructive criticism. My plan may not be an easy one to put into operation or to see through to the end, but at least I have a plan, so please do not tell me mine is wrong without putting forward one of your own!

Appendix Two:
Animal Liberation

An End to Isolationism!

by Ronnie Lee

(originally published on August 9, 2014)

One of the difficulties with us humans is that we have (or certainly most of us seem to have) a deeply engrained tendency to fail to see the bigger picture.

Sadly, this is a tendency that has been ruthlessly encouraged and exploited in their own interests by capitalists and the Right, who have had little difficulty in encouraging people to consider their own wellbeing and that of their families, nations and ethnic groups to be more important than that of other individuals, nations and races.

So instead of a far-sighted community, based on caring and sharing, equality, fairness and selflessness, we have a myopic society, where greed, competition, selfishness, lack of concern, prejudice, division and appalling inequality between rich and poor hold sway.

Of course, this same failure to see the bigger picture has also been exploited to cause appalling suffering and slaughter of other animals, by those who profit financially and otherwise from such abuse.

However, it's not just ordinary members of the public who fail to see the bigger picture, but animal liberationists too—and by animal liberationists I'm talking about all of us who want to see an end to the oppression of other animals by humans, not just those folks who take direct action against laboratories, etc.

Seeing the bigger picture in relation to the animal liberation struggle is coming to understand that we will not succeed in obtaining the widespread emancipation of other animals from human tyranny, unless we rid a large percentage of the general public of human supremacist attitudes.

This changing of people's attitudes can only be done through vegan education, according to the broad definition of veganism, as meaning opposition to the use of other animals for any purpose, but starting with diet, because the food industry is by far and away the largest area of animal abuse that is bought into by ordinary people.

Doing such education isn't exciting and very rarely yields immediate results, as it tends to take a while with people for the vegan message to sink in and you're really not going to get a "eureka" moment at the info table of a meat-eater immediately vowing to go vegan!

This means that difficulty in seeing the bigger picture tends to draw animal protectionists towards taking part in and supporting activities, such as animal rescue, Sea Shepherd, hunt sabs and even the ALF, which yield much more immediate results.

Now all these "immediate results" activities are extremely praiseworthy and honorable, because they have saved a huge number of animals from death and suffering and continue to do so. However, I would describe such activities and the groups who carry them out (even the direct action ones) as "rescuist," rather than "liberationist," as they seek to save individual animals without attempting to change fundamental human supremacist attitudes which prevent animal liberation from being brought about.

And it isn't just that vegan education can bring about an eventual widespread change in human attitudes that rescuist activities cannot, it's also the case that persuading people to be vegan can spare more animals in the short-term than rescuism, through the reduction in the demand for animals to be reared or caught for slaughter that will occur as veganism increases.

A microcosm of this situation occurred just a few years ago when I worked as National Co-ordinator for a UK greyhound protection group called Greyhound Action (GA).

Now GA courted controversy by refusing to get involved, as an organization, with rescuing greyhounds (although, as individuals, those of us who ran the group all had rescued ex-racing dogs in our homes). Instead we concentrated totally on educating the public to boycott greyhound racing, because we saw the bigger picture and understood that rescues would be having to desperately try to snatch what discarded dogs they could from the death needle or gun provided for them by the racing industry until the seas froze over, unless concerted action was taken to bring that industry to an end.

So we picketed the tracks and staged info stalls in city centers—and through the reduction in public attendance at and betting on greyhound races this caused, helped shrink the industry to such an extent that more dogs were spared from suffering and slaughter than all the rescue people, who were much more numerous than us, could ever have saved.

This was a lesson for me in the importance of seeing the bigger picture and tackling the root of a problem, rather than just dealing with the symptoms, that I've carried with me into the campaigning I do today.

In addition to not having sight of the bigger picture, rescuist activities are isolationist in that they tend to just involve the activists and the animals they seek to rescue with little or no dialogue or interaction with ordinary members of the public. In fact, I believe that is what attracts many animal protectionists to them, because there is no need for any involvement with those "nasty ordinary people who eat meat and don't care about animals."

It's interesting to note that nearly all the ex-ALF activists I know who are still working for animal protection do so in the world of rescue, rather than as campaigners or educators who have involvement with the public, which I feel is a continuation of the isolationist mindset that attracted them to the ALF in the first place.

Another form of isolationism exists within the vegan community, where there are so many groups that just spend their time swapping recipes, telling one another about the latest new vegan product in Morrisons and scoffing vegan cake, without any real attempt to get out there and educate ordinary people to be vegan.

Thirdly, there is the widespread isolation of the animal liberation movement from other movements for radical and progressive social change, whom we need to make alliances with if ever we are to create a decent world for all its inhabitants, both human and non-human alike. This form of isolationism is very eloquently challenged by Dr. Steve Best in his excellent Total Liberation talk.

Here in Britain, I feel that one of the best ways animal liberationists can ally themselves with members of other progressive movements is through involvement with the Green Party, where they can work to eventually bring about a government that will pass strong and far-reaching legislation for social justice and animal protection (see my previous article for more on this).

With over 30 rescued animals of various species in my home, I am certainly not opposed to animal rescue and I salute the brave activists of Sea Shepherd, the ALF and the Hunt Saboteurs Association, all of which groups I have helped, either actively or financially in years gone by.

I also love being in the company of other vegans and feeling the camaraderie of people who have the same compassion in their hearts for other animals as I do, and the consuming of delicious vegan food (including cake!) is wonderful too.

But the bottom line is this—unless far far more of us become involved in vegan education in the world of ordinary people and unless our movement becomes integrated as part of the Left, animal liberation will continue to be a far-off dream.

There comes a time to see the bigger picture and to end our isolationism—and that time is now!

Appendix Three:
Putting an End
to Animal Exploitation

Interview with Ronnie Lee
(originally published in *Ballast* magazine,
January 26, 2016)

Ballast: Do you remember when you thought that the education system and pedagogy wouldn't be enough to change people's ideas about animal rights?

Ronnie Lee: What made me think about this was, when some years ago, people campaigning against Huntingdon Life Sciences (HLS) animal research laboratory almost succeeded in forcing the place to close. Campaigners from Stop Huntingdon Animal Cruelty managed to convince most suppliers and all the UK commercial banks to withdraw services from HLS.

However, the government at the time, a Labour one, stepped in and took the previously unheard of action of allowing the lab to have banking facilities with the Bank of England, thus allowing HLS to remain in business. Then the government passed new legislation to make it harder for people to campaign against animal experimentation.

They also encouraged the police and prosecution service to arrest and prosecute campaigners under laws that were never originally intended for that purpose. The aim was to put anti-vivisection campaigners in jail, and many people were given long periods of imprisonment for SHAC activities, with one person receiving an 11 year sentence.

I came to the conclusion that although the government were the major culprits, animal rights campaigners were also to blame for this situation, because we were not involved in political campaigning to try to prevent a pro-vivisection government from coming to power. I formed the view that animal liberationists had to become more involved in politics, because if we did not do our best to get a decent government into power, we could hardly complain when we ended up with a bad one.

B: To fight the government response, in terms of actions, which one was the most fruitful and successful that you have organised on the ground?

RL: It's difficult to evaluate. In the past, going back 30 years or so, I was involved in many direct actions and some of them did result in animal abuse establishments closing down and going out of business.

There was one campaign in particular in London against a lab called Biorex, where they carried out all sort of horrific experiments on animals. This was a long and very varied campaign, with people doing sit-ins, direct action, demonstrations outside, etc., and, in the end, the lab closed down and the building was taken over by Greenpeace and became their head-quarters in the UK. So it went from an appalling place for animals to offices used by people to protect the environment and the animals living in it.

However, although direct action has undoubtedly saved thousands of animals from suffering and slaughter, I came to the conclusion that if we wanted to bring about the widespread liberation of other animals from oppression by humans, we had to change the fundamental attitude towards non-human animals of a very large number of people and that could only be done by vegan education.

When you consider there are more animals directly killed by humans every hour (the overwhelming majority by the food industry) than the total victims of the Nazi holocaust, it becomes obvious that there has to be a major in-depth change in society to put an end to this horrific situation.

I can't see direct action being able to play a major part in bringing about that social change, because I don't think enough people will be pre-pared to carry out the large number of actions required to do it. Therefore, we must turn to vegan education as the major strategy for bringing about animal liberation. However the question arises of how to deal with people who refuse to be educated.

If such people are still allowed to operate freely, they will continue to be involved in animal abuse, which is a situation that obviously cannot be tolerated. We already have situations in this country where the majority of the population is opposed to a particular form of animal abuse but the people that carry out that abuse are still allowed to do so because govern-ments won't legislate against it.

Like fox hunting for example. For decades a considerable majority of the population has been opposed to it, but it was still allowed to continue because nothing was done by the government to outlaw it. The reason for that was because of the attitude of Members of Parliament, with the majority not wanting fox hunting banned or not considering it an important enough issue for legislation. There is a law against it now, but it is not very strong and not properly enforced. It's the same thing with animal experimentation, where most people are opposed to cruel experiments, but such tests are still allowed to continue because the government does not have the will to take action.

Therefore, it needs more than people opposing something to make it stop. And, in order to make that happen, we have to become involved in political activity to make sure we get people in power who will pass strong and far-reaching animal protection legislation.

If people are educated to be vegan, the number of animals killed for food and other reasons will be massively reduced, but it will not end altogether because some people will still want to consume animal products etc. So, in addition to education, political campaigning needs to form part of our struggle, if we want to totally end animal abuse.

B: Most people, even politicised ones, think human rights come before animal rights and believe it isn't possible to struggle for both at the same time, as if the desire for emancipation can't be extended to all lives. What do you answer to that?

RL: Where people are focused on struggling against capitalism, for instance, they don't say that to fight against racism, sexism or homophobia is wrong. They support these struggles and see them as compatible with their struggle against capitalism. For instance, they don't say "we have no time to stand up for the rights of gay people because we must focus on fighting against capitalism."

At one time I think there were some anti-capitalists who believed that fighting against sexism, etc., was "diversionary," but I don't believe such people exist these days. It doesn't make sense to say that to also struggle against speciesism is not compatible with those other struggles, because it is totally compatible. There is no reason why we can't fight against all these things. Indeed, they're connected, because we're talking about prejudice.

Racism, sexism, homophobia, etc., are all forms of prejudice, and speciesism is also a form of prejudice against those that are considered to be different. People just have to extend their thinking.

It's only a few hundred years ago, perhaps less than that, when black people weren't considered to have rights and were generally believed to be inferior to white people. Therefore it was believed legitimate to oppress black people and use them as slaves.

There has obviously been a big change in thinking on that issue, brought about through campaigning and people coming to realise that racial prejudice is wrong. It's the same with speciesism, where we have to fight to overcome that form of prejudice and to teach people that all forms of prejudice are linked.

B: That was actually our next question: do you think the animal rights struggle should be connected to other social and anti-capitalist struggles?

RL: Yes, absolutely, because it's part of the same continuum. It's a struggle against prejudice and exploitation and the struggle against speciesism is linked to all of those other struggles.

B: Animal rights seem to be still something the majority of people don't understand. Even being a vegetarian or a vegan, a non-activist one, seems to cause hostile reactions. What drives you? Where do you get your energy from?

RL: Regarding the first part of your question, about hostility towards vegetarians and vegans, I think it's becoming much less these days, because as the popularity of vegetarianism and of veganism increases, more and more people are ending or reducing their consumption of animal products.

Re, what drives me. To be honest, it's mainly anger. Anger at the injustice of animal persecution. What we are seeing is an extreme form of bullying. This comes with any form of prejudice, but most particularly with the ill-treatment of animals, because it's the strong persecuting the weak.

That makes me feel angry and it's from this anger that I get the energy to fight. I do think though, that such anger has to be controlled and used as a fuel, rather than it being allowed to dominate, because people don't do things in the most sensible way if they are driven by uncontrolled anger. You have to try to use the anger as a fuel that drives you in a direction that is determined by calm thought and analysis, which is what I try to do.

B: The "Cahiers antispécistes" in France compares the way we treat animals—in terms of logistics, techniques—to apartheid in South Africa or to the Nazi's extermination camps. Does it seem to you a relevant argument, that can make people understand?

RL: I think it is absolutely relevant because what we are talking about is supremacism and imperialism. The Nazis, for instance, regarded themselves as superior to other races. Their ideology was that the Aryan race was superior to all others. Because of this ideology they believed it was right and proper to persecute people of other races and put them into concentration camps and to even do experiments on them, and to drive them off their land and occupy it.

The Nazis had a policy called Lebensraum, which means "living space," and that policy was to drive people of other races off their land, use them as slaves or send them to concentration camps, and then to occupy that land with the Aryan race. That's very similar to what humans have done to other animals. We have our own policy of Lebensraum where we take the territories of other animals and use those for our own purposes. Then the animals are persecuted in various ways whether it's for food, experimentation, etc., etc.

There is a very close parallel between how the Nazis treated other races and how the human species treats other animal species. The human species behaves like a bunch of fascists and imperialists in terms of the way it treats other animals.

B: When we interviewed other animal rights campaigners for the magazine, they all promoted legal and non-violent actions. Some of them think it would be enough to show people slaughterhouse videos to make a change, in a peaceful way. They say use of violence is counter-productive and that it turns away public opinion from this cause. We know you've been asked a lot about it, but if you don't mind again, for our readers who don't know the subject…

RL: Well I can understand what they are saying and I think overwhelmingly the most important thing is education because it's about changing the way that ordinary people behave.

For two reasons: firstly because their current behaviour in itself supports the persecution of other animals. If people buy animal products, go to the zoo, to the circus, etc., then obviously that supports, encourages and finances the abuse of other animals; that's the first reason.

And secondly, when it comes to trying to create a political system where animals are properly treated—in other words to have a government that will pass the legislation you need to protect animals—so those people will vote in the right way. The nature of a government depends on how people vote, so it's very important that people are educated to vote for the best party for animal protection.

It's really important to educate people to change their behaviour as consumers, but secondly also to change the way they behave politically. That's something of vital importance. And political campaigning is connected to that.

What I'd say about the question of violence is that first of all it depends how violence is defined, because damage to property is often called "violence" where nobody is physically injured. Personally I wouldn't call that violence. For me, violence is when a person is physically attacked.

I think whether or not violence is a good thing is a question of tactics, with regard to what is the best way to move forward in terms of really changing things big time. And I believe that has to be largely through education.

When direct action takes place, there is sometimes outrage in the media, but does that represent the general opinion of ordinary people? I tend to feel most of the fuss is caused by people who want to abuse animals just shouting more loudly because they're upset about animal liberation activities. I don't believe it's a reflection of how the average person feels.

If you or I were to see somebody in the street beating a dog, and we said "please don't beat your dog," but he carried on beating the dog, we would have to use some force—which could be defined as violence—to stop that from happening. Now would that be wrong? I'd say of course it wouldn't. And I don't see the difference, in moral terms, between someone beating their dog in the street and somebody torturing an animal in a laboratory.

So if someone did go into a laboratory and used violence, or used force I'd prefer to say, to stop that from happening, I wouldn't criticize that person anymore than I'd criticize a person who used force to stop someone from beating a dog in the street. To me, there's no difference between those two things. People have to be very careful before they condemn others for carrying out that sort of direct action.

So, I think it's not so much a question of what is ethically right or wrong, but more a question of tactics, because we have to think tactically about what's the best thing we can do to bring about animal liberation. I could go right now to a laboratory and physically attack somebody carrying out an animal experiment to stop them from doing so, and I don't think my action would be morally wrong, even if it resulted in serious injury or death to the vivisector.

But if I think about it tactically, and ask myself what is the best way for me to go about trying to stop animal experiments, attacking the vivisector appears not to be the best option. Is it better to physically attack a vivisector and end up in prison, thereby greatly reducing my ability to campaign for animal liberation? Or is it preferable to do education and political action and remain able to campaign for many years to stop vivisection as a whole?

I think it's a question of thinking more long term. If you think short term, such as "that animal is being tortured now, I need to save the animal, I'll go in there and I'll use force and I'll stop it," I don't think that's morally wrong and it's far better than turning a blind eye and not doing anything at all. But if you think more tactically, in a more strategic way, about how we actually stop this whole system of persecution, then the route of education and political action is the way to go.

If someone went and used "violence" to try to stop animal abuse, I wouldn't condemn them for doing that, because the people truly deserving of condemnation are the animal abusers and all those people who are doing nothing to stop animal persecution, but I'd see such "violence" as perhaps not being the best thing to do tactically. We are fighting a long war against human imperialism and to win a war, you have to think long-term and have a long-term strategy that will bring eventual victory.

I believe in being ruthless in pursuit of animal liberation, certainly in terms of carefully analysing the situation, formulating the strategy most likely to succeed, and steadfastly sticking to it. When faced with the nightmare of human imperialism, ruthless is the only way to be. I do not want people to think for a second that my favouring of education and political campaigning, rather than direct-action, as the main way forward for animal liberation, is a sign that I have become less ruthless. It is because I have become more so.

B: Did you think about this long-term strategy while in prison? This is where you created the magazine *Arkangel*. What role do you give to writing and promoting your ideas?

RL: I think my change of emphasis in terms of political campaigning—and also to a large extent with education as well—came later. Arkangel was still, in a sense, very much promoting direct action in the best way it could, while trying to minimise the risk of prosecution.

One of the main reasons I was put in prison was because I was judged to be the publisher of the ALF Supporters Group newsletter, which went out every couple of months to people who signed up as supporters of the ALF. Inside the newsletter there was a lot of stuff encouraging people to do direct action and to get involved in the ALF and it was very blatant— we even had a kind of cartoon strip in one of the issues that actually showed people how to break into somewhere, how to disable alarms and all that kind of thing. It was very much up front in its encouragement of illegal action and we just got away with it for quite a long time.

And they said I was the publisher of that. I wasn't actually the publisher, but that was believed in court and was one of the reasons I ended up being put in prison, for encouraging people to carry out ALF actions and cause criminal damage. With ArkangeI, I felt we had to be very careful to do things in a way where we could avoid being prosecuted.

My idea for the magazine was for it to be like a substitute for the ALFSG newsletter, but more cleverly written. So it wasn't totally along the lines of how I think now, but nevertheless, I think there was a lot of useful stuff in Arkangel.

B: Do you consider ALF prisoners—or prisoners from any other similar movement—as political prisoners?

RL: Absolutely yes, they are political prisoners. Whether that means those prisoners should be treated any differently to other prisoners is another question. But yes, I think they are political prisoners.

B: You were imprisoned in 1986 and released six years later. In what way did your time in prison influence your beliefs and your route for the future?

RL: Because I knew I would be so closely watched in everything I did, I came out of jail thinking that it was going to be very very difficult for me to be involved in direct action and I wondered what else I could do to promote the cause of animal liberation.

It was at that stage I started thinking about going out on the streets and doing stalls to educate people. This was difficult for me at first, because I had never previously had very much involvement with the ordinary public, but I gained confidence by helping people who were already doing street stalls, so that eventually I was able to organise and do them myself.

B: Joining the Green Party in the UK was one of these routes?

RL: Yes, but that came a lot later because I was just involved in education for several years after I came out of prison.

Then for about 13 years, my wife and I ran a campaign, called Greyhound Action, to protect greyhounds. This all started after we adopted a greyhound and became involved with a greyhound rescue organization, which we mainly helped by transporting the dogs to their new homes. This made us look into the situation of greyhounds and how many were killed and abused because of the greyhound racing industry.

I don't think you have greyhound racing in France but in certain countries—USA, Australia, the UK and Ireland—it takes place on a commercial level. About 10,000 greyhounds a year are killed because of the UK dog racing industry industry, with the situation in Australia probably the worst of all.

So we started campaigning against the greyhound racing industry, trying to put a stop to it by working to close down greyhounds tracks. It started in a small way. Initially we thought of it as a small part of everything we did, but it grew to be so big that it took over and I was spending about 80 hours a week on the campaign, which gave me very little time to do other things.

While I was involved in the Greyhound Action campaign, the business I've mentioned already, about the government bringing in new laws against anti-vivisection campaigners, was going on. So, I thought to myself, that as a movement, we do have to get involved in politics to try to stop that sort of thing from happening.

It had become very much a trend in the animal rights movement to not be involved in politics. There had previously been attempts to make a political connection, like when the Labour Government was elected in 1997. Before the election the Labour Party made lots of promises with regard to animal protection, which enticed a lot of animal rights campaigners to support Labour and to work to get them elected. Before that, animal rights campaigners weren't really involved in politics.

Labour did get elected and they did eventually pass some legislation to protect animals, but they also went back on a lot of promises. One of the big promises they made was to begin an investigation of animal experimentation—to really look into it. So there was a big hope that they would at least reduce the number of animal experiments. But they didn't do that.

And there was a guy called Barry Horne, an animal liberation activist, who was serving a long prison sentence for ALF activities. Barry went on hunger strike to try to force the government to live up to their promise to set up a Royal Commission to look into animal experimentation. They refused to do so and Barry ended up dying from the effects of his hunger strikes.

This caused a lot of animal rights campaigners to believe that involvement in politics was a big mistake, because politicians were not to be trusted to keep their promises. Then there was the government repression against SHAC, where a lot of people got put in prison for long periods of time.

These things caused me to think in the opposite way to many other animal rights campaigners, because I formed the opinion that, realistically, whether we like it or not, we are always going to have a form of government, at least for the foreseeable future, so if we don't do anything to influence what that government is like, we can hardly be surprised when the government we get is one that supports animal abuse.

The biggest area of animal suffering and slaughter is the food industry, especially factory farming and industrialised fishing. More than eight billion animals a year are consumed in the UK, which far exceeds the number killed by any other industry of animal abuse.

Under successive governments, including Labour ones, this has got worse, with big subsidies being given to these animal slaughter industries, so we have to work to eventually get a government elected that will turn that situation around. I came to the conclusion that if we didn't try to get the best possible government, we could hardly complain when we got the worst possible one.

So when I had more time, after I was no longer running the greyhound campaign, one of the things I wanted to do was to get involved in politics, at least to some extent. And I thought to myself: what's the best way to do this? Because governments are formed by political parties, I asked myself what was the best political party to try to get into government?

I thought it has to be the Green Party, because they have by far the best policies on animal protection. Those policies aren't perfect, by any means, but Green Party policy is to abolish factory farming and hugely reduce industrialised fishing, which are by far the two biggest areas of animal abuse.

To me there were really two possibilities: one was getting involved in the Labour Party and trying to radically change them; the other one was to join the Greens and try to get them into power. I couldn't see how Labour could really be changed. Of course things are perhaps a little bit different now. The current leader, Jeremy Corbyn, is a big supporter of animal protection and has appointed a vegan, Kerry McCarthy, as shadow environment minister. The problem is, though, that most Labour MPs don't support Jeremy Corbyn. He's good, but most of the others aren't. I think that's a huge problem and what will eventually happen, I don't know.

Anyway, I decided to get involved with the Green Party, and together with some other people, formed a group called Greens for Animal Protection (GAP) which campaigns within the party to further improve its policies on animals and to persuade it to give a higher priority to animal protection. Although the Greens have got good policies on animal protection, they don't advertise or promote those policies sufficiently and that needs to be changed. GAP is involved in the policy-making process within the party and holds stalls at green party conferences, vegan fairs etc.

I outlined my current thinking re vegan education and political campaigning in January 2014 in a blog article entitled "A Greenprint for Animal Liberation" which has been translated into French.

B: A French anti-capitalist and ecologist thinker, Paul Ariès, has written a book that is violently opposed to anti-speciesism and the ALF, whom he has accused of being anti-human. What is your opinion about that?

RL: To say that animal liberationists are anti-human is like saying if you are against the Nazis, you are anti–German, isn't it?

For me the term animal liberationist applies to anyone who wants other animals liberated from oppression at the hands of the human species. The term doesn't just apply to the ALF, nor to followers of Peter Singer who wrote the book called "Animal Liberation."

And animal liberation is on the same continuum as black liberation, women's liberation and gay liberation, where people are struggling to gain the freedom of oppressed groups from prejudice and persecution. Animal liberation isn't in opposition to human beings as such, it is in opposition to the behaviour of human beings when they oppress and persecute other animals.

I would describe the behaviour of humans towards other animals on this Earth as human imperialism. The human species, in general, behaves in an imperialistic, supremacist, and speciesist way towards non-human animals, which can be equated to racism, sexism etc. To compare the behaviour of the human species to the behaviour of the Nazis isn't saying that all humans are Nazis; it's actually saying that the regime set up by the human species on Earth, in relation to other animals, is similar to the regime the Nazis wanted to set up in relation to other races.

To say we're opposed to Nazism isn't saying we're opposed to all Germans. The two aren't the same. So what Ariès says doesn't make sense to me. To be opposed to human imperialism isn't to be opposed towards all humans, it's to be opposed to the regime that has been set up. And really it's not mainly about ordinary people, it is about the type of leadership we have, because most people follow leaders.

Ordinary people have been brainwashed: born into a system and a society where they are constantly told that humans are superior to other animals. Similar to the situation of somebody born a few hundred years ago, when it was generally believed that black people were inferior to whites. Most people just accepted that and didn't challenge it, because it was the norm to believe that.

If the Nazis had triumphed and been able to spread and enforce their policies, a German child of the Aryan race growing up today would be brought up to believe they were superior to people of other races and that it was right and just to exploit those people. There would be very little challenge to that, because people would be brought up in that system.

The people who promote and push the current human supremacist system are people who have a personal or commercial interest in animal abuse and the political leaders who support them. Those are the people driving human imperialism, it's not ordinary members of the public. So, it's not so much ordinary people that animal liberationists should be opposed to, but rather those people in positions of power and influence who promote human supremacism.

B: What role has religion, and more particularly Christianity, played in our perception of other animals?

RL: I think it's a problem, because a lot of religions, and particularly Christianity, have the attitude that humans are made in the image of God and we're the most important species and the ones that should dominate the earth. That's very much embedded in Christianity and most other religions and it obviously encourages speciesism.

As an atheist, I dislike religion. I believe religions to be irrational and harmful. That's not to say that all religious people are bad. I've known a lot of good religious people, but I don't think they're good because they're religious. I think they're good people who just happened to be religious and that religion doesn't actually do anyone any good.

I think veganism and animal liberation are rational concepts, and I dislike anything I perceive to be irrational, probably for that reason. Although I've known some Christians who have been excellent campaigners for animal protection, I would say that's despite their Christianity, rather than because of it, because I think Christianity as a whole has encouraged the persecution of other animals.

Index